The House on Jefferson Street

BOOKS BY HORACE GREGORY

Poetry

Chelsea Rooming House
A Wreath for Margery
No Retreat
Chorus for Survival
Poems 1930–1940

Selected Poems
Medusa in Gramercy Park
Alphabet for Joanna
Collected Poems

Prose

Pilgrim of the Apocalypse: A Study of D. H. Lawrence
The Shield of Achilles: Essays on Beliefs in Poetry
A History of American Poetry 1900–1940 (in collaboration with Marya Zaturenska)

Amy Lowell: Portrait of the Poet in Her Time
The World of James McNeill Whistler
The Dying Gladiators and Other Essays
Dorothy Richardson: An Adventure in Self-Discovery

Translations

The Poems of Catullus
Ovid's Metamorphoses

Love Poems of Ovid

Editor

New Letters in America
The Triumph of Life: An Anthology of Devotional and Elegiac Verse
The Portable Sherwood Anderson
The Snake Lady and Other Stories of Vernon Lee
Selected Poems of Robert Browning (Rinehart Editions)
Evangeline and Other Poems by Henry Wadsworth Longfellow

Selected Poems of E. E. Cummings
The Mentor Book of Religious Verse (in collaboration with Marya Zaturenska)
The Crystal Cabinet: An Invitation to Poetry (in collaboration with Marya Zaturenska)
The Silver Swan: Poems of Romance and Mystery (in collaboration with Marya Zaturenska)
Selected Poems of George Gordon, Lord Byron

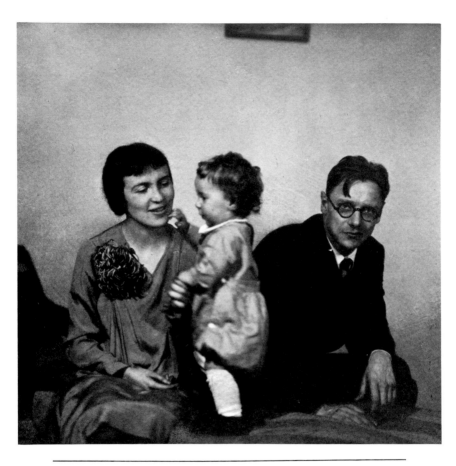

Marya Zaturenska, Joanna, and Horace Gregory in 1928.

Horace Gregory

THE HOUSE ON
JEFFERSON STREET

A Cycle of Memories

"IT IS DANGEROUS TO LIVE,
BUT TO WRITE IS MUCH MORE SO."
—*Wyndham Lewis*

Holt, Rinehart and Winston

NEW YORK · CHICAGO · SAN FRANCISCO

T O

Norman Holmes Pearson

"What is a book . . . ," so wrote Wyndham Lewis,

"but a long letter to some friend?"

Acknowledgment

In the writing of this book, I am deeply grateful to all who
have helped me during the past ten years. Among the many, I
wish to thank Marya Zaturenska and Patrick Bolton Gregory
for their criticisms, advice, and warnings; Dr. Howard A.
Rusk, Dr. John Prutting, and Dr. Cushman Haagensen, who
extended my life so I could complete the manuscript; Stanley
Burnshaw for his insistence that I write the book at all; James
Henry Gregory for information on obscure points in family
history; Glenway Wescott for his *Goodbye, Wisconsin* and
for details in the story of Grace Lusk; Dudley Fitts whose examples of courage and wit so often sustained me when things
looked dark; and Alison Bond for her final reading of the
manuscript. None of all these is responsible for errors.

H . G .

April 9, 1970
Palisades,
Rockland County,
New York

CONTENTS

The House on Jefferson Street

1

Wellspring: Childhood

MY GRANDFATHER'S HOUSE, at 717 Jefferson Street, stood sideways on the tip of a sharply rising hill. On its left, the land sloped into a tilted street that ran downward into a red and smoky sunset view of a factory-littered valley. The brick facade had been a mistake, for it gave what had once been a sturdy old frame house a top-heavy and pretentious air: if one faced the house and stared up at it, one had the illusion it was about to pitch its tall, three stories forward across the street, its turreted, cream-colored façade split wide, spewing bricks.

Moreover, the white façade seemed to deny the warmth within the house, its many book-lined walls, its red-brick, coal-burning fireplaces, and green-domed student gas lamps on desks, on tables. Several generations of deeply worn Victorian furniture ranged through the rooms. One was forced to make one's way around massive tables and immobile chairs. The rooms, each on a slightly different level—one step down into the library, one step up into the front parlor—invited intimacy and seclusion. On table or sofa, the latest issue of the *Atlantic Monthly* or the *Living Age* was well within reach, as were the latest novels of F. Marion Crawford and Henry James.

At the time of my earliest visits to this house in Milwaukee, my uncle, John Goadby Gregory, his wife Victoria, and his four children, Marian, Caro, Paul, and Elizabeth, had long settled there. And though I enjoyed its air of domestic intimacy, I felt conscious of being away from home, for Uncle John was my father's elder brother and the principal heir of my grandfather's continually dwindling estate. My grandfather had died at ninety-six in 1883, fifteen years before I was born. In his house, I knew his presence only as that of a vigorous-looking man with gray hair, a high, pointed white collar and black stock wrapped round his neck; these details in an oval-framed, oil portrait that hung in my Aunt Victoria's front parlor. It was not until much later that I realized how powerful, yet subtle, that presence was; how deeply it influenced the members of my family, including myself. Every family, with its deep enclosures, is a wellspring of being for its heirs.

The earliest visit to that front parlor must have been when I was nearly three years old. It was a frozen, cloudy day in March, and the occasion, my Cousin Elizabeth's birthday. Someone had carried me there, probably my father from our house, a great distance away. I was set on the parlor rug and swiftly unbuttoned and unbound from my winter wrappings by my aunt. Elizabeth, four years older than I, was first on my list of friends. Her hair was extremely fine, platinum-gold, very straight and long, either gathered up with hairpins on top of her head—the way she wore it after a bath—or in neatly braided pigtails down her back. Her eyes were Cornish blue with light behind them, and she had a small, slightly hooked, Norman nose. Her cheerfulness was contagious, and

[2]

in these early days, I never saw her out of temper. I remember my mother murmuring that Elizabeth was spoiled, that Victoria was alternately too strict, and then suddenly, too lax with her.

Whenever my attention strayed from Elizabeth, I was absorbed by the things that surrounded her. The first object of wonder in that front parlor was a larger-than-life-size alabaster bas-relief, resting on an oak easel, and so placed—as in an artist's studio—to catch the light from the opposite window. The relief showed the profile, neck and shoulders bare, of a still youthful woman. Rumor had it that the profile was of my aunt, and that it was the work of an itinerant Roman craftsman who had once paid a call on my Uncle John. My uncle, as editor-in-chief of the *Evening Wisconsin*, Milwaukee's most influential newspaper, was evidently thought a man worth cultivating. The Italian, so the story went, was so enchanted by the sight of my aunt—by her fair skin, gray-blue eyes, and chestnut hair—that he could not resist the temptation to sketch her then and there. A month after the sculptor's visit a huge van rolled up to the door of the house, and two moving men set up the heavy easel and the bas-relief in my aunt's front parlor. My aunt and uncle were both flattered and bewildered by the gift, which was, of course, too large, too prominent. To reject it would have insulted the sculptor; the sale of such a conspicuous object in a small city was certain to reach the artist's ears. Moreover my aunt's heart, and feminine vanity, were touched, for in spite of the austerities of plain living and high thinking she had acquired in her readings of Emerson, she could not bring herself to store the bas-relief and its easel away in the attic.

Objectively viewed—the more one looked at the bas-relief, the less it resembled my aunt—it could pass as an idealized portrait of any one of the sculptor's women friends. It was clear that the alabaster woman had her hair arranged in a

Greek coiffure, a style that my aunt was not known to have worn at any time. People entering the room swiftly moved their way around the easel, and seldom glanced at the white, faintly smiling profile. And during the years I gazed up at it, neither my aunt, nor my uncle, could be lured into talking about it at all.

My aunt's front parlor seemed to hold a unique attraction for stray objects of art. Placed on a large, black-letter edition of the Bible in German, was a minutely sculptured—every feather distinct—North American Indian in black bronze, his spear in hand, one knee raised, fixed in an eternal war-dance. Yet the warrior's ferocity and gestures seemed unconvincing. The little statue had obviously been done by someone whose image of Indians was derived from memories of the tame savages in Buffalo Bill's Wild West Show. This too, I learned, was a gift my aunt did not dare refuse—from the formidable, red-faced, black-garbed proprietress of the *Evening Wisconsin*. One day I was held up to shake hands with her as she leaned her bulk toward me from her carriage. "You're an infidel," she said, dropping my hand, and falling back against her seat. I was utterly mystified by her remark, for "infidel" was a word I had never heard in conversation. I concluded that she did not like my face. Later, I was told that she was a Roman Catholic, and that she had probably heard that my father was not, and that this was her way of showing, crudely enough, her disapproval of her editor-in-chief's family. To me, *she* seemed rather heathenish, and her gift, in that sense, was not inappropriate.

More in keeping with my Aunt Victoria's taste, were two other objects in the room. The larger one was a square, flat-topped, magnificently japanned, black piano; and on its glossy top stood a column of black-veined, gray and lavender marble, out of which was carved the opening petals of a rose. One saw a darkened reflection of its shape in the polished piano-

[4]

top. These gave her parlor an air of distinction, and so did the pictures she had chosen for its walls. Near the portrait of my grandfather was a miniature in oil of his second wife, my English, London-born grandmother. She had been twenty-five when he married her, some forty years younger than her husband, and as if to accentuate the disparity in age between them, the portrait revealed a fair-haired, eleven-year-old child, who looked very like my Cousin Elizabeth. The miniature was painted, I believe, by a follower of Hayter. A fall of light, a halo, seemed to form above the child's golden hair. As my grandmother—the first Elizabeth in my family—so often told me, she sat for her portrait the same week Samuel Rogers, the banker-poet and friend of Lord Byron—as well as of her father—treated her to an evening at the theater. (And it was this indirect family acquaintance with Lord Byron that probably led me to read his poems at the age of nine.)

Near my grandmother's portrait there was another miniature, that of a servant girl in a white mobcap, shielding a candle with one hand, light flowing upward across her smiling face. I suspect that the picture came from the sentimental fancies of an obscure nineteenth-century German painter, yet I found the girl irresistible. I was always tempted to smile back at her. Above the piano hung a large and faithfully colored reproduction of Whistler's *At the Piano*. On the adjacent wall was a print of a brilliant-hued Delacroix tiger.

The Whistler, the Delacroix, the square piano, with its top like a great, deep refectory table's, the sculptured rose, all belonged, so I thought, exclusively to my Aunt Victoria's world.

And emerging from this setting was the figure of Aunt Victoria herself: her dresses carelessly buttoned and hooked, seemed to swallow up her thin body within their folds; and her hat pinned on back to front—or front to back? She was never quite certain of how it arrived where it was. Even so, she was precise in her movements. Like many, who are slightly deaf, she had a disconcerting manner of raising her head and smiling into space. Hers was an Emersonian smile of divine abstraction, which was, of course, often irrelevant to the conversations going on around her. At moments, her gray eyes were a translucent blue, and whenever they glanced in my direction, they seemed ineffably kind and friendly. Within the spheres of her influence—her women's club, the Unitarian Church, and the Gregory family—she encouraged appreciation of the arts. In this she was fervent, and so transparently sincere, that in the cultural circles of the growing city, she gained a modest degree of respect. She denied herself many small luxuries, and practiced penny-pinching so as to send the two daughters of my uncle's first wife to boarding schools in the East, the elder, Marian, to an art school in New York, and Caro to a training school for librarians in Pennsylvania. It was my aunt's favorite illusion that she, and only she, was the "practical" member of the household at 717 Jefferson Street. It was she, truly enough, who kept household accounts and struggled with arrears in paying bills. Even when I was far too young to understand the weight of her responsibilities, she would say to me, "Your poor dear Uncle John is a professional man, and a darling. But *I* have to take care of things, or we'd all starve. Think of it! Only yesterday, a horrible drunken beggar came to the back door, and your uncle calmly handed him a half dollar. Your uncle said he couldn't help it. The man was hungry and was much too dirty to ask in for a meal. Now, that would never happen to *your* father; unlike your father, your uncle is *not* a businessman, and couldn't be, no matter how hard he tried. He has to be himself, and that means that he's just a great big old dear!"

From my aunt's front parlor, one stepped down into my uncle's study. Except for the space above the fireplace, which was filled by an enormous smoke-darkened portrait of my aunt's great-aunt, a painfully plain-featured woman in a very low-cut gown, the walls were covered with books: innumerable volumes of poems, and bound collections of British quarterlies and weeklies, dating back to Dr. Johnson's *The Rambler* and *The Gentleman's Magazine*.

In later years, while showing me the curiosities of his library, my uncle's portly manner was that of a genial, ruddy-faced, spectacled, Irish schoolmaster. Like my father, my Uncle John retained and cultivated what must have been their father's Trinity College, Dublin accent. And whenever my uncle had the merest hint of beer or whiskey on his breath, the accent grew more pronounced. His way of speaking, his Regency diction, were among the invisible legacies my grandfather had left behind him. They also distinguished the Gregorys from most other families in the city, for the Gregorys felt, with unreasonable assurance and pride, that they were foreigners, living at the center of a horde of barbarians, in the American Middle West.

It was my uncle's fault, my grandmother confessed, that visible proof of our superiority was not at hand. First of all, there had been thin rumors of Gregory descent from King Duncan of Scotland, who was once supposed to have been murdered by Macbeth. Two family trees, hers, of the Goadby line, and my grandfather's, their branches intact, had been faithfully transcribed upon a large sheet of paper, which fell into my uncle's hands—he was then two years old—and had been torn to bits. All that was left was a scattering of legends, from which a few elderly facts could be discerned. These included my grandfather's cousinship to the Gregorys of Coole, and his connections at Trinity College. He was reputed to have designed the bridges in Phoenix Park, Dublin, and in his fragment of an autobiography, he revealed that he had hopes of being appointed Astronomer Royal. That he had been handsome, eloquent, impressive, I have no doubt; for how otherwise could he, then a man more than sixty, have taken, even temporarily, the fancy of a young woman scarcely turned twenty-five? It was evident that in the house he had built on Jefferson Street, memory of his voice and legend haunted his descendants to reemerge in their dreams.

My uncle, aside from his narrow chin and dark blue eyes, did not inherit my grandfather's features. His straight nose, his iron-gray curls, had come from his mother's father, Dr. Henry Addison Goadby. There was something vaguely clerical, even priest-like, about his appearance. He wore old-fashioned, straight, stand-up white collars, and thick, glittering eyeglasses, framed in black gun metal. Like his mother, he was frighteningly nearsighted, and preternaturally serene. I often wondered if their nearsightedness were the actual cause of their serenity, for, in their view, the wicked world was at several removes, fading into a mirage of sunlight, or the rise of a parti-colored fog. Those who met my uncle for the first time, took note of his elaborate courtesies, the raising of his hat, the pursing of his lips, and then, the sudden broadness of his smile. Often, they concluded wrongly that the man drank heavily, and did not realize that he scarcely saw them at all. To him, they were little more than targets for a well-directed formal bow. Yet some were not far wrong in thinking him intoxicated, for he was so shamelessly immoderate in the reading of everything that came his way, that he seemed dazed whenever he stepped outside his library.

He had so arranged his day that visits to his office were brief. These were between seven-thirty and eleven in the morning, six days a week. Since the *Evening Wisconsin* was an afternoon paper, his editorials were handed in at eight, and then, for three hours or so, he directed his staff. When these chores were completed, he walked swiftly, for he walked as fast as he wrote, through the city in a semi-circular route, back to Jefferson Street and the books in his library. There, in a cloud of cigar smoke, he would read till dinner at eight. Three quarters of an hour later, with a bow, and a boyish wave of the hand, he stepped away from the dining table, out of the room, out of the front door of the house, down two blocks at a right angle to Jefferson Street into an old-fashioned *Bierstube,* behind which was a *Garten,* where, on summer evenings, swaying steins and voices were raised in a chorus of "Deutschland, Deutschland, über Alles."

Within twenty minutes, he was back in his study, with a pitcher of cold, tap-drawn beer on the table at his side, his writing board on his raised left knee, while under his swiftly guided pencil, square sheets of copy paper were streaked with slanting words, and then dropped to the floor. In another half-hour his stint was done, the papers scooped up from where they had fallen, shuffled into order, and fastened together with a metal clip, so as to be ready for the Linotype next morning.

My uncle was then free to recite, to whatever guests were in the room, either his own verse (this by request only, for he was at once shy, vain, and proud), or selections from his favorite poets, all the way from Sir Philip Sidney to Sir William Watson and Kipling. In this list, there was always special stress placed upon poets his father might well have admired—Alexander Pope, Oliver Goldsmith, Thomas Moore, and Barham of *The Ingoldsby Legends.* My uncle loved to declaim at length. His recitations often broke down the cheerful serenity of his demeanor for in declaiming verse, his emotions were all too easily aroused: his voice shook dangerously, and even comic verse would move him close to tears. On these occasions, my father would whisper in my ear, "Poor John, poor John." And strangers in the room would again think my uncle had been drinking far too much for his own good. The moment his guests left he would light up a corncob pipe, and resume his reading into the small hours of the next morning.

One night, his solitary vigils in the library brought him a quarter-hour of melodrama. At half-past two, or thereabouts, my uncle felt the mouth of a revolver pressed against the back of his neck, and received instructions to empty all his pockets quietly. The voice he heard was that of his first wife's brother, mad Parke Paul, a handsome, vigorous man of six-foot-four, who had been locked away in a sanatorium after threatening to murder his mother. He had now escaped and was in need of train fare to transport him out of Wisconsin. My uncle had enough money in his clothes to send Parke on his way. Ten years later, during the First World War, my uncle learned that his brother-in-law had enlisted in the United States Army, been cited for bravery, and had died in action, "somewhere in France."

When my uncle took charge of the house on Jefferson Street, he had come a long way up from being a "printer's devil," and one of the founders of the first printers' union in the city. He had been an unusually bright reporter on a morning paper, and soon after he joined the staff of the *Evening Wisconsin*, he was appointed secretary to the man whose widow now employed him as editor-in-chief. Even so, my uncle was not rich, and there was a haze of mystery hanging over the fact that he had amassed a huge, overflowing library. From my aunt, I had been given to understand that bibliomania was a rich man's passion, that, in the collecting of books, the poor had better be sane, that books attracted dust, and that the books in my uncle's library had not been properly dusted for many years. There was little doubt that in acquiring his books, my uncle had pitched himself beyond his means. His household expenses were vulnerable to the slightest rise in the cost of groceries—and on my aunt's dining table, margarine would often take the place of butter. Yet the entry of books into the house never ceased. Each Saturday afternoon, my uncle bought, for a quarter a load, armfuls of books that had been given away to the Salvation Army. This he regarded as the exercise of great—and secret—economy.

Behind my uncle's buying of books, which overflowed the rooms on the ground floor of the house and eventually had to be stored in empty quarters on the third floor, was a social phenomenon. In the years between 1910 and 1918, something called a "country club" civilization had been increasing its hold on the well-to-do families of the city. The donors of books to the Salvation Army were young, were those who never read a book, if they could help it; they belonged to a "fast set," sets that played bridge, tennis, and golf, drove racing cars, and bought mink coats for their girls, drank more than they could carry, and gaily diminished the millions their grandfathers had made. Thorstein Veblen had gazed at these spenders of Midwestern wealth with an appraising and prophetic eye. He was a social moralist who looked around him, and was soon possessed by the desire to displease. He had a penetrating, if turgid, gift for ironic observation; and if he could not set things right, he could point, with justified disgust, at things gone wrong. At first glance, it may have seemed odd that this austere critic and lecturer almost ruined his academic career by having love affairs with his women students. Yet his domestic conduct was consistent, in its confusions, with his turgid prose, his ironic insights, his violent hatred of smooth thinking.

My Uncle John, had he thought it worth the trouble, would have attacked Veblen as a dangerous immoralist and crank, and Veblen, had he cared to look in my uncle's direction, would have dismissed him as an ineffectual servant of the rich, one who merely survived on the spoils of "conspicuous wealth."

Though in his later years, my uncle acquired a certain local notoriety as one of Wisconsin's "official" historians, it was impossible to associate his image with those of frontier shrewdness and resourcefulness. His provincialism was of a different order; it never relinquished its curious, yet cordial Dublin gloss. So far as the geography of his native city, Milwaukee, was concerned, he was severely pedantic; yet even this sternness vanished with the slightest shift in conversation.

The years I spent Saturday afternoons and evenings in the house on Jefferson Street were, of course, long before I ever heard of Veblen, or knew that books such as *Theory of the Leisure Class* could possibly exist. My awareness of money was extremely limited. When I went visiting my Cousin Elizabeth, I was given a silver quarter, with the understanding that in return for my aunt's hospitality, I was to offer Elizabeth a treat. (In a roundabout fashion that I could never quite unravel, my aunt would remind me that while I was rich, Elizabeth was poor—with the result that I would always put my silver quarter into Elizabeth's cool, clean, upturned palm.) She would then offer to guide me out of the house, steady me down the steps, and across the street. To my right, up Jefferson Street, I always noted the high gray-brick walls of a convent, from which I could almost believe I heard the sound of singing. To wake me from this brief reverie, Elizabeth would slide an arm across my shoulder and gently steer me down an incline until we stood in front of a drug store. As I remember these afternoons, the month was always August, the time was always three o'clock, the glare and heat intolerable. We longed for a cooling drink. Now a soda clerk leaned over us. Elizabeth straightened her back, her fist that held the quarter reached toward the clerk, her voice recited the formula: "Two strawberry ice-cream sodas," and the quarter was dropped into his hand. A few minutes later, head slightly bent over her straw, her round blue eyes looked deeply into mine, the change from the quarter, uncounted, tucked out of sight. The money, handed out so eagerly, had disappeared.

My visits to Jefferson Street aside, drug stores were a not infrequent subject of conversation in my father's household, for at fourteen he had been apprenticed as boy chemist in a large wholesale drug house. Even in my day, its warehouses, block-long and smoke-stained, had an ugly, dark, intractable look. Their backs turned to a brown, oily river that wound its way through the business section of the city, and whenever I passed them, there was the smell of chemicals and spices in the air. The smells and the sight of so much unrelieved, bleak ugliness always made me feel a trifle sick. Beggars and drunks, long past redemption, slept, huddled and folded up in the shallow, stone-faced thresholds, against locked and bolted iron-bound doors. I half-suspect, for he never said so, that my father was rather proud of his connection with those huge, ungainly buildings that had marked the origins of his career in business, and in fact, there was reason for him to be proud of his early accomplishments. With the books that my grandfather's library had provided, and a mere two years of grade school behind him, he had taught himself Latin and mathematics, and in this fashion, had laid the groundwork for his training as a chemist. His lighter readings were in Fielding, Smollett, Charles Lever, Samuel Lover, Sir Walter Scott, Dickens, and through the public library, where as a boy he worked at night, the novels of Thomas Hardy, and later *Jude the Obscure* were among his favorites. As I grew older, he loved to catch me off guard with sudden disclosures of his reading in poetry. One day, while seated at the wheel of his car, driving us home from his office, he intoned the first stanza of Tennyson's "The Lady of Shalott"—he knew I had elected a year's study of Tennyson at college—then he continued with, "How can you read that filthy catamite?" I had never thought of my father reading Victoria's laureate, and as for his knowing gossip concerning the poet's life, that idea was furthest from my mind. In his middle years, the only twentieth-century writer who won his approval was Bernard Shaw. With the exceptions of Mark Twain and Hawthorne—and all the way from Whitman to the present—he dismissed American writers as "egoists" and "barbarians." "Trash" was what they wrote, and if, by chance, he would spend a half-hour of an evening reading the latest number of *The Saturday Evening Post*, often as not, he would suddenly fling the paper over his head behind him, or toss it emphatically into a distant corner of the room.

In one of his extremely rare confidential moods, my father told me that when I was one or two (I believe in 1900) the drug store era of his life began to recede into the past. I was partly the cause, so he said, of that great change. At nineteen, he had married his first wife, who had just turned sixteen, and by whom he eventually had three children, two boys and a girl. At twenty-one, he had set up, for his employers, the first commercial laboratory in the city. A year later, when his second son was expected, he decided to form a partnership with a young man who had also been an apprentice in the firm, and to open two retail drug stores under their names, "Richardson & Gregory." Soon after the birth of this son, her third child, his young wife died. Within a few months of her death, my uncle's first wife was also dead, and the two young widowers, with three small children apiece, settled into the large house on Jefferson Street. To take charge of the household—and its six children—my mother, a native of the lake country north of the city, was hired as housekeeper, while she, in turn, employed two servant girls. This was not an easy assignment, and I still marvel at my mother's tact, and evenly balanced temper, in carrying it off so well. My uncle's marriage to my Aunt Victoria soon relieved my mother of her extraordinary duties. My aunt took over the care of my uncle's children, and soon had a child of her own

—Elizabeth—while my father married my mother, and they, with my father's children, moved into an apartment over one of his two drug stores where I, a seven-month's child, was born. My frail health, with its attendant heavy medical expenses,* made my father conscious of how little money his newly founded drug stores actually brought in. He tried to increase his income by taking "flyers" on the stock market, and while he raised considerable cash this way, he also threatened "Richardson & Gregory" with bankruptcy. He then discovered that Richardson, a sad-eyed, low-voiced, lethargic man, was an alcoholic.

The high cost of keeping me alive forced my father to find more secure, more independent means of supporting his family. He dissolved his partnership with Richardson and took over from the drug stores heavy chemicals, paints and oils, spices, and flavoring extracts. With this peculiar stock of goods he founded a business that was quite his own, supplying manufacturers with paint and acids, and bakers with sugar, nuts, machinery, spices, and canned fruits. Slowly, his business matured, and with each little step for the better, he moved his family into more prosperous residential sections of the city. In a year or two we had moved out of the gray-brick, traffic-noisy, corner building in which I was born.

Of my earliest memories, even the fragments are broken. I remember a rocking horse with a straw-colored mane and tail, and an iron figurine—a fireman in a red uniform whom I dearly loved, for I made up stories of his great heroism. The most startling memory of this early period, one that haunted me for many years, was of a relic from one of my father's drug stores. I remember climbing—I could not have been more than three—to an attic storeroom, dimly lit by a dusty

* During early infancy I had contracted tuberculosis of the bone, affecting the upper vertebrae of the spine, which, in turn, caused paralysis of the left hand and foot, as well as a slight tremor in the right hand.

dormer window, where a few stray objects, salvaged from the dispersal of drug store furnishings, still survived. Near the threshold, facing me, stood a five-foot high wooden China-man, a mechanical creature, wound up to action by a key in his back, who used to stand (so I heard afterwards), behind the plate glass window of my father's store, facing the street, nodding at all who passed and sipping from a wooden cup countless invisible cupfuls of medicinal tea. In the attic, where I first met him, he had become soot-streaked, his long mus-taches and pigtail grown iron-gray with dust, yet as he in-clined his head to sip his tea, his smile was as sweet and fright-ening as ever. For a reason I could not explain, his dusty cheerfulness inspired horror.

One dark afternoon, probably in winter, I hoisted myself up the attic stairs, only to discover my fifteen-year-old half brother, Johnny, sawing the Chinaman in two for firewood. I began to scream, and still screaming with terror until rescued by my mother, I was carried downstairs.

Another early—but very pleasant—picture is of a Christ-mas morning, when I was set down by my mother before a grate, which contained large lumps of coal, with thin green and red flames shooting up around them. To this was added a side image of my mother giving me, from a spoon, a few drops of coffee, cooled with milk. And somehow associated with this, there is a turn to horror again. The memory here is of a book, bound in shining, irritating bright blue cloth. It was a book I shied away from whenever I saw it on a table, or in a bookcase. Like the Chinaman, the book, in its garish blue binding, inspired fear. How and why it did so, was a story told by my mother to her friends.

It is because of my mother's telling of the story that I can reconstruct the entire incident. As she told it, her voice, a soft soprano, held a note of awe. She was still young, and was easily carried away whenever she spoke of unusual experiences.

Part of my mother's great charm was in her air of country-girl truthfulness—it was difficult to doubt her word. She was of Schleswig and Bavarian parentage, and brought up in the dairy farm section of Wisconsin, an idyllic countryside of blue skies and lakes, and rolling pastures.

Her story was of a time before I could talk, when I rested in crib and baby carriage, or was carried in the curve of her left arm. According to her, I was a tractable and quiet baby: very early, within a few months after my birth, she had formed the habit of cradling me in one arm, and reading poetry aloud to me. Her favorite poets were Longfellow and Bryant and—a peculiar choice—Thomas Hood. This last, I believe, was made through my father's mother, a loyal Londoner, who could well remember the London of Hood's day.

It may well have been that Hood's verse held a half-morbid attraction for my mother, but whether the attraction was morbid or not, she picked up the bright blue book, and from it read "The Song of the Shirt" aloud to me. With the passionate and drum-like beat of its rhythms in my ears, I began to scream, and I screamed until she had placed the book aside. Of course, I was much too young to have understood the words, yet I was overwhelmed by the presence of terror and doom. There was no doubt that my protest also overwhelmed my mother. In the future she was careful to avoid readings that inspired fear. She swiftly eluded any requests to read *Grimm's Fairy Tales* aloud, and she visibly shrank away from the recital of brutalities and scenes of sadism.

About five years later I read Tennyson's *The May Queen*, which filled me with something of the same dread that attended my mother's reading of "The Song of the Shirt." But in this latter case, my feelings were more complex: I am certain that nothing less than morbid curiosity impelled my reading of the poem, for I sensed, in its opening line—" 'If you're waking, call me early, call me early, Mother dear . . .' "—

the predestined and mawkish death of its young heroine. My feeling of dread was quickly replaced by that of anger, for I felt I had been tricked by Tennyson into responses of false pity and terror.

"How could he know what Thomas Hood meant?" my mother asked her friends. There were times when she believed I had second sight. At the very least, she held a calm faith in the rightness of my intuitions. In proof of this, she would tell an anecdote of one of my earliest responses to fear. I was in my crib, flat on my back, when suddenly a great, round, bald-headed, smiling face leaned over me, and breathed heavily into mine. Again I cried until it disappeared. Several years later, I learned that the face belonged to the bridegroom of one of my mother's handsome sisters. Others had seen a big, ruddy, round-faced, loud-talking fellow, who at the slightest invitation had always been ready to sing, or dance. I was the one who knew he was not to be trusted, and who had given the first warning that he was to desert his wife a few months after marrying her. So much for my mother's confident memory of my encounter with him. All I remember is the terror I felt when a large, round, smiling face leaned close to mine. Was his the mechanical smile that later was to frighten me on the face of the wooden Chinaman?

I have still one other memory built up this time from associations of my mother's talk about our neighbors. I must have been six or seven. The central figure of this episode was not myself, but the sallow, stout, slow-moving, angelic-looking little boy, Billy, who was exactly my age, who had large, and magnificently colored, gold and light blue toy soldiers—and who lived, across a well-cut plot of grass, next door. To the rear of the lawn, between our houses, was a neatly boxed-in area of clean sand, where Billy and I built forts in which to house our armies.

The cleanliness of our houses and lawns was typical of that

section of the city, its South Side settled at that time by the sons and daughters of industrious German immigrants. Our neighbors were resolute in maintaining the outward semblance of respectability. Few were poor, and those few disguised their poverty so effectively, that when they sank from prosperity into bankruptcy, and from there into oblivion, they left no traces of their distress behind them. If anyone was tactless enough to inquire where they had gone, the reply was that they had "moved away." And other families that looked remarkably like them moved in. Housewives directed their campaigns of "spring cleaning" every thirty days. With sleeves rolled up, and aprons crisply ironed, diamond rings glittering on their fingers, one saw them spread rugs and blankets on their lawns, and saw their round arms flashing out of open windows to commandeer a sluggish housemaid, or laggard handyman in the back yard. Billy's mother, a pretty, generous-breasted, red-cheeked, brown-haired, blue-eyed young woman, was a housewife of that kind. Wherever she walked, a whirlwind seemed to rise behind her skirts. Her voice was a sometimes brilliant, sometimes dreamy contralto.

Her sturdy and supremely well-fed little Billy was even more docile than I was: he never complained, and almost never wept; he was ridiculously easy to command. Therefore, as we played together, it was I who ordered *his* toy soldiers about, and it was I who designed the forts, and laid out the battlefields. At a kind word, or an affectionate gesture in his direction, his face would broaden into a flushed smile. He was a child of very few words.

One day, I overheard my mother talking to a friend about Billy's mother. The curious fact was that that young woman was away from home almost every afternoon. Billy went to school only on fine days, and only in the morning. On afternoons, while his mother was out of the house, he would lie in his crib the entire five or six hours. My mother asked her

that old neighborhood, the skies seem high and cloudless, the air refreshing and filled with sunlight. Then the place disappears, and my father's increasing prosperity shifts us to a slightly more fashionable section of the city.

Of the furnishings that had moved with us from house to house, none was more characteristic than a black-framed series of six oval portraits of middle-aged men, dimly smiling through growths of sideburns, or amply-tailored beards. These were America's poets: Whitman and Emerson, Whittier and Bryant, Lowell and Longfellow, and they hung above the French, glass-cased clock on the mantelpiece. Though these gentlemen held an exalted place in our new living room, though my mother seldom modified her high opinion of their writings, their bearded visages did not meet with my mother's approval. Her dislike of their tonsorial styles, so I think, had a concealed origin, for the portraits had been a gift to my father from my Aunt Victoria, and in the presence of my aunt, my mother was never entirely at ease. The shadow of a scarcely visible antagonism fell between them. Christmas gifts from my aunt—which so often stressed the nature of her cultural pretensions—always alerted my mother's sense of the inept and the ridiculous. Yet she was enough impressed by my aunt's tone of authority never to oppose her openly—therefore the American poets, for many years, remained enshrined above our mantelpiece. Then on a sun-shining day of vigorous "spring cleaning" the poets disappeared, and were never seen again.

About the time of their disappearance, my mother told me how I acquired my name. On the day of my birth, under Aries, April 10, 1898, a notice appeared in the *Evening Wisconsin* announcing the arrival of Horace Victor Gregory, a son, to Mr. and Mrs. Henry Bolton Gregory. My Aunt Victoria had appointed herself my godmother, and had invented my name—which came as a surprise to my mother and father. With a half-apologetic air for her officiousness in naming their son without their permission, she told my parents she could not resist the temptation, "because Horace Victor Gregory has such a lovely Latin sound." Though she herself had not studied Latin, and was aware of the poet, Horace, only through Alexander Pope's "Imitations of Horace," she was loyally conscious of a streak of Latinity in her husband's family. She was proud of the fact that my father had taught himself Latin from the books in his father's library. My aunt's initiative in my naming was evidence of her invasion of a province that belonged to my parents, and it was proof that her transcendentalism had its moments of ruthless aggression.

My aunt's officiousness again exerted itself when she decided my family needed cabinet photographs of me—with my dog. To effect this end, she called upon the assistance of her tall, sweet-tempered, younger unmarried sister, Maud Smalley, who had a touch of brilliance in her skills at portrait photography. Maud was the largest woman I had ever seen; and her word, though softly spoken, was always law. With Maud in the room, my usual self-consciousness disappeared, and even Jippy, my self-willed, intelligent, black-and-tan terrier, responded submissively to her dominance. For five years or so, Jippy was my treasured companion, a creature who, since he had spent his first year in a German household, was bilingual. His great flaw was his almost Prussian conduct out-of-doors; he was insulting to other dogs, even those larger than he, and he viciously snapped at the heels of all—men, women, dogs, or cats—who passed our door. To my grief, he was brutally murdered by an angry neighbor. But his death came long after the period when Maud Smalley, with her great smile and tomboyish enthusiasms would command my family, even my mother, and my young sister, Josephine, to sit before the lens of her cloth-draped camera.

[23]

There was little doubt that, from time to time, my mother needed protection from Aunt Victoria's aggressiveness, and this came from my English grandmother—who loved my mother, but looked on her eldest son's wife, Victoria, with severe disfavor. Though small in stature—she was scarcely more than five feet tall—my grandmother was formidable. She never allowed others to forget that she was the daughter of the noted entomologist Dr. Henry Addison Goadby, professor at the University of London, and author of *Animal and Vegetable Physiology*, who had received a gold medal for his researches from the hands of Queen Victoria and contributed, with Owen and Darwin, to *The Bridgewater Treatises*.

Henry Goadby's career was both promising and tragic, truncated by death in early middle years. Before he had started his researches at the university he had been trained at law, and for a brief time, practiced as a solicitor. During this early interval, he had won a litigation suit for his clients, two daughters of a certain Bishop Geddes who, many years before, had been a drinking companion of Robert Burns. The two ladies had little cash, so in payment for young Goadby's services they offered him relics of their father's friendship with the poet: a copy of the first edition, interlined with corrections for the second, of Burns's *Poems, Chiefly in the Scottish Dialect*, and a whiskey-toddy ladle used by Burns on winter evenings. These my great-grandfather gallantly accepted in lieu of cash, and he reverentially treasured them.

His young wife, my grandmother's mother, died of a "consumption" when her daughter was barely seven, and for a year or so, her two children, a boy and a girl, were brought up by her husband's mother, where all four lived together in Holburn. "A dreadful time" for her, so my grandmother often told me, for whenever her father left the house, he entrusted her with the key to the door of the room that he had converted into a laboratory—with the instructions that she was to forbid entrance to it of *her* grandmother, his mother. The terrified little girl had become the guardian of her father's collection of unsightly creatures: East Indian insects, grown to enormous size, great hairy spiders; wild bats, nesting in corners and behind bookcases; large, brown rats, suspended from the ceiling in cages—and worst of all huge, fat centipedes, suddenly overturning their bottles, where they slept in alcohol on their high shelves, threatening to tip over and drop down the back of one's neck.

Her release came when her father unexpectedly packed her off to a boarding school on the Continent, near Le Havre, there to learn a lady's accomplishments: needlework and drawing, water-color painting, and French and German. At eighteen, she was "finished," and returned to London where, as her boat moved toward its wharf in the Thames, her father seized the end of a rope tossed to him by a sailor on deck and leaped aboard. "Father was then so wonderfully agile," she would tell me, "so graceful, so light on his feet, so happy to see me, to hold his Lizzie in his arms, and I was wild with joy to see Father again!" By this time, he was nearly certain of becoming a famous man, and for five years, his prospects were in the ascendancy. I have a daguerreotype of Dr. Goadby as he was then—and the portrait shows him seated, as were sitters for the great Octavius Hill, leaning toward a book held in his left hand. The head is framed by masses of crisp, ringleted chestnut hair; the high forehead is vertically creased in a slight frown, the eyes below it open in an unworldly stare, the corners of the mouth drawn down severely, and below the face, there is a stylishly high white pointed collar, tightly bound in a black silk stock; the figure, from shoulder to waist, alert, and tensely held. One could easily imagine a flow of electric energy pouring from the image in the daguerreotype. Certainly, Dr. Goadby looked like a serious young man, perhaps one of genius, mounting the first steps of a hill to the future.

The probable date of the picture is 1842—five years before he suffered a mysterious accident, or breakdown.

Temporary blindness was the beginning of Dr. Goadby's series of disasters. In order to restore his health he undertook a sea voyage—across the Atlantic to Boston, taking with him for companionship his daughter, Elizabeth. Once aboard ship Dr. Goadby struck up an acquaintance with an Irishman, John Gregory, with a Trinity College accent, who, like himself, was a widower. Gregory was accompanied by a grown son, George, a few years older than Elizabeth, and toward whom she turned with innocent confidence and admiration. This attraction had swift and unexpected consequences. Dr. Goadby insisted that she marry the young man's father. "Better," he told her, "to be an old man's darling than a young man's slave." As soon as the party of four landed in Boston, Elizabeth yielded to her father's will. This was a moment of weakness she soon regretted. John Gregory, good-looking and impressive as he was, had far less money than his manner led one to assume. His social graces were coupled with a wild sense of irony and farce—attributes that Dr. Goadby, with his intense seriousness and devotion to biology, completely lacked. Yet the two men had one negative trait in common—a lack of business acumen so profound that it resembled a drive toward self-destruction.

Dr. Goadby had earned a touch of fame in his researches into physiology. John Gregory was known in Dublin as a resourceful engineer and author of several textbooks on elementary mathematics and astronomy. Both men felt that their talents had received inadequate rewards, yet John Gregory, the more optimistic of the two, was sustained by the fact that he had been commissioned, back in Dublin, to write a book telling indigent Irishmen where to settle in America. Both earned their way from Boston to the Middle West by delivering lectures on the sciences they represented. The start of their careers in the Middle West was promising enough; at Milwaukee, in the offices of the city's first mayor, Solomon Juneau, a French-Canadian Indian, John Gregory secured the post of civil engineer. He immediately began work on his commissioned book, later published in Dublin, *The Industrial Resources of Wisconsin*. At the newly founded University of Michigan, Dr. Goadby accepted a professorship in the department of science. In imitation of his elderly son-in-law, he married a woman young enough to be his daughter. Within a few years, both men, surrounded by shrewd provincials in a rough environment, felt trapped and discontented.

John Gregory was commissioned to drain water from a large ditch in the street leading to a clapboard courthouse. He complied by presenting the Milwaukee city council with a blueprint of a scheme to divert the ditch water into Lake Michigan. His blueprint was scarcely less elaborate than a diagram of the sewer system of Paris. He then advised his fellow councilmen, much to their dismay, that his plan would be the greatest engineering feat ever attempted on the North American continent, and that Milwaukee would be the honored site of its achievement. It was obvious that Mr. Gregory never thought of anything in petty terms—but was it less than certain that he was not trying to make fools of his fellow administrators? His manner was always courteous, his appearance imposing, and his abundant flow of words eloquent and often ambiguous. Even his enemies on the city council could not question his veracity; they knew he was much too proud to tell lies (and too lacking in discretion). Yet his elaborate mode of exposing facts often seemed to encase them in a dreamlike aura of unreality.

In his fragmentary autobiographical sketches an air of fantasy prevails. He has written that in his early years in Dublin, he enjoyed the patronage, advice, and casual friendship of Spring-Rice, Lord Monteagle, Chancellor of the (British)

Exchequer. It was through Monteagle's influence that he had hoped to obtain a post in the office of the Astronomer Royal, and it was against his patron's advice that he had agreed to take over the presidency of The Dublin Academical Institution. Monteagle had warned: "You will regret what you have done all the days of your life; you have seen how many projects have lately ended in your city in a bottle of smoke; and yours may end in the same way. . . . The situation of Assistant Astronomer Royal, with a positive certainty of promotion, was not beneath any man. In such a position you could provide for all your relatives and friends."

Of course, Monteagle's prophecy was not far wrong, for John Gregory was peculiarly unfit to run an establishment of any kind. He could not secure patrons and endowments fast enough to finance a teaching staff and pay the rent on a building large enough to house it, and though the Academical Institution hopefully changed its name to College of Engineering, the venture was doomed, and John Gregory began to feel that in Dublin, at least, he had made more enemies than friends. His wife had died, and the famine years of the 1840s in Ireland had begun—all he possessed was the gift of talk and a flair for setting words down on paper. Friends commissioned the book that he might write to help those even less fortunate than he—the starving Irish sailing to America. He had been proud of his mission; he saw himself as a gentleman-author, engaged in securing the welfare of his countrymen—a philanthropist of sorts, whose *Industrial Resources of Wisconsin* was to be bestowed on future generations of Irish emigrants. The book actually attracted a few Protestant Dubliners to Milwaukee, soon to be outnumbered by the many liberal-minded Germans who fled Europe at the collapse of the 1848 revolutions.

Earnest and businesslike pioneers were not drawn to men of John Gregory's ironic humors, nor did they care to understand his strange bursts of levity and self-criticism. He chose to identify himself with the more unusual settlers in Wisconsin of whom he wrote biographical sketches in his unfinished autobiography. One of these was Thaddeus Pound, lieutenant governor of Wisconsin, and grandfather of Ezra Pound. The most extraordinary and moving of these sketches is undoubtedly the one he wrote of his son, George, who had died a few years after the two had arrived in the Middle West. In this piece, John Gregory wrote of himself in the third person, and with a show of stoicism, charged with irony, blamed himself—his curse of talking out of order and too much—for the ruin of his son's career. He implied that he should have left the graceful, mild-mannered young man behind him in Dublin. George's only flaws were "extravagant habits"—which he himself possessed: money always ran through the open hands of father and son.

John Gregory's marriage to Elizabeth Goadby had been a mistake. Her father had always been her idol. Her rules of highly virtuous, Church of England conduct were too rigorously sustained to allow tolerance of her husband's extravagances, his fits of boredom, his ill-timed Regency jokes—even his apparently inexhaustible reserves of optimism. She felt he lacked the will to protect her—or their three sons, born in the span of four uneasy years.

When her second boy was born, so my grandmother told me, she began to have premonitions of disaster. To her horror, the baby had red hair. With the child in her arms, she marched into her husband's presence. "Mr. Gregory," she said—she always addressed him formally when out of temper—"what's the matter with this child? No one in my family ever had red hair!"

"I did, my dear," said he, with a smile, and a bow from the waist, "I am one of the red MacGregors!" In telling me this tale, the memory of an ancient wrong came over her and she stamped her foot in anger—"His hair was *white* when I married him!"

I also gathered from her, as well as from my reticent father, that there had been trouble over giving the red-haired baby a name: she had insisted upon "Blaine," and he upon "Bulwer Lytton," for he claimed that Bulwer-Lytton had been one of his cherished friends. Certainly Bulwer Lytton Gregory had a magnificent ring, but he and his name disappeared from family memory. (When I was fifteen, and rummaging through family keepsakes, I found a yellowed clipping from a St. Louis newspaper—to the effect that Bulwer Lytton Gregory was on a lecture tour of the country entertaining large audiences with anecdotes of his father's friendship with the noted novelist.)

Elizabeth Goadby's sense of coming misfortunes was a truthful portent of events. When her young stepmother shipped Dr. Goadby, an angry, speechless victim of a stroke, from Ann Arbor to Milwaukee, to be cared for by his daughter, John Gregory raised a beautifully shaped white hand to put on his hat, and left the house. He did not return, for the modest house had grown too small to accommodate an overburdened wife, himself, three active boys, and the enormity of his father-in-law's disaster. In any case, he had had enough of domesticity.

Dr. Goadby was not a passive invalid. My father remembered him as a violent old man, propped up in a chair, with a poker in his right hand raised to strike or lunge at his grandsons who danced in a semi-circle around him, just out of reach. He would stare at them with blood-shot, bewildered eyes.

My grandmother countered my grandfather's desertion of the home by forbidding him ever to reenter the house or to have any contact with the boys—the implication being that his very presence would contaminate them. My father recalls that one May morning, when my grandmother had gone out on an errand and the little house, set in the middle of a small orchard was suddenly fragrant with spring, he turned to see his father's face smiling in at him through an open window. The old gentleman solemnly raised his hat—which had been tilted at a jaunty angle—in salutation to his invalid father-in-law seated across the room, and then requested the boys to hand him the fire tongs, between the blackened grips of which he thrust a roll of money. As he extended the bills to them, he informed the boys that the money was for household expenses, and cautioned them, in a jovial voice tinged with irony, to remind their mother that he had not so much as shaken their hands. Then he again raised his tall hat, and vanished.

For about twelve years John Gregory was to his family scarcely more than a cheerful apparition. And his appearances were always timed to fit the hour his wife was away from the house, and never longer than the few minutes required to thrust a roll of money at the tong's length into the hands of the boys. It was eventually learned that my grandfather had built a fine, big, three-story house for himself at 717 Jefferson Street, and that the orchard house was now in the sole possession of his wife.

Fortunately, Dr. Goadby's martyrdom was not long sustained. Within a year or two he was dead, and his courageous daughter, still struggling to free herself from her husband's patronage, his smiles, his blandishments, his sometimes generous, but always irregular gifts of money, decided to take a teaching job in a local public school. Although her salary was piteously small, she was declaring her independence, and her right to bring up her sons as she saw fit. She increased her income by working late at night, translating short stories from the French for the feature section of a daily paper—and it is through her nocturnal efforts that Milwaukee readers were among the first in America to enjoy Turgenev's *Sportsman's Sketches*.

The Elizabeth Goadby Gregory who was my mother's protector, teacher, and guide had acquired great skills in defeating such upstart opponents as my Aunt Victoria. It is highly probable that her distrust of John Gregory's smiling flow of talk and masculine nonchalance had stiffened her adherence to a particularly hardened brand of Victorian feminism. She worshipped Queen Victoria with the same idolatry that her husband had for Robert Emmet, Lord Monteagle, the Duke of Devonshire, and Bulwer-Lytton. She retained in her library bound volumes of *The Youth's Magazine, or Evangelical Miscellany*—where I first read a few of Wordsworth's and Southey's shorter poems—*Chambers's Miscellany*—with its brightly colored cardboard covers, and its glowing brief biographies of Rembrandt and George Washington—Maria Edgeworth's *The Parent's Assistant: or Stories for Children* and Thomas Day's *The History of Sandford and Merton*. To these classics of Regency and early Victorian childhood, she had added one of Queen Victoria's great favorites, the many-volumed *The Lives of the Queens of England* by the sisters Strickland, who, when they visited Oxford, were greeted by hordes of undergraduates chanting, "The queens, the queens, the queens!"

Exiled as my grandmother was to a little Germanic city in the American Middle West, whenever she stepped out-of-doors, she defiantly reaffirmed the universality of London's rainy climate in her dress. However fair and dry the weather, however hot the sun shone down, her feet were encased in rubber overshoes, her right hand gripped an umbrella—and from her left wrist swung a waterproofed reticule. Her bonnets, trimmed with violets, her black shawls and dresses, her many-tiered petticoats, were chosen in imitation of the Queen's wardrobe. For she, too, was a small woman, inclined to portliness—and as she grew older, her resemblance to photographs of Victoria Regina was too marked to be ignored. Dressed in black, she wore the hardships and wreckage of her marriage with something of the same pride and dignity that her Queen wore her widow's weeds. If, during an exchange of conversation—in a parlor, or at the dining table—an English place name floated to the surface of the talk, she would occasionally break into tears, and a pause of embarrassed silence would be banished by the swift, apologetic smile that crossed her tear-stained face.

When I was first taken to visit her, she lived five doors to the right of 717 Jefferson Street in a gray clapboard cottage that her husband had willed to her. Settled here, in comparative security, on an income supplied by my father and my uncle, she cultivated a Victorian variety of interests. Her long devotion to pencil-sketching had given way to a passion for photography, which then made necessary an esoteric knowledge of how to perform wonders in a darkroom as well as the art of hypnotizing relatives who had promised not to move while sitting for a portrait. Like Maud Smalley's, her voice carried authority. Her own large camera, with its long-legged tripod, was supplemented by a portable Kodak carried in her reticule whenever she walked abroad.

Another of her delights was the collecting of rare botanical specimens, plants of all nations and climates, and they pullulated, creeping and climbing, pinkish, or white, green, yellow, and brown, rising out of water-filled plates, and saucers, and earthen jars set near the windows of her overheated five room tropical grotto, and her living room was shaded by vines, trained to mount its walls, and guided by stretches of white twine. From behind a spray of ferns, and above their tallest

[*33*]

fronds, came the trill of a canary, swaying on his perch, in a brass wire cage. Through the rooms there was the combined smell of mold, damp earth, newly brewed green tea, coal gas— and slightly fermenting strawberry jam—the jam stored away in the locked kneehole cubicle of a mahogany Chippendale desk that had once belonged to Dr. Goadby's mother. On top of a round, isinglassed, coal-burning stove, stood a teapot, heated, and perpetually at hand—while a cup and saucer waited on a nearby table, next to a half-loaf of bread, and a quarter pound of cheese.

With the serene conviction that the sun never set on the limitless reaches of Victoria's Empire, Elizabeth Goadby, probably influenced by her childhood readings in *Line upon Line* as well as in numbers of *Evangelical Miscellanies*, cited events in Biblical history as though they referred to scenes that had taken place between the warring natives of a British colony. Her air was magnanimous; her interests were so wide-spread that the little pioneer city of her exile had become a mere pinpoint on the map. Not unlike her Queen, she approved of Disraeli; she assured her grandchildren that his people were the remarkable tribe of the Bible—and that knowledge of their customs was an important feature of a child's education. During March and April she would illustrate the solemnity of the Passover Feast by serving large squares of matzoth with unsweetened, creamless tea. This was her manner of "Sunday School" instruction, and it was both colorful and effective.

With equal persuasiveness she would quote episodes (not without her sudden nostalgic tears) from Macaulay's *History of England*, and so eloquent was she in her praise (which by the way was in direct political contradiction to her fondness for the pro-Stuart *The Lives of the Queens of England*) that she inspired my mother with enthusiasm for his writings. My mother memorized whole pages of his *History*, and during the latter months that she awaited my birth, she transcribed the greater part of his collected works.

During her long exile till her death at ninety-four, my grandmother kept herself to herself and made few friends. In her general mistrust of people around her she made two exceptions: one was my mother, and the other was a shy, Protestant-Irish spinster, a Miss Henrietta Bolton, whose brother had been a close friend of my grandmother's brother. (Rumors were that the two men had become cotton brokers in New Orleans, and during the Civil War, had been officers in the Confederate Army.) And in her genial art of shying away from her neighbors, in "the making of her own bed and lying in it," in her habit of drinking countless cups of Irish kitchen tea—instead of coffee such as Germans drank around her—Miss Henrietta could well have passed for my grandmother's sister. Miss Henrietta had been my father's godmother, and whenever she announced this fact to one of his children, her thin shoulders straightened, and her very blue eyes took on a visionary stare, as though she had just received a special award of merit. This was followed by the brightest of her smiles, and one was suddenly aware that there was the faintest, most delicate touch of burlesque in her manner.

I remember her youthful figure as being perpetually dressed in gray: in spring, gray tailored suits; in summer, gray dotted Swiss tea-dresses. She had the gift, though not the means, of looking stylishly turned out. She wore her wide and stiff-brimmed sailor hats tilted at a smart, yet modest angle. In summer, I was often invited to tea in the front parlor of her little house, around the corner from Jefferson Street, a few steps from my grandmother's. On those occasions, it always seemed my grandmother did the talking, and, at appropriate intervals, Miss Henrietta would swiftly nod her head, then sit at attention again, as though my grandmother were the sibyl at Delphi.

It was rumored that Miss Henrietta's small income came from a rarely visible nephew who wore long yellow hair and lived in a distant city. Then—and to me, without warning—Miss Henrietta disappeared. My grandmother, however questioned, refused to discuss her absence.

At last, my father drew me aside: a month ago, a delivery boy had knocked at Miss Henrietta's front door, and as it opened, he received a stream of obscene language in his face. The police were called, and Miss Henrietta, still screaming and enraged, was committed to an asylum on the outskirts of the city. It was not unlikely that my grandmother visited her in her new home—and it was probably for loyalty's sake that she never spoke of Miss Henrietta again. Virginal Henrietta! Her fate was that of Wordsworth's sister, Dorothy, whose old age was darkened by the same affliction, and a sense of loss was felt, as though there were a fall of brightness from the air.

So far my memory carries me. The years between 1903 and 1910 are in a haze of distance and datelessness—or is that haze a premonition of eternity? I find it impossible to impose upon them a true order of chronology. I heard rumors of my father's small business prospering, and on a Sunday morning when I accompanied him to his office—for in the many years of his long life, he would visit the office on Sunday for an hour or two to look at the bookkeeping and to feed a family of cats he had stationed there, I heard of a great San Francisco earthquake. In much the same fashion, I overheard my father speak to a friend of the Panic of 1907, and how fortunately his business had weathered it. I remember scraps of conversation about a social democratic party, and of Victor L. Berger, who founded it, and of Emil Seidel, a bland-faced, spectacled man, loved by the city's German population; there was also David Rose, a Democratic mayor of the city, a less dangerous reformer than the others because he was a great ladies' man, and encouraged a flourishing theater-bath-house-red-light district.

One summer Sunday afternoon, I was carried in my father's arms to meet David Rose, a spruce, yellow-gloved, robin-breasted little man with graying red hair, culminating in a red mustache and goatee. The occasion was the unveiling of a bronze monument to Robert Burns in a small city park where my Uncle John had been invited to declaim a piece of verse he had written in memory of the Scottish bard. The day fell furiously hot, out of a dazzling whitish blue sky, and the usual breezes from Lake Michigan refused to blow. Under the stilled trees of the park about a hundred middle-aged people, mostly women armed with parasols and paper fans, sat on iron benches. My uncle mounted a small, bunting-draped platform—it looked none too steady—and with a very red face, began to read his verse. Whether the poem was good or bad I can't say, but it seemed endless, and my uncle's voice rose in emotional violence as the reading went on. My father began to whisper, "Poor John, poor John"—then, suddenly, tears streaming down his face, my uncle stopped, bowed from the waist—and the audience, taken by surprise, gave him several rounds of applause. During the applause, he had vanished from the platform; the mayor took over with a few cooling platitudes; cut the silk cord that had held the shrouds of the statue in place, and revealed the latest gift of liberal-minded German millionaires to a grateful city.

Although, between ourselves, my father and I affected embarrassment at my uncle's performance, we were secretly proud of his public accomplishments. After all, he still represented a connection of the Gregorys with civic virtues as well as with (through his editorial page) the world outside the city. This pride was, of course, a family weakness, for it had a trick of exaggerating our claims to importance, and inflating our sense of superiority to our neighbors. It encouraged my Aunt Victoria to patronize almost everyone she met, and my father to regard the majority of his business associates as "mere tradesmen."

Of the great world outside of Milwaukee, I picked up fragments of information from several sources. Heated discussions between my uncle and father were the first of these; the second was the pages of *The New York Evening Sun*, and *The Boston Evening Transcript*, that were always to be found on my uncle's study table. Still other sources were *St. Nicholas* (where Elizabeth won prizes for her verse, submitted to "The St. Nicholas League" columns), and old stacks of *The Strand Magazine* and *The Pall Mall Magazine*, both from London, and the *Ladies' Home Journal* in the attic. According to my uncle and father, who were Republicans of the old school, Democrats were dangerous animals, but more dangerous than these night-roving creatures, were the renegades, Theodore Roosevelt and Robert M. La Follette, who posed as Republicans, but were actually Progressives. They were far worse than Berger and Seidel, who were out-and-out Socialists—at least you knew where they stood, with their talk about Marx and Henry George, and because they were Germans, they were not likely to let their ideas run away with a sense of practicality.

In spite of my father's opinions, Roosevelt had become my hero. I had read Richard Harding Davis's account of how Roosevelt and his Rough Riders had charged at San Juan Hill. I had read Roosevelt's own *African Game Trails* with passion and admiration. On rainy days in the attic, I had followed my hero's career in The White House by reading a column he dictated once a month—while shaving—to Edward Bok, an editor of the Curtis Publications, for the *Ladies' Home Journal*. Lying flat on my stomach, with aging back numbers of the magazine spread open on the floor, I read Roosevelt's exhortations to American womanhood. So far as I know, he was among the first to take full advantage of the idea that Americans lived and prospered within the voluminous, loosely woven bonds of a matriarchy, and to this authority, he made a direct appeal. To women he talked of the need for forest conservation, of our grave responsibilities as a first-class world power, and of our need to increase the birthrate of this country. To young women (and here the image of a Gibson girl, chaste, yet large breasted and wide hipped, would flash through my mind), he spoke out loudly against the evils of "race suicide."

These weighty topics often baffled, yet excited me, for I had come to the tenuous conclusion that "race suicide" had some connection with "white slave traffic," a subject illustrated by photographs of girls in near-undress in the feature sections of the Hearst Sunday papers. The difficulty was that all such warnings of social harms were never explicit—or clear enough through the smoke of their heated rhetoric to tell me of things I wished to learn. Roughly I pieced together what I read of "race suicide" and the "white slave traffic" with information I tried to assemble from Darwin's *On the Origin of Species*— which, at nine, was extremely heavy and prolix reading. I traced—not without moments of turgid distaste and fear— embryonic evolution from the tadpole to the child in its mother's womb. My labors were sustained by two compulsive forces: one was, of course, sexual curiosity; the other was pride. Since I was a great-grandson of the entomologist, Dr. Goadby, I could not admit myself defeated by Darwin's text. With a dictionary at my side, I plunged onward. What emerged at last was a confused array of graphic images loosely attached to abstract conclusions. Since I was house-bound by uncertain health, there were no boys of my own age I could question, and I did not dare to speak of what I had mislearned to my parents, or even my elder half brother, Johnny. I was left mystified and wordless.

The nearest approach to solving the mystery (which remained unsolved for many years) came from a very different quarter. This was on several of the afternoons during a long, sultry summer that my Cousin Elizabeth joined me on rainy day visits to our attic. There was always an air of secrecy surrounding her ascent with me to the top of the house.

My Aunt Victoria had decided to prohibit her young daughter's use of slang, and for that reason she forbade Elizabeth the reading of the garishly colored comic sections that came with Sunday editions of the newspapers. This happened at a time when my cousin had become almost tearfully concerned with the week-to-week misadventures of Happy Hooligan. Happy was a character after Elizabeth's own heart: he was so deeply inept, guileless, and generous that he inevitably fell victim to the violence of the world. Wrapped in gauze bandage from foot to neck, he could still offer words of hope for his sympathetic readers: "Cheer up! The worst is yet to come!" Each Monday, I carefully refolded the comic section of yesterday's paper and stored it in a box in the attic. Elizabeth had, of course (since I had told her), full knowledge of the riches of my attic library. She decided it would not do to disobey the letter of her mother's commandment: she would, therefore, never look at a comic sheet again. Yet she could permit me to tell her—in exact detail—what Happy Hooligan's latest adventures were.

Quietly, we climbed the attic stairs, Elizabeth helping me up the top high step. The attic was dusty, stuffy, and hot, and her face was pink with the exertion of the climb. We moved toward a dormer window, and as I seated myself on a large cushion, I saw that she was serenely removing her clothes: her feet and legs were already bare—with a swift gesture, she stepped out of her drawers, and then calmly lifted her dress over her head, and off. She sat down opposite me and smiled; her pale body seemed to glow with light in the dusty air. To look at her filled me with wordless pleasure and excitement; I thought she looked extraordinarily beautiful, and I was far from being unmoved by the delightful naughtiness of her act. She then folded her legs under her, and told me to tell her all about Happy Hooligan. And while I recited his latest disasters, she seemed to radiate coolness and ease. As soon as I reached the end of the week's installment, and without the least coyness, or embarrassment, she lightly slipped on her clothes again, stood up, and was suddenly impatient to rush downstairs. She would have to hurry, for she feared her mother would wonder where she was, and would begin to look for her.

On one of the last of these attic visits, as she seated herself contentedly before me, she offered the information that we could never marry—for we were cousins. She had investigated this point carefully, she said, and though, in the attic, we never joined hands or kissed, we were slightly saddened at the prospect of being forever separated.

It was not until I went to school some half-dozen years later that I learned more of the biological facts that had eluded me. When asked questions by elders who might have enlightened me, I foolishly pretended I understood what I had read in Darwin's writings—which was, of course, half self-deception.

Meanwhile, my admiration of Theodore Roosevelt continued. I had heard that in his boyhood he had been unusually frail, that he had made himself fit by ignoring his handicaps, even to hiring ex-prizefighters to teach him how to box. I also learned that in addition to his skill in the making of phrases, he had an eye and ear for poetry—rare qualities in an American President! Much was made of his friendship, however casual, with Edwin Arlington Robinson, an intractable poet, vastly unknown when Roosevelt discovered him, and difficult to befriend. Against the advice of professional poetry critics, Roosevelt became a champion of Robinson's books of poems.

Roosevelt's patronage lifted the poet from the extremes of poverty and obscurity to public notice, and for a brief time he persuaded Robinson to accept the sinecure of a minor post in the United States Custom House, and when the poet's ethical scruples—since he felt himself a burden on the taxpayer—forced his resignation, the President respected his decision. In his relationship to Robinson, Roosevelt's conduct was Jeffersonian; as I was to realize later, he belonged to a tradition that had its beginnings in Thomas Jefferson, the man in high office, who was also one of worldly culture, an aristocrat and a liberal.

My boyhood worship of Roosevelt took still another turning; it tilted me, I think, away from the joys of Barnum and Bailey's Circus to the more exotic pleasures of going to Buffalo Bill's Wild West Show. Colonel Cody's more dandified image had become superimposed upon that of the roughriding Roosevelt, and was all the more compelling because it was visible in the flesh. Cody's graceful figure, his expertly tailored deerskin suit, his tanned face, long white hair, mustache, and goatee had magical qualities, and when he shook hands with small boys (including myself) in his audience, he had the manner of an accomplished actor. His elegant postures were in direct contrast to the stained backdrops of the tent behind him, his tawdry bareback riding girls, his troupe of ragged, dusty Indian boys who were the supernumeraries of the show. I saw little of the frontier-plainsman-Indian-fighter in Cody; every flourish of his horsemanship carried with it an aristocratic aura. And this enhanced his attraction for me.

Almost fifty years later, when I visited Rome, and was wandering near the Spanish Steps—that famous haunt of tourists—I dropped into Greco's Coffee House. On its walls, lined up with pictures of former patrons (including John Keats and Mark Twain), were signed and framed photographs of Colonel Cody. There he was, in his deerskin jacket, looking as smart and gay as I remembered him, standing in an ill-swept sawdust ring. Alongside of the photographs were yellowed and framed newspaper clippings telling how brilliantly he had conquered Roman society. A few hours later while dining with Prince Caetani, I spoke to him of my amusement at encountering Buffalo Bill in a Roman café. The Prince, an octogenarian, who still dressed in a high Edwardian fashion—as though he had stepped out of a portrait by Sargent—suddenly beamed at me. "Ah, yes," he said, "a magnificent fellow, Colonel Cody—he knew a horse when he saw one! He taught me, and a crowd of us boys, how to ride bareback up and down the Corso!"

Perhaps my early liking for entertainment beyond the resources of the circus and the zoo, was also conditioned by the kindness of my mother's brother, my Uncle George, who worked in the offices of a farm machinery plant. From the age of six until I was twelve, my Uncle George would take me (at first, literally carry me) to a Saturday matinee each week. As I remember them most of these were "girlie shows" or musicals, George M. Cohan productions, and such popular road shows as *The Wizard of Oz* and *Babes in Toyland*. In the company of this kind of fare, *The Chocolate Soldier* was a work of deep and mysterious probity. Good, bad, noisy or shrill, deep or shallow, I saw and heard them all as they trouped by on their traveling circuits. On these Saturday afternoons, the spirit of holiday prevailed.

It was my Uncle George, a bachelor of course, who provided the holiday. He had startlingly black hair, and round, dark brown, childlike eyes, full lips, and a long hooked nose; close shaven as he was, his chin and jaw showed hint of a deep blue shadow beneath the skin. His gestures and the innocent expression of his eyes gave him a serio-comic-melancholy air. His straw boater—or in winter and fall, his derby—was tilted to the left side of his head. I seem to remember him best during intermissions of the show, in the lobby of the theater,

[*43*]

flourishing his frequently relit, long cigar, and urging me to drink up my lemonade. From his pockets he would produce, as if by the grace of everlasting boyhood, bags of hot popcorn and peanuts, and boxes of Cracker Jack. On these occasions, he was Bounty itself, confiding to me that he always smoked big cigars, because smoking cigarettes looked *cheap*. He was unconcerned about money and his most endearing trait was his ability to live completely within the present. For him, tomorrows did not exist—all the world had become a stage where endless chorus lines of girls tripped and swayed to the tinny blare of "Alexander's Ragtime Band."

Though these entertainments delighted me, and I was grateful for his kindness to a very young nephew, as I traveled through the city on his shoulder, and later, at his side, I began to learn that there were other kinds of theater. I was greatly attracted by huge gaudy posters plastered on the sides of buildings showing girls and fair-haired young men in wild distress—heroes and heroines roped to railroad tracks, or to conveyer belts under whirring buzz saws—black-haired villains in top hats were also in the picture. There were posters of scantily clad, barelegged girls, clutching naked children, "turned adrift" into a snow storm, or of ruddy-faced, yellow-whiskered British tars clasping hands. I remember such titles as *Hearts of Oak*, *Never Too Late to Mend*, and *Orphans of the Storm*, in large letters across the top of the posters. By a show of interest in what the posters promised, I hinted that George take me to see the plays they advertised. With equal gentleness, and tactful evasion, he replied that my tastes were morbid, and that watching girls toss their legs in the air was healthful exercise. He clinched his argument by reminding me that the shows we saw never played to a cold or empty house.

Then as well as later, the theater had become a special and often hidden source of inspiration for me. Though poetry touched my emotions in a more direct manner, the theater gave me the sense of living in a world that was more orderly and less precarious than the one that I encountered in my everyday existence. In the make-believe world of the theater, my physical disabilities vanished, and my repressed thoughts and gestures found dramatic and eloquent expression.

My Uncle George's refusal to indulge me in a taste for melodrama had results in future action. For me, at least, it was a turning point—and I was approaching seven—in my theatrical affairs. I was thrown upon my own resources of invention: from a single episode, so brightly lithographed in a big poster, I was forced to reconstruct a three-act play. Since my hands were not steady enough to control a pencil, I had to carry the scenario and lines of the play in my head, till I found occasion to direct the action and recite the speeches of its characters. My actors were the wooden, slightly mobile, puppets of a Germanic-looking "Humpty-Dumpty Circus," and their stage was the green-carpeted floor of my nursery-bedroom. It was I who moved them into each other's arms, who intoned their controversies in courtroom scenes, I who whispered the dying words of a blue-eyed heroine—who though given up for lost, would spring up to life again. The moment anyone stepped into my room—even Cousin Elizabeth—the play would cease. It was as though a curtain had actually dropped to the floor, yet one that rose again a few seconds after my visitor would leave me, for I was sole audience as well as the entire dramatis personae—the phrase "dramatis personae" I had proudly acquired from my Aunt Victoria.

These performances, inspired by the sight of a new poster each Saturday, usually ran the length of an afternoon. Except from the intelligence of my mother's youngest sister, Martha, they were kept secret from all members of my family, for Martha often brought me a graham cracker and a glass of milk at four in the afternoon. Of my relations, Martha alone

[45]

held my profoundest trust: she, I knew, would never betray me by laughing at my oddities, for she, herself, was slightly out of the world of everyday affairs and grown-up people. Martha was short and thin, scarcely taller than an eleven-year-old child, and, as if to stress her difference from other young women of her generation, she wore a pair of gold-rimmed deep blue spectacles, which made strangers think she had gone blind.

Whenever she took me out for a short walk, she held my arm and hand with exquisite tact, as though I provided her with wide-seeing eyes, while she, with her straight, up-and-down posture, gave me a model of steadiness and lightness in learning how to walk. This exchange of protectiveness was at the root of our long-sustained friendship, and throughout my early boyhood she was my single confidante. At our house, she was a frequent afternoon visitor, and on days when my mother stepped out, Martha would stay with me till dinner time.

My visits to her flat were far less frequent, for her rooms were at the top of a steep, highly polished flight of stairs. There were curious details of her house-furnishings that held fascination for me. One was a framed lithograph of Holman Hunt's *The Light of the World,* which dimly loomed through the shadows cast by an art nouveau lamp. To me, the literal-mindedness of Hunt's Christ with a lantern—like the image of a railway brakeman—was a kind of torture. It had the perversity of making me feel anti-religious and depressed. And because the reasons for my feelings were obscure, my discomfort increased as I gazed at it. Other curiosities on her walls were verse and mottoes burnt into or painted in glowing red on wood, or printed on thick paper; lines such as "The Moving Finger writes; and, having writ . . ." illustrated by Elihu Vedder's faceless, hooded figures and convoluted draperies, glazed and framed, became the objects of my youthful skepticism. As I read and reread Kipling's "If" behind glass, his demands became increasingly unreal, and I, "a good child," according to my parents, was filled with impulses, however vague, to go astray. In my eyes, "A man's a man for a' that," burnt into wood, became a wild non sequitur, and though I liked Burns's songs, I could make nothing of it. Why was it, I asked myself, that hand-sewn cross-stitched mottoes in farm houses I visited with my mother during summer vacations inspired less disrespect? The question was too complex, too large for me to answer.

Though my visits to Martha's flat filled me with doubts, I accepted her differences in taste from mine as the superficial realities they were, and I associated them, not with our friendship, but with the city where we lived—particularly, her neighborhood, less prosperous in appearance than mine. In this respect, my instincts were related to my general feeling that the house on Jefferson Street did not *belong* in Milwaukee at all, that it was a family fortress whose brick façade was a bulwark raised against its own environment.

In my eyes, Milwaukee was, the more I saw of it, a foreign city. I had been told that its German newspaper had an increasing number of readers. This conviction was borne out during my summer Sunday-morning airings through the city, along Lake Michigan to Whitefish Bay. My father, my mother, and I, traveled in a modest "buggy," behind a slow-moving chestnut mare called "Bessie"—who was the quietest, most even-tempered animal I had ever met. (My father had become so fond of her, he refused to buy a car until her death.) These weekly drives, prescribed by a doctor because of my failing health, gave me a detached, yet leisurely view of my native grounds and their surroundings. How German the city looked! In front of the public library stood a dark green bronze statue of George Washington, looking slightly threatening and distinctly Teutonic in feature. Along the drive eastward to the north rose high stone castles, imported, I was told, stone by stone, from the Rhine to provide shelter for German brewery millionaires and their families, nursemaids, gardeners, cooks, and chauffeurs. If one looked down, and into the distance, surely enough, on the white beaches, one saw children and nursemaids, small and animate as tiny mechanical toys, "Made in Germany," playing near the waves.

Our destination was an open-air restaurant set on grass terraces leading down to the lake. White-jacketed waiters mounted and descended the terraces, carrying aloft trays weighted with large glass mugs of overflowing beer. Sousa's marches poured from a rollicking, sun-glittering brass band, and the blue waters of the lake seemed transformed into the waves of the River Rhine that I had seen in pictures in German beer saloons where, on rare occasions, my father had carried me, he to drink two fingers of whiskey, and I, a tall, frosted glass of lemonade. At Whitefish Bay the treat was, not lemonade, but fresh from the lake and the broiler, browned and smoking on a white pine plank, the whitefish. Though the open air had been prescribed to stir my appetite, the sight of food—even the whitefish—made me feel faint and remote. Only the breeze from the lake seemed refreshing. From the haze surrounding me, punctuated by sounds of the band, and shouts of waiters, I heard German gutturals and expletives.

No matter how often my father took me for rides behind the ambling flanks of Bessie—for she never achieved a trot, but something close to a ladylike lope—I could not shake off my curious lassitude. A climax of sorts was reached while on a visit to my grandmother's cottage on Jefferson Street. Quite without warning I fell to the floor of her parlor in a deep faint. When I came to, I found myself on a sofa in the rear of the room, my mother leaning over me. Through the rest of summer, through the fall and into mid-December, I was watched over carefully: someone, usually my mother, or Martha, was always near me, always within call of my nursery-bedroom, where I would be inventing new plays for my actors. Then suddenly, I was very ill, and moved to my mother's and father's double bed—or was this an illusion of my illness? The very walls seemed to vanish in blackness, then reappear. Just beneath the surface of my sleep, I heard, as though it were far distant thunder, the sound of voices, and a word or two: . . . appendicitis . . . his temperature has dropped to zero . . . peritonitis. . . . Then unearthly quiet. I could feel myself being carried downstairs into blackness. I was in something that moved. This must have been a primitive motor ambulance that hurt me fearfully with the noise of chains that clanked around me. Again a voice. It was my father's; he had crowded himself into the narrow spaces above me and at my sides, and seemed to be hanging on by his hands and knees. He was pleading with me to live, to survive the moment of the threat of death, telling me that I could not fail him.

I then half-remembered that I had been told how he had saved my life a few seconds after I was born, how he put his lips to mine and breathed life into me, then kept me alive by feeding me patented foods with a medicine dropper. Now, he had renewed his efforts: I was willed to live. A wave of darkest sleep came over me.

2

Wellspring: Youth

M Y STAY AT the hospital and my six-month recovery at home were like the reenactment of a death and slow rebirth. It was important that I resume the lengthy process of learning how to walk. This did not worry me as much as it did my elders, for I was sure that I could not fail in doing so, and I welcomed everything I saw around me with new eyes. I felt taller and more at ease, as though I had put merely childish things behind me. I had outgrown most of my toys, and stuffed animals, dolls, and building blocks were left to collect dust on the white enameled shelf that ran as a ledge across and around the green walls of my room. I deserted my room for the family library where, from time to time, I overheard whispered references to the problem of my education.

What now seemed many ages ago, I had been taught by my mother how to read, and her method, so it seemed to me at least, was a lively and ingenious one. Since she loved reading poems aloud, she recited them, and taught me by my repeating each line of verse after her until I had memorized it. When I had memorized the poem, I was asked to "read" the poem from the book she handed me. Seated on her lap or at her side, I learned by both of us reading the same page together, and after poems were read, together, we would attempt a page or two of prose. My first lesson consisted of the last nine lines of William Cullen Bryant's "Thanatopsis." Since she was young, death had no immediate terrors for her, and I can only suppose that a youthful love of sententious rhetoric on the subject of a peaceful death guided her choice. Certainly, I was neither moved nor frightened by it. When I came to "Like one who wraps the drapery of his couch/About him," I amused myself by conjuring up the image of a stout Arabian settling in for an afternoon nap. And I believe that this Oriental touch had been suggested by the image of a "quarry-slave at night/Scourged to his dungeon," for I had heard that Turks captured Christians and made slaves of them. All this was, of course, far away from anything Bryant had intended.

From Bryant, we went on to Whittier and Longfellow—and because of his shorter pieces, Longfellow held my mother's deepest affections. Though conscious of the fact that "The Village Blacksmith" had been recited several thousands of times too often, she enjoyed its music, and she was utterly charmed by his "Maidenhood." "Maidenhood," as I saw it in the illustrated edition of Longfellow we read together, was accompanied by a line cut of a barefooted, lightly dressed, possibly blushing, little country girl about to cross a stream, "Standing, with reluctant feet/Where the brook and river meet," a sensuous vision, not too far, I think, from that in Longfellow's imagination. I immediately associated the picture with my mother, a portrait of her before she came to the city and married my father. Even in this somewhat sentimental, abstracted piece of verse, its music had a touch of Longfellow's magic, his light, almost effeminate awareness of the mysteries of life, which has given the best of his poetry to immortality. If I was too young to realize all of this then, instinctively, I responded to the magic of his sensuous rhythms.

After a few months of reading verse together, my mother expanded my efforts by applying the same technique to *David Copperfield:* that is, she would read aloud while my eyes would keep step by following the printed words on the page. The memorizing of verse had given me enough of a vocabulary to increase my speed in reading prose: soon, I took the book from her hands and began reading it aloud to her. We were both delighted.

She also applied a rhythm to the teaching of arithmetic, and taught me the singsong of the multiplication table as well as a series of subtractions. Unfortunately, as I was soon to discover, she failed to make clear to me certain practical consequences of those exercises, and I was never able to associate the Arabic numerals with money. "Mental arithmetic," the kind used in the rapid making of change, was far beyond whatever skills I possessed. Rapid subtractions from dollars, quarters, and dimes confused and annoyed me. In my distraction, and sense of failure, I was willing to toss money out of the window, or give it away to anyone who took responsibility for it. Moreover, I was all too well aware that these impulses were unheroic. Yet I could neither explain nor defend them. To be unheroic was a loss of prestige in my own eyes, therefore, I avoided as best I could, all trials and uses of "mental arithmetic." To make up for this deficiency, I became a perfectionist in my recitals of the multiplication table.

During my long convalescence, my reading expanded at a tremendous rate. Starting early on Sunday morning in bed, and inspired by my Aunt Victoria's gift of the Temple edition of Shakespeare—intimate little volumes, bound in flexible red imitation leather, easy to hold, pretty to look on—my week began. Quite unaware that my Temple edition of *A*

Midsummer-Night's Dream was a predigested, bowdlerized version of the play, I was wholly caught up within it, and the coverlet of my bed assumed the contours of Shakespeare's enchanted forest. On those Sundays when my half sister, Florence, decided she could not take me to services at St. James's, the slender, high-vaulted Episcopal Church we attended, I would stay abed to reread *A Midsummer-Night's Dream, Julius Caesar,* or Shakespeare's *Sonnets.* The delight and freshness of these Sundays is always associated in my memory with the early morning light, and the poplar tree outside my window, fluttering its leaves from green to silver. Sometimes, before the household had awakened, I would fall asleep again over my book and the music of the plays and sonnets would echo mysteriously in my dreams.

The rest of the week I devoted to other poets: evenings, and sometimes nights till midnight, were given over to Dickens, Thackeray, and the historical novels of G. A. Henty and Sir Walter Scott. To anyone watching me, the shapes of my wide readings must have seemed amorphous, and certainly undisciplined, for within forty-eight hours I would shift from George Eliot's *The Mill on the Floss* to Kipling's *Stalky & Co.* Yet reading did not occupy all my time. Secretly, I wrote fragments of verse on scraps of paper, which I then concealed under the blotter on my desk. Undoubtedly my furtiveness was due to my reluctance to expose these outpourings to the hard light of adult criticism, and when my mother eventually did discover them, I only gave her my permission to collect them and to store them away in a cardboard box—on the topmost shelf of my closet—after she had solemnly promised not to read them.

My Aunt Victoria did not need to be told that I was writing verse: she simply assumed as much—just as she had assumed that my parents would accept the propriety of her choosing a name for me. Certainly she must have known of my interest in poetry, for she and my uncle gave me a leather-bound Keats, a volume of Landor's love lyrics (which I read at odd moments everywhere, for it was compact enough to carry in a pocket), and the selected poems of Swinburne.

About this same time I discovered *The Adventures of Huckleberry Finn.* The book was a gift from my father, for he had heard that a committee, representing the women's clubs of the Middle West, had had the book removed from circulation in public and school libraries, and were attempting to suppress its sale in bookstores throughout the Middle Western states. However conservative my father's convictions were, he opposed all forms of literary censorship. The rhythms of Huck Finn's narrations carried me close to the shores of poetry—closer, I thought, in pulse-beat and feeling, than had the more weighted movements of Whitman's *Leaves of Grass.* I had to confess, if only to myself, that too many acres of *Leaves of Grass* induced me to fall asleep. Aside from his great elegy, "When lilacs last in the dooryard bloomed," I found most of Whitman boring and unmemorable. Even more unhappily, I found the other writings by Mark Twain a disappointment.

Forty years later, over lunch with T. S. Eliot in a New York restaurant, I heard that prohibition of *The Adventures of Huckleberry Finn* extended from Milwaukee to St. Louis. With a wistful gaze from his brown eyes, he told me how much he regretted having to wait till middle age to enjoy the book; both he and his elder brother, Henry, had been forbidden to read it. Recently he learned that Henry had disobeyed their mother, and thought that he had too—and spoke highly of the book to him. T. S. then remarked: "If only I had read it when I was young. Now I read it as a critic does."

Though I found pleasure in long days of reading, I began to sense a lack of direction in my learning—as well as a specific need for knowing how to spell. Beneath the outward show of aimlessness, a need to write had taken form within me, and simultaneously awakened a desire to be a graphic artist. I suspect, but of course cannot prove, that the pictures in my Aunt Victoria's front parlor had some bearing on this desire: I wanted to be like Whistler and Delacroix, both artists, as I somehow discovered, who had written books; and if I failed in that ambition, I would try to accept, with the best grace I could, the place of Thackeray, whose role as a writer obviously dominated his talents as an artist. No one I knew had ambitions quite like mine; in having them, I felt unique, lonely, both superior and freakish—and inarticulate. I wanted to paint the best of pictures and write the best of poems.

My first sight of a poet proved to be a disillusionment. He was James Whitcomb Riley—a man with a round face that loomed pale, like a new moon, over a tightly-buttoned black frock coat. He was probably wearied by having read his "child rhymes" several times too often to audiences, such as my mother and I belonged to, of clubwomen and small children. His manner was perfunctory, and to me his Hoosier dialect sounded affected. It was also possible, as rumor had it, that the man was drunk. For it was assumed, and not without reason, that Riley, however well-dressed he may have been for the occasion, had a poet's vices. Anyway, Milwaukee audiences were difficult to please—and I, used to the professional skills of my Uncle George's Saturday afternoon musical comedy matinees, was hypercritical.

But a few years later there were other reasons for my discontent with the performance. Young as I was—I was no more than eleven—I had had the time to have grown weary of hearing his verses recited by, among others, my Uncle John. To me Riley's dialect had become baby talk. I had already struck up an acquaintance with the poems of Keats and Byron, and if I was too young to understand them, I began to realize that these represented poetry of a higher order: to me they were written in the language of true feeling. A few years later, when my Aunt Victoria gave me James Russell Lowell's *Complete Poetical Works*, I discovered that Riley's Hoosier dialect was first cousin to the dialect of "The Biglow Papers," and I was certain that his devices in representing speech were close to being an unctuous fraud. This was the beginning of my later distrust of the "homespun manner" in American verse.

My acquaintanceship with boys in my neighborhood had grown extremely tenuous: I did not share their experiences at school; I could not, because of my physical disabilities, join them in outdoor games. If I so much as hinted to them that I liked poetry and painting, I knew they would dismiss me as a "sissy." Even had I confessed an admiration for Huckleberry Finn—since he was only fictional—I would have been met with the blank stare of ignorance mixed with contempt. They were interested in "real things," like automobiles and sports. With them in mind, I became a close reader of the sporting pages of the local daily paper, and I buttressed this with reading the New York papers in my uncle's study. Within a month or so, I became a small authority on the toughest of the sports—prizefighting. Against this, I balanced a secondhand knowledge of billiards, that most elegant of indoor sports, where the successful trajectory of a ball across the green field of a billiard table held an analogy to art.

Armed with the information I had acquired from the sports pages, I began to voice opinions on the merits of heavyweight champions and their contenders—opinions, which because I voiced them, were met by denials and catcalls. One day, in the face of laughter and mock-solemnity, I announced that Jack Johnson would win the heavyweight title fight, and even offered to support my opinion with a half dollar bet. Johnson was not the favorite, and my wager was readily accepted. Three days later Johnson won the bout—but the boys I bet with refused to pay up, on the grounds that I had them at an unfair advantage because I read so much, and knew about Johnson from out-of-town newspapers. Instead of having won their esteem, I was made to look like a prig, and temporarily I felt like one. After this experience, I no longer attempted to court the friendship of the neighborhood boys, though I continued to read the sports pages for my own amusement.

I did however strike up a slight acquaintanceship with a boy who lived across the city from me, among the millionaires and the newly rich, in a neighborhood only one stage below the best. The Augustus Powerses, as I shall call them, belonged to my parents' weekly bridge club, and Augustus Powers also belonged to that very small company of Catholic-Irish in the city who had become miraculously—and flashily—rich overnight. Augustus was a florid-looking man, with a large, drooping yellow mustache and a deep voice that he used effectively to shout oaths at his employees. He owned and operated a huge foundry. His wife was a thin, dyspeptic little woman from Central Europe, who at any social gathering always sought out the most remote corner of the room, where she seated herself apologetically on the edge of the most uncomfortable chair. Her frail voice trailed into whispers, and her dark hair, piled on her head, seemed ready to fall to her shoulders. Her clothes, usually lacy in texture, dark brown or black, looked as though they had been made for a much larger woman, as did the lavish jewelry she wore, diamond necklaces, rings, and bracelets. It was said her husband bought her dresses and jewels, marched home with them, and then flung them at her, across the bedroom. Weeping, she would then summon a maid to drape the finery over her trembling body. She seemed fearful of everyone, including her five sons and daughter.

To me, the Powers family formed an early, exaggerated, not very flattering picture of what the millionaire rich in the Middle West were like. Later, other impressions were superimposed upon it, modifying my opinions, shifting my prejudices, yet, at its center remains the figure of Joseph Powers, the boy in the family nearest my age, a few years older than I. No matter how unreliable Joseph proved to be, one could never resist his charm, his air of wide-eyed innocence. Our infrequent meetings were surrounded by an atmosphere of the unexpected, for they were usually occasioned by his having been sent home—with special urgency—from one of the many Eastern preparatory schools that had hopefully taken him in charge. He dressed like the juvenile lead in a George M. Cohan musical show: blazer and white flannel trousers, newly cleaned and pressed. He addressed his elders respectfully as "M'am" and "Sir," and in their presence was constantly performing small, courtly acts of politeness—rushing forward to open doors, or moving chairs in their direction. His desire to please seemed inexhaustible, and when he pressed his attentions on his father, the elder Powers's disdainful rejection of them always seemed gratuitous and boorish.

With me as audience, Joseph always had a great deal to say for himself, and in these accounts, his heroism, ingenuity, and daring loomed large. Most of his stories were concerned with his various expulsions from school, and there was one that had the flavor of being a schoolboy classic, of how he had lured a chorus girl into his dormitory, and into his bed, and how both had been discovered there by the headmaster early next morning. Another tale had something to do with lobster pots, and small boats in a storm off the coast of Maine, and his absence from school without permission. He was forever rescuing young women in distress, and for some reason or other plying them with huge sums of money.

One day I overheard his mother asking him what had become of a large cut-glass punch bowl that had mysteriously disappeared. I heard the murmuring of Joseph's soothing voice, his reverential "M'am's"—and then his mother's wail, "Joseph, Joseph, why do you always lie to me?"

How many millions, real or fictitious, Augustus Powers actually amassed I never knew, but I do remember hearing, some thirty years later, that soon after his death his foundry was no longer owned by his heirs, that his wealth had melted away.

About this time, I became conscious of my personal finances. For the purpose of buying books of poems, I hoarded all the gifts of money that came my way—stray dimes and quarters went into my treasury as well as birthday windfalls of one or more dollar bills. These accumulated against the days when I would visit a bookshop, bills in my right trouser-pocket, change in my left, all carefully counted and the total well in mind, to sound the limits of my debauch. My favorite bookstore had, on a fine, windy autumn day, the smell of Lake Michigan's blue waters coursing through its open door and windows. It was an overcrowded, overflowing shop, books stacked from floor to tables, and shelved from floor to ceiling, and there, in the center of the shop's confusion, stood the bookseller's chief clerk, his wife. She had shining black hair, gathered in a knot at the back of her head, and the luminous white skin of a mermaid, generously exposed to view—for the black velvet dress that she habitually wore in the shop was cut so low and so tentatively attached to her shoulders that one would think a single shrug of these shoulders would bring it fluttering to the floor. When I would mention the title of a book I wanted, an expression of half-amused bewilderment would cross her face: "If ever I had that book, I've clean forgotten it," she would say with a dreamy smile, and I would be obliged to seek it out myself from amidst the tide of volumes that seemed to engulf her. As if moving under water, she would slowly extend a gleaming white arm to receive the money.

Under such benign influence and confused emotions I would spend every cent I had saved. It was from her shelves and tables that I bought my Alexander Pope, my Robert

Burns, my Shelley, my Kipling, my Masefield, and the *Collected Poems* of Thomas Hardy. With growing infrequency, my visits to this bookshop continued through many years. Though the merest flicker of gray appeared in the velvet-gowned mermaid's hair, her opulent figure never lost its youthful curves and suppleness.

Since I slept lightly and woke early, I sustained reading on Sunday mornings long beyond the period of my convalescence, in the little, square, red leather Shakespeares—and when later, I saw some of them on the stage, half their beauty seemed to have melted away. This applied to the comedies but not to *Hamlet*. Through one of her rare moments of impulsive kindness, my half sister, Florence, hurried me off to see a matinee performance of Forbes-Robertson as the Danish prince. Florence was then a red-haired girl of nineteen who looked like a discontented cousin of Rossetti's "blessed damozel." Once seated in the balcony, and the curtain up, the restless girl grew monumentally bored, while I was gradually and gloriously overwhelmed by Shakespeare's music, as intoned by Forbes-Robertson's magnificent voice. After the final curtain, Florence leaped to her feet. As she was helping me into my coat she suddenly seemed to notice that I had grown unusually quiet; perhaps I looked a bit dazed. I saw her frightened face peering into mine: was I ill? Did I feel well enough to walk home? Actually, I was feeling marvelous—enveloped in a dream that lifted me above and beyond the violet glow of the arc-lights that lined the streets on our journey home that winter evening.

Overnight, so it seemed, I had outgrown my Uncle George's musical show matinees; I now demanded something richer, deeper, more lasting in theatrical experience. Curiously enough, I found what I was looking for at the Orpheum Circuit Vaudeville. These were matinee performances, both on "farewell tours," of Pavlova and Sarah Bernhardt. After an afternoon chiefly engaged in looking at trained dogs and horses, Japanese tumblers, and hearing the screams of broken-down ex-music-hall stars, the appearance of these two great performers of the recent past seemed to touch on the miraculous.

Pavlova performed an excerpt from *Swan Lake:* my concentration on her was so intense that she seemed to loom up from the stage larger than life, a glowing apparition of flowing limbs. And from this vision came the transformation of the dancer into a swan.

No less memorable (but for me, a frightening contrast) was the sight of Sarah Bernhardt in an abbreviated version of her title role in *L'Aiglon,* dressed as that doomed young man, in a gold-spangled, pale blue velvet uniform, her small face topped by a wig of bright yellow curls. She swayed stiffly, then plunged slowly across the stage. It was all too clear that she held herself erect by grasping furniture and dragging forward an artificial foot and leg. Evidently she did not dare sit down. Her voice, unsexed and shrill, was that of a molting peacock in a city zoo. Had she offered up for sale her loss of talent and her loss of youth? Some kind of spiritual death was in the air. In this display, she had stepped beyond the purges of tears and the sense of tragic loss, into the region of the grotesque. The magic of the footlights had dropped away. It was as though I had caught sight of her amid the disorder of her dressing-room: suddenly I was aware of the dual nature of mimetic art, of the close juxtaposition of sordidness, and the fading glory of her performance.

These experiences at the theater brought me into direct contact with the world of "Art." So too did my visits, in the company of my Aunt Victoria, to the Sunday afternoon poetry recitals of The Wisconsin Players, which took place in an old mansion, not far from Jefferson Street, and in a quarter of the city that still maintained a faint aura of fashionable patronage by dint of its proximity to certain "chic" restaurants and teashops. The atmosphere at The Wisconsin Players, as reflected in its audience, was less "bohemian" than —discreetly—avant-garde, and perhaps a trifle dilettantish. As might be expected, The Wisconsin Players was a target of ridicule for the city's solid middle-class citizens, yet for a half-dozen seasons or so, the theater held its ground, and introduced young poets, playwrights, even short story writers such as Sherwood Anderson, to the young people of the city.

My Aunt Victoria presented me to the moving spirit and courageous patroness of The Wisconsin Players, Mrs. Laura Sherry, best remembered today for her production of Wallace Stevens's play, *Carlos among the Candles*, at a time when only the few, among them her friend—Miss Harriet Monroe of *Poetry*—had championed or even read his verse. A glimpse of Mrs. Sherry's welcoming, enthusiastic temperament is shown in a letter to Stevens that compared his writings for the stage with those of "Synge, Verhaeren, Tchekov, Andreyev . . . von Hofmannsthal, Shaw's 'Androcles and the Lion,' Schnitzler, Hauptmann's naturalistic plays, Duhamel and Dunsany." The list of names is interesting because it so fully represents the fashionable reading of 1917, a few years after I had met her.

I saw in Mrs. Sherry a reincarnation of the stately Ceres, sowing good will among those who admired and wished to participate in the very recent arts, and who also happened to belong to the Junior League, as well as to the city's Yacht and Tennis Clubs. From my Aunt Victoria I learned we were fortunate to have her here at all, for Mr. Sherry, in marrying her, transported her from New York where she had been an actress. There was also a hint that she might not be with us long; it was said the big city held fascinations for her that our city could not provide. In those days my picture of New York was drawn largely from the illustrations in *St. Nicholas:* to me it was a place where the rich, in dinner jackets and evening gowns, were *tremendously* rich, and the poor, in rags, stood begging in the midst of plenty; where the Hotel Plaza was a dazzling white wedding cake; and where the squirrels in Central Park were fed by a benevolent William Dean Howells. Though I knew even then that these fancies of New York were somewhat childish, they were revived whenever I thought of Mrs. Sherry. Certainly, I found it impossible to fit her into another image of the city—which I called from some source different from *St. Nicholas*—where actresses in pink tights quaffed champagne out of slippers along Broadway's "Great White Way."

Of my Sunday afternoon visits to The Wisconsin Players I remember a rectangular hall with a small stage or podium at the far end; the audiences, consisting mostly of women, were seated on fragile, comfortless folding chairs. The precarious seating usually—and unless he was very good—divided attention with the speaker. When Carl Sandburg read something that sounded to me like "I got hair under my arms," I had to struggle to suppress my laughter. Yet I felt behind his graceless manner a purpose larger than Riley's, perhaps a larger one than Sandburg's words actually conveyed. Most of his lines were hard to remember; they slipped away and blurred into a succession of homemade homilies.

Vachel Lindsay's recital was no less informal, but of a very different character. That Sunday fell on an ice-coated, intractable day in February. The rectangular auditorium of The Wisconsin Players was filled with blasts of wind from the northern pine forests of upper Wisconsin. As he mounted the little stage, Lindsay looked impervious to the weather. The Lindsay that I saw was very like an Illinois farm boy turned Evangelical preacher; his navy blue serge suit seemed to have been bought and fitted in a country general store, but was

[*63*]

scrupulously clean and pressed. A shock of lank yellow hair fell across one corner of his forehead. His presence was arresting. His announcement that he was about to recite a sermon, "King Solomon and His Wives," was accompanied by the sudden appearance on stage of a dozen Junior League ladies in classic dress, their bare feet, thighs, and torsos exposed to the winds of February. (It was afterwards rumored that they had been trained by Paul Swan, then visiting the city, in the uninhibited pleasures of the modern dance.) With old-fashioned country politeness, Lindsay bowed from the waist at the ladies, drew himself up full height, threw his head back, closed his eyes—and chanted. The women echoed the refrain, "King Solomon had a million wives," and leaped about in unison in a manner befitting novice Bacchantes; most of them looked a bit embarrassed and uncomfortably cold. Since his eyes were closed throughout the recital Lindsay's voice seemed to issue from a dream. He seemed to be studiously, mercifully unconscious of the women swaying precariously around him.

When he came to the end of his performance, he opened his eyes, and bowed to the women, and with disarming simplicity he thanked them all for sharing in the music and the rhythm of his poems. The women vanished in a rush to the warmth of their dressing rooms.

The Lindsay recital was cause enough for gossip, yet Lindsay's innocence was so clearly in evidence that small share of the blame fell to his lot. Paul Swan and Laura Sherry were considered evil or dubious influences. Some thought Lindsay a trifle mad, and the more mature, such as my Aunt Victoria, regarded him as decidedly *strange;* but she accepted him as part of Chicago's "literary renaissance" ("a Robin's Egg Renaissance," as Sherwood Anderson was to call it.) It was soon fairly well established that the very institution of The Wisconsin Players provided a valuable lifeline to the aesthetic activity that flowed between Chicago and New York. Poets from the East were attracted to read their poems in Chicago, and on their way south or back home again, they were persuaded to drop by at The Wisconsin Players. One of these was Robert Frost.

To me Robert Frost and the reading of his verse were revelations in the way poetry should be offered to its audience. The poet wore a dinner jacket and black tie; his manner was as formal as his dress. As he stepped behind a lectern, he seemed younger than the hint of gray in his hair foretold, and as he read aloud his dramatic narratives from *North of Boston,* his voice, often dropping to a whisper, had lyrical qualities that modulated rather than stressed whatever histrionics his lines required. If some few of the characters in his pastorals were distinctly rural, the poet himself did not stoop to the use of ungainly rustic mannerisms. Frost gave his characters the graces of dignity and understatement, as well as an air of mystery. This was in great contrast to the noisier demonstrations of poetry I had recently heard. What a relief it was to encounter a poet who spoke in the accents of a sensitive and civilized man!

Perhaps the foregoing comments on my early memories of Frost require a word or two of explanation. I had known nothing of him before this reading: I did not know he had recently returned from a two-year stay in England; nor did I know that he had spent six years teaching in New Hampshire, reason enough for his poise behind a lectern. Other poets I had heard at The Wisconsin Players lacked his complexity, his experience, his years of non-success, his ability (in a remarkably short time) to make friends in England and to influence them, as well as to exert a classical discipline over his poetry. The slender, engaging young man I saw was to be replaced by several mutations of his personality, and through these changes, he at last emerged as his own conception of

[65]

"The Good Gray Poet," homespun, relaxed, scattering gnostic shreds of wisdom wherever he went. Behind this exterior (which seemed false to me), was a discerning critic, a wary raconteur, alert in his dispraise—a host who ignored the clock and held his guests enchanted until the early hours of the morning. All these were qualities of one who had had to make his own way in the world: beneath the suface he was hard, resilient, and deliberately untruthful. In my last memory of him—this is situated in the late 1950s—he is standing before me on a college campus, his mortarboard tilted back on a matting of white hair, his black gown fluttering in the wind, while in a lowered voice—so no one but ourselves could hear—he talked of the strange predicament of being both poet and teacher—and of the trials of raising a family. He had the air of a witty, searching, and not unkindly fortune teller.

My Sunday afternoons at The Wisconsin Players extended far beyond the winter my Aunt Victoria introduced me to Laura Sherry. My mother had bought a "town car," a glossy, glassed-in, black carriage, steered with a handlebar, and powered by electric batteries. The Electric was a decorous machine, high-slung, slow-moving, stately, and so easy to control that even I could drive it. For some half-dozen years the Electric carried me to The Wisconsin Players. There, on a gray-dark, rainy day, in a second-floor parlor, I was introduced to Emmanuel Carnivalli and Sherwood Anderson. The room was chill, and the Italian poet, who looked like a waif, wore a heavy wool muffler around his neck. On that dreary afternoon, his unhappiness seemed deeper than the sea, and his frail voice (he had probably caught cold) reiterated his worries over how long Mrs. Sherry would tolerate him as a house guest. The worries were like small refrains in his complaint—would she let him stay another night or two? or send him back to Chicago? or, if not Chicago, where? Where could he go? And yet, the brutal climate was killing him. It was clear that Anderson, dark-eyed and troubled, had been trying to soothe him as if he were consoling a child.

As Carnivalli moved to a corner of the room, Anderson turned to me, and then with a friendliness that overcame my shyness, told me he had read a one-act sketch I had submitted to Mrs. Sherry, and recommended that she put it on with several other experiments of that kind. I was flattered and a little bit dazed by the news, for by that time my ardor for the sketch had cooled. I felt I had grown far beyond it, for in the life of the young, six months' time is half eternity. My little experiment was something not be repeated; it had been a boyish attempt to emulate Jean Cocteau's sketches in *Vanity Fair*, which was all very well for the moment, but nothing that I felt was quite my own. Yet I was tremendously grateful for Sherwood Anderson's gift to my self-esteem; for his praise had made me bold enough—a year or two later—to hand over several of my poems to Mrs. Sherry, who gave them to Harriet Monroe—and thus initiate my appearance in *Poetry* (Chicago).

The use of my mother's car gave me greater steadiness of hand, but the problem of a formal education was still unsolved. My sense of loneliness increased. Within my immediate family circle, I occupied a detached, middle position: I was too young to join in the activities of my elder half sister and brother, and too old to join those of my own sister Josephine and brother James. When family quarrels took place, my position was that of a neutral witness. My daydreams carried me away to the London of my grandmother's childhood, and to the New York of *St. Nicholas* magazine. The four years' difference in our ages had also separated me from Cousin Elizabeth; our worlds had grown amazingly far apart. When I saw her, she was often tearful, awkward, and sullen; she hated books; she refused to go to school—and I began to think my mother had been correct in saying my Aunt Victoria was both too strict and too lax in bringing her up. Elizabeth was no longer the amiable child I knew. It remained a mystery why my aunt so successfully educated her stepdaughters, and yet seemed to neglect the care of her own child, all the more strange because of her general interest in education, including mine. Or, was Elizabeth attached to the "practical" side of my aunt's imagination, the side that insisted that the discontented child go to "business school" to learn typing and stenography? Or was my aunt simply too weak to stand up to the force of her young daughter's will?

In any case, the "practical" side of my aunt's imagination was of unusual shape and character. Since the house on Jefferson Street was large enough to shelter more than a half-dozen human beings, and since my uncle's earnings often fell behind household expenses, her imagination seized on the idea of taking in "paying guests." Hers, however, was not to be an ordinary lodging house; it was to attract "people of quality," those who knew and enjoyed the advantages of culture, those who could appreciate the arts. With them in mind, she bought and placed a piano in each of her four spare rooms, and had plumbers add four new bathrooms, an investment that kept my uncle in debt for the next ten years, long after the last paying guest had departed. So far as money was concerned the scheme was, of course, a wild disaster, but in all other respects it was successful beyond her dearest hopes. In their passage back and forth between Chicago and New York, journalists, including one or two future members of the staff of *The New Republic*, novelists, and actors stopped over for a few days at the house on Jefferson Street, for these were years when my uncle enjoyed local celebrity, and my aunt felt at last she had created a salon in her front parlor. Although the cuisine on Jefferson Street left much to be desired—my aunt's specialties were creamed chicken on salted crackers, minced

[68]

fish, and chopped raw vegetables—dinner conversation was lofty and spirited, ranging from discussions of William James's *Varieties of Religious Experience* to Sir William Watson's stanzas on "the woman with the serpent's tongue." If the boiled potatoes smelled burnt, and the coffee cream sour, such trivialities were forgotten in controversies over the respective merits of Shaw, Barrie, and Maeterlinck. And if guests of liberal persuasion regarded my uncle as a reactionary, he quickly disarmed them by his extravagant optimism.

It was from within this circle of her "paying guests" that my aunt discerned a solution for my lack of formal schooling. Among the guests was Grace Lusk, distinguished for her career as an educator. She had been commissioned by the University of Wisconsin to spend a year in Europe, gathering information for a report on secondary school education abroad. She returned to the university, completed her report, and promptly collapsed. She was then about thirty: it was as though the strain of being an academic paragon, raised on a poverty-stricken farm in Wisconsin, and sustained from there onward by scholarships, had suddenly taken its toll. Her trouble was diagnosed as "a nervous breakdown," and with her doctor's permission she spent the first six months of her convalescence under my aunt's care. To steady her nerves—particularly, the tremor in her hands—her doctor suggested that she take up target-shooting. She bought a revolver, and with her usual proficiency in learning, she became "a dead shot," as expert, so she said to me later, as Buffalo Bill. Certainly, it was an intriguing sight to see her tall figure, gaily sweeping down the back lawn of the house on Jefferson Street, placing a tin can on top of the high wooden fence; then racing back up the lawn, her long skirts lifted above her ankles, to where a clump of lilac trees stood, and wheeling smartly about, her right hand outstretched, firing the revolver with an explosion that shook the air. These sessions of target practice took on the air of a frivolous, childish game, performed with precision and much girlish laughter. In spring the smells of gunpowder and of lilacs floated through the back yard and into the house.

At the time my aunt advanced her name as my possible tutor, Miss Lusk had returned to her flat in a little town some seventy miles northwest of the city. Riding through its leaf-green shaded streets, one caught glimpses of freshly cut lawns, and brilliantly white, jigsaw-fretted façades of houses. A nearby lake provided a setting for a few large summer estates, one of which belonged to our friends, the Augustus Powerses, with whom we spent an occasional weekend. At the far end of the lake was a gaudy little amusement park, from where, on Sunday afternoons, a bone-thin woman with curly blond hair, attired in soiled white tights, would ascend in a balloon. As she approached the basket, with every indication of reluctance in her face, her cries of "No, no, no, I can't g-g-go up. God save me, I can't go up," never failed to draw a crowd. She wept open-mouthed, her grease paint wet with tears. Five minutes later, as the balloon swung over the lake, she would leap from the basket into the water and swim triumphantly ashore. Aside from this brief interval once a week, both town and lake seemed wrapped in warm and sunlit domestic sleep.

It was arranged that Miss Lusk was to travel to my house once a week to gather up the stray ends of my wide readings and to put them into some sort of order. One morning, early in September, my mother introduced me to the tall, sandy-haired young woman who wore an extremely low-cut white blouse, and a long, ankle-length tweed skirt. At a single glance, she looked not unlike a small boy's caricature of a school-teacher: black-ribboned pince-nez, sturdy walking boots, untidy hair gathered loosely in a twist at the back of her head. So she seemed till she seated herself opposite me at the card table we had requisitioned to support our books, pencils, and papers. Suddenly her intimate, closely enveloping charm began to work. The blue eyes behind her pince-nez would change their expression with the slightest turn of thought and feeling, and her generous, sensual mouth would often curve into a half-questioning, half-critical smile. Though her exterior remained that of the archetypical "old maid," her humor, her wit, her intuitive sympathy with whomever she wished to please, projected a kind of beauty that drew me, as it lured my Aunt Victoria, into her net.

The two hours a week she questioned and lectured at me were filled with excitement. Arithmetic, grammar, geography, and history were caught up in an exchange of inquiry, information, and commentary: each session closed with a ten to fifteen minute discussion of poetry. Through Robert Browning's dramatic portraits, she introduced me to Italy and France, and turned my face to look eastward, across the Atlantic, beyond the British Isles.

She could not, of course, entirely dispel my moments of panic before taking written examinations, moments during which I half-convinced myself that I was wholly ignorant of everything, and that my spelling was so hopelessly bad I could never learn to write. Yet at the end of a year, Grace Lusk pronounced me ready to enter The German-English Academy, a preparatory school, chiefly for Yale, where she had advised my parents to send me. She warned me that I would be two years older than most of my classmates—but this would be no great loss, for I would find schoolwork less difficult to do than they would. (Her prophecy turned out to be correct.)

At our last session across the card table, she was supremely elated. She had just taken on, so she said, an amusing job, something quite new. Near her flat in the country town lived a man who had made a fortune manufacturing a patent medicine for cows. "A funny, old-fashioned-looking man," she said, "fat and jolly," who wore big, black mustaches, such as barbers and bartenders used to wear; he was extremely proud of his success and had made up his mind to compose a book on the breeding of cattle. Of course, he couldn't write, but his name on the title page of a book would give his patent medicine wider sales and more prestige. She had agreed to "collaborate" on the writing of the book, and in preparation for her new venture, she had immersed herself in texts on animal husbandry. I wondered why she seemed so eager to launch herself into such an absurd and awkward adventure.

During my last few months of Grace Lusk's tutelage I began to attend classes at a local school of fine arts. Not unlike Grace's motives for taking target practice, my parents' reasons for sending me to art school were therapeutic—drawing and painting, they thought, would increase my manual efficiency. Underlying my own motives was a passionate regard for painting itself, yet every time I attempted to draw or paint, the results were so far short of the visions haunting my imagination that I would fall into half-hours of despair, tinged with a nameless sense of guilt. It was as though I had betrayed a sacred impulse of the spirit. I hated the compromise my ineptness forced upon me, yet the joy of looking at paintings survived my rejection of whatever I placed on paper and canvas.

Because my walking was still unsteady, my Cousin Marian, in training for the teaching of art in secondary schools, would pilot me to my art classes, and on red-letter days, accompany me to Chicago to visit the Art Institute on Michigan Boulevard. Bespectacled, expansive, full of instructions, she would guide me through dark streets under "The Loop" onto the breezy thoroughfare where the Institute stood. Because of the flow of traffic up and down the boulevard, crossing over it was always regarded as a special feat of skill, delayed by several false starts and rapid retreats, usually ending in a reckless sprint to the opposite curb. Once in the Institute we were safe, and there I would visit the South Seas with Gauguin, and stand for hours before his imaginings of half-naked, mindless women facing me with folded arms. And there was a scene of a southern swampland, painted by George Inness, which caught me up in its air of tropical mystery. I had found, vicariously enough, an escape into a haven far away from my failures in a classroom.

One noon, on the way back from our visit to the Institute, where I had seen Gauguin's woodblock prints in red and black, small masterpieces, so I thought, of his craftsmanship, Marian and I stepped into a deeply shaded restaurant. We were wrapped in cool, submarine, semi-darkness. As we sat down, I happened to glance into a far corner of the room and there, seated at a table, was Grace Lusk, waving a hand at me. I walked to her table while Marian, overcome with shyness, stayed behind, her face shielded by a menu. Opposite to Miss Lusk sat her employer, the man with black mustaches, who looked up at me with a truculent stare—he was not as jolly as she said he was; he looked merely vulgar and possessive. I returned to Marian as quickly as I could.

At this encounter neither Marian nor I could shake off a vague feeling of embarrassment, and for reasons I could not have explained, I decided not to speak of our meeting Miss Lusk in Chicago to my parents. For the time being, Miss Lusk and her employer dropped from my mind.

My father's fortunes had taken another brief rise; we had moved to an elaborate, fretted and towered, three-story mansion, with porte-cochère and carriage house to shelter my father's Buick and my mother's stately Electric. To my mother's despair, the place demanded more servants than she could manage, yet the house with its ample lawns, large rooms, woodburning fireplaces (even a completely furnished billiard room, next to my third-story bedroom) delighted my father. All this was on a grander scale than that achieved by the house on Jefferson Street. He had come a long way up from the child who for six days a week lived on molasses and broken crackers, trundled home in a baby carriage from the cracker factory, and on Sunday had a small piece of beef for dinner. He was also a long way up from the humiliated boy whose father, after large, drunken promises, had failed to get him a job as errand boy in The First National Bank; he had come up far from the adolescent who, for a half dollar tip, delivered to his father at 717 Jefferson Street, each Saturday evening, two gallon jugs of whiskey, one ordinary, the other, excellent sour mash. The old man would salute him politely as he handed him the tip. The ownership of the big rambling house on the west side, across the city from Jefferson Street, was proof of the distance traveled by my father from youth to middle age. He refrained from boasting to his friends and business associates; his twelve–hour day at work, five days a week, and half days at his office, Saturdays and Sundays, remained the same, yet to his immediate family—though nothing explicit was ever said—he radiated an aura of wealth. In his quiet way, he gloried in the luxuries his large house provided: the neat rooms for servants he could not quite afford, the grandfather's clock in the front hall, the bay windows looking out to a broad avenue lined with elms, the spacious dining room where, from a decanter on the sideboard, he helped himself to a double bourbon neat before his six o'clock breakfast of oatmeal.

As for myself, my walking had gradually improved enough to permit my making my way through the city alone. I was now properly enrolled at The German-English Academy. And I had acquired skill at the billiard table. Though my hands still revealed an obvious tremor, I felt confident enough to challenge acquaintances to a round at pool; to their amazement I often managed to press them to the very edge of defeat; and on rare occasions I won the game. These small victories had the same unsatisfactory results as my earlier knowledge of prizefighting. They won me no respect for my shoddy skills, and even lay bare in too demanding a manner my eagerness to make friends. It became clear to me that my time would be better spent in developing my own personal talents and interests, rather than in trying to conform to those of others.

The German-English Academy occupied a nest of Victorian Gothic buildings ending on one side in a plate-glassed, "modern" annex. Across the street was an elderly brewery, from which poured the medicinal, if nourishing smell of malt. (In those days most of my tonics were flavored with malt, and this is probably why, even today, I cannot fully enjoy a glass of beer, and why I cannot tolerate the smell of beer in a restaurant or bar.)

The school was conducted on the plan of a German *Gymnasium*—before one entered the senior class of the upper school, one had to pass Yale College entrance examinations; indeed, many of the seniors went on from the Academy to Yale. The principal of the upper school, Dr. Pratt, a rotund, grizzled widower with an innocent smile under his short mustache, had been a "Yale man" in the distant past. He was nearsighted, but because he was an ardent vegetarian and Christian Scientist, he felt it unbecoming to wear eyeglasses. The mist that drifted before his eyes seemed to obscure all signs of evil.

Many of Dr. Pratt's pupils were heirs of some of the wealthiest families in the city, and every few years or so, a gaudy, firm-jawed girl would invade his office to announce her pregnancy, and to claim that one of his seniors was the father of her unborn child. He would receive this news with such convincing unbelief, such dignity and righteous anger, that the girls would leave his office visibly shaken in the belief of their own truthfulness—or lies.

Dr. Pratt was a staunch enemy of frauds and falsehoods

[75]

and in his management of the school his high-mindedness exacted good behavior from some of the most unruly and cynical of spoiled rich boys—and the fact that he refused to believe in the worst of their conduct somehow made their exploits seem childish rather than gloriously wicked. The Academy had become Dr. Pratt's second wife: the books he loved—which comprised an extensive, and, in part, erudite library in the Latin classics—he gave to the school. If in his presence, a boy would let drop a coarse word or gesture, Dr. Pratt's silence would evoke the boy's instant "Beg pardon, sir, forgive me."

In the world outside the Academy Dr. Pratt's authority was soon to melt away. In the eyes of well-to-do trustees and parent-teacher associations, he was an eccentric, nearsighted, aging man who looked like a sadly diminished version of William Howard Taft. His salary was low. His dress was untidy; and in his feeble pretensions to neatness he seemed even less presentable—his black jackets and striped trousers looked as though they had been rented from a second-hand store. He lurched into his office—ate lettuce sandwiches from a paper bag; and though plump, always had the air of being vaguely hungry. It was clear that he could not raise money for the school; the sight of his torn gray gloves alone was enough to condemn his efforts as a fund raiser. After the trustees had discharged him from his duties, his hatred of fraud did not prevent him from investing his savings in dubious stocks. He lost whatever remained of his small fortune.

Whenever the weather was fair, I was permitted to make my way to school alone, and to lunch at any restaurant within walking distance of the school. Going out to lunch was far more exciting than sharing a couple of noon hours with my classmates. I delighted in my newfound freedom. My walking was still precarious, but I found that the best way to cope with the handicap was to ignore it.

Across the street from a city hall was Martini's, my chosen restaurant, an old-fashioned café with tiled floor, marble-topped tables, and wire-backed chairs. Its menu included Vienna rolls with sweet butter, freshly brewed coffee and a 'variety of coffee cakes which were served by a troop of silent, red-cheeked, adventurous-looking waitresses in starched white uniforms. In the rear of the high-ceilinged, large, mirrored café, sat a group of old men, the elderly brewers, tanners, and bankers of the city, playing Schaff's Kopf or a very slow game of chess. It was said that as these old men took their places, the wealth of the city was assembled—and there they were, the stout and the lean, in white waistcoats, and dark gray morning jackets, some smoothly shaven and bald, others with closely cropped, upstanding hair and waxed, up-pointed, white mustaches. Their grandsons and great-grandsons were my fellow students at the Academy.

In these small excursions, I gained an exhilarating sense of being on my own—of liberty, both from parental care and the possible ridicule of boys near my own age. And there was still one other freedom, the greatest of all, which came on Wednesday afternoons. At the Academy, if one's grades were above eighty-six, one was free of school from Wednesday noon till nine the following morning, and though we were also free from Friday evening till Monday morning, it was the midweek recess that I prized. It allowed me to make use of my season ticket for each Wednesday matinee of the Russell-Janney Players at the Pabst Theater, a few steps away from where I had just finished lunching at Martini's.

It was at 717 Jefferson Street that I first heard of the Players from Cyril Yapp, a character actor and one of my aunt's paying guests, who had received praise from the critics for his role of the Cat in Maeterlinck's *The Blue Bird*. Indeed, the little man's appearance was remarkably feline. His gestures were quick, his conversation caustic, and he talked rapidly as he padded about the room. Yapp was well-read, as actors sometimes are, and erudite in details of theatrical gossip. He told me of Cathleen Nesbit, an Irish actress now stranded in America because of the Kaiser's War, who had been a cherished friend of the poet, Rupert Brooke. In London he had met them together—and she had recently joined the Russell-Janney troupe. He urged me to see her.

The Janney troupe was subsidized by a group of civic-minded Milwaukee millionaires, and housed in the Pabst Theater. To the Pabst I went, and when the curtain rose on Shaw's *You Never Can Tell* and on Cathleen Nesbit, I fell—so far as imagination could plunge me—in love, and remained so for two years of Wednesday matinees. A ludicrous aspect of the situation was that I was far too shy to ask Yapp to introduce me to Miss Nesbit. A foolish mixture of diffidence and pride stood in my way—and, of course, this half-realization of my ineptness increased my awkwardness and loss of confidence. My vicarious love affair was a well-kept secret, half-acknowledged by myself alone—the images of beauty glimpsed at in her blue eyes, black hair, wide mouth, and slightly up-tilted nose charmed me through the entire repertoire of Shaw, Wilde, Masefield, Sheldon, Galsworthy, Wedekind, and Schnitzler. To me Cathleen Nesbit and the spirit of the modern stage were one—and three years later when I read Lucretius on the nature of love, I knew what he meant when he spoke of love's idols and images that haunt human imagination and desires; certainly he did not underrate the powers of Venus: "Birth-gendering Venus, mistress of gods and men/ And where you walk, sweet-smelling flowers rise."

It so happened that I had found the almost perfect setting for my infatuation, for the interior of the Pabst Theater had the decor of a Viennese opera house—a great crystal chandelier hanging from a distant ceiling, red brocade lining the boxes and the walls; one was surrounded by an ocean of old rose plush-covered seats. To my left and right were a few heavily jeweled elderly women attended by young men—and from these small circles rose bursts of high falsetto voices. Behind us was a deep semi-circle of empty seats, and the empty boxes with their gilt trimmings seemed to hang like golden cages, when the lights were dimmed, in vacuous air. Although these sparsely attended matinees may well have been a strain on the nerves of the players, I was appreciative of the fact of counting myself among "the happy few" who were free to gaze upon Miss Nesbit, and to admire her flights of gaiety and swift turns of laughter. My attendance in this select company of theater-goers provided me with armor against the snobbery of wealth practiced by classmates at the Academy. I developed a snobbery of adolescent intellectual superiority: I assumed myself the only one in the city who had cherished the significance of Swinburne's death; and prided myself on the knowledge that I was among the few who read E. M.'s early volumes of *Georgian Poetry*.

It was also clear that the millionaires who played chess at Martini's and subsidized the Russell-Janney Players had higher and less provincial standards of culture than some of their offspring, who also happened to be my classmates. This did not mean that these meticulously dressed old men were other than the dogmatic, shrewd, arrogant businessmen they appeared to be. The difference was that they were two generations closer to a European culture than their grandsons were. They felt rather than knew that the plays shown at their theater had more substance than the latest film sent into their city from Hollywood. Their tastes in painting were as well-defined, but less shrewd, and less alert. As patrons of the city's art museum, they would rather have admired a Bouguereau (which they did) of blind Homer being led by an attractively undressed, barefooted little boy, than be talked into buying a Renoir.

[79]

If during the first two years of the Kaiser's War I was not greatly shaken by news of the "Front" it was because I shared with those around me a sense of remoteness concerning the conflict. The city was divided into pro-German and pro-English camps, and newspapers to quiet open enmities made a point of toning down news from the battlefronts and doing the best they could to make local events seem of first importance. To find exciting local news was often difficult, for to all outward appearances, the city was so serene in its middle-class, Social-Democratic complacencies that it seemed virtually asleep—after business hours. All signs of evil and distress were swept discreetly out of sight. Even murderers had little claim to notoriety, for Wisconsin had abolished capital punishment.

It was therefore all the more startling for me to see Grace Lusk's name in the thick black type of a newspaper headline. She had killed her employer's wife. In the quiet little town where she lived, northwest of the city, Miss Lusk had invited the woman over to her second-story flat for tea. Revolver in hand, she stood on the second-floor landing awaiting her guest. The moment the woman had closed the door behind her and turned to face the stairway, Miss Lusk opened fire. Her year of target practice under the lilacs in the back yard of the house on Jefferson Street had not been wasted. When the fatally wounded woman dropped to the floor, Miss Lusk had a moment of panic; she held the nozzle of the gun against her own chest, and fired again; the bullet passed, almost harmlessly, through her thin body; there was a slight flow of blood, yet in the passion of the moment, little pain. She recovered self-control, stepped to the phone: first called her doctor, then the police. She told the patrolman that she wanted them to remove the dead body of a woman from her front hall; and she went on to explain that she had rid the community of an undesirable element—a worthless creature who did nothing all day long but play cards and gossip about the love affair she, Grace Lusk, was having with her husband. Miss Lusk admitted that the police would have to put her under arrest, but she assured them that she had done no wrong.

Throughout her trial, she sustained an air of righteous calm and insisted, over and over again, that she had performed a service that would benefit the entire community. She puzzled the jurors, who, with great reluctance, found her guilty of murder; and the judge, who sentenced her to life-imprisonment, could not suppress certain signs of admiration. It was as though Grace Lusk had been engaged in a campaign for moral reform—and had almost won. The sincerity of her convictions went unquestioned. Her trial carried with it vague overtones of triumphant Feminism—as though certain plays of Ibsen—*Hedda Gabler, Rosmersholm, A Doll's House*—had belatedly come to life on Wisconsin soil. And it seemed fitting that Miss Lusk was of Scandinavian descent.

A few months after the trial, I heard that Miss Lusk, committed for life at Waupun, had won the friendship of the head warden, and was now engaged in reforming the educational system in state prisons. And one evening a few months after this I was called to the phone where I heard her voice inviting me to come visit her the following afternoon at a sanatorium that could be easily reached by trolley car from my house. Though my parents seemed cool to the invitation, they granted permission for my visit, and with new poems in my pocket to show her, I arrived for tea at her suite in the sanatorium. As she talked, her room was aglow with the afternoon light, pouring in from windows all around us. She told me firmly that prison life was making her ill, that she had written an appeal to Governor LaFollette who had had her transported here as a prelude to her release. She was flushed and nervous, and warned me that this last piece of news was to be kept as a secret between us. She was quick-witted as ever and both kind and sharp as she questioned me about my writings and how I was getting along at school, and then, with infinite tact, so quickly I had no time to feel self-conscious, she took me in her arms, kissed me goodbye, and steered me out of her suite. I never saw her again.

Through my Aunt Victoria, I later heard rumors of how Grace Lusk had left Wisconsin behind her, had married in Boston, and had written articles, either anonymously or under an assumed name, on prison reform for the *Atlantic Monthly*. I never made certain as to the truth of these rumors, for my aunt mentioned them casually, swiftly, so as to cut short further discussion, and before I could raise a query, she was safely launched on another topic of conversation. When she chose to employ them, my aunt for all her sincerity had a genius for the fine arts of evasion. It was with some difficulty that I managed to extract fragmentary replies as to what happened to the man who had made patent medicine for cows. He in turn had been imprisoned for violation of the Mann Act, an anti-"white slave" law, forbidding a man to cross state lines with a woman with whom he intends to spend the night. Miss Lusk's employer had thus been obliged to serve twenty years' hard labor—which, so I heard later, he did with ill-temper and sullenness. Everyone seemed to have forgotten the fate of his poor wife—a bloodstained, pathetically hopeless shade, wandering in limbo.

Slowly, from its great distance, the Kaiser's War began to penetrate the fastness of my city's isolation. The name of my school was abruptly changed from the more honestly descriptive "The German-English Academy" to the colorless "Milwaukee University School," which committed it to nothing whatsoever.

In my own family, strange fissures came to light. I remember, early in the war, the red evening sunlight shining through

the windows of my Uncle John's library, and my uncle rushing into the room to announce that Paris had been saved, and
then breaking into tears. At this, my aunt turned to my father
and said, "Though he looks English, John is much more temperamental and Irish than you are, Henry. I sometimes wish
he weren't." On this occasion, and because all of us shared in
his great joy, my uncle's tears were quickly forgiven, and yet
we felt slightly guilty, because so many people outside our
family circle were openly pro-German. In this delicate balance
between convictions, we still felt that everything we loved—
and civilization itself—had to be saved from the destructive,
invincible Huns.

My father's attitude, though outwardly one of calm, was
buffeted by contradictions. Shortly before the war, my father
confided to me that the Germans were the actual rulers of the
world, that the English were decadent; that German cutlery
and surgical supplies were far superior to those of English
make—the trouble being that the English had too many unions!
As the war grew deeper, and loss of life more terrifying, my
father was caught up, not merely in the isolationist spirit of
the Middle West, but in the ambiguities of feeling in his
family relationships. All his mother's devotion had been con-
centrated in her protection of her eldest son, John; her younger
son, my father, had been the recipient of her unconscious
cruelty. Until he was twelve, he remained unchristened, unnamed, and was known only as "Baby"; until twelve, he remained at home to "take care of the house," and was not
permitted to go to school with his two brothers. It is not
surprising that his attitude toward the English had been influenced by his mother's treatment of him. Nor did the image
of his father fill the vacuum left by her neglect. In his eyes
the fecklessness of the Irish was typified by his father's conduct. In his family, he had been "the odd child out," unwanted
by the Irish as well as the English—and as for Germans, he

was half-convinced that they were nothing more than highly skilled and educated brutes. Yet the two women he had married, his girlish first wife as well as my mother, were of German parentage, and there had never been any question of his faithfulness to them.

My mother echoed, with only the slightest difference, my father's ambiguous attitude towards the war. During her childhood in a German-Lutheran school she had been savagely scolded by a Lutheran minister. She left the school, she left the Lutheran communion, and after she had grown up and married, she attended services in the Episcopal church. She also reflected the views of my English grandmother, who looked down her nose at the Kaiser with the same air of patronage that *his* grandmother, Queen Victoria, bestowed on him.

By 1917, when the United States had at last entered the war, my family's detachment from the opinions of those around us became extremely difficult. Because the majority of my father's customers were pro-German, and because my father had refused to contribute to a German War Relief Fund, bakers decided to boycott The H. B. Gregory Company. Because my father refused to invest as deeply in Liberty Bonds as local bankers in charge of bond drives demanded, his credit was curtailed. He rode this storm with admirable poise. He told the bankers that his patriotism was so well-established that it needed no support from wild investments of money he could ill afford to withhold from the running of his business. To the bakers he expressed the doubt that much of their fund would ever reach German soil, and indeed, most of it never left the United States. Within six months, his precariously sustained neutrality had fortunate results. Among the bankers the most violent of his persecutors had been discovered hoarding sugar, and my father, in his stead, was then appointed by the federal government to distribute food. My father's customers, disillusioned by the maldistribution of the German War Relief Fund, returned to his fold, and under his benevolent tyranny shared in the rise of his business ventures. His business prospered as never before.

The war also exerted its influence on the drifting character of my school friendships, and in these the pro-German elements became less friendly. I was drawn closer to a boy whose health was nearly as precariously balanced as mine, and whose family had something of the same tinge of Anglican heritage that mine possessed. The family was of recent arrival in the city, and my friend Jack's father had come west from New York to be chief executive of a hand-grenade manufacturing plant that had sprung up, like a brick and iron clad mushroom, outside the city limits. Jack's father was also one of Woodrow Wilson's advisers, a dollar-a-year man who spent as much time in Washington as in Milwaukee.

No less interesting than her husband was Jack's mother, who had abnormally dark skin and, I fancied, Negroid features. She composed light music, and seemed to spend large portions of the day reclining on a chaise-longue. The atmosphere she created around her was one of singular passivity and quiet. All clocks were out of sight, yet great punctuality was observed; servants appeared noiselessly, and vanished in silence. Adjacent to the modest house was a vine-shaded porte-cochère that sheltered a maroon-colored Pierce-Arrow and a gray-uniformed chauffeur. In Milwaukee, their more ostentatious, and in some cases, even wealthier neighbors, felt themselves snubbed by Jack's family—which, I suspect, they were.

Jack's mother's companion was the very music teacher who had given my sister Josephine piano lessons—a plump, perpetually optimistic woman, usually to be found at her post behind her friend's chaise-longue. One had the impression that she was kept close at hand to rescue Jack's mother from those deep seas of melancholia into which she was apt to fall, and to bring her back to surfaces of rippling music. To me, there was something mysterious in their relationship, and as the music teacher twisted, between restless fingers, the strands of pearls that dangled over her breasts, I sensed a vague aura of hysteria in the air.

On the few weekends during the year that Jack's father spent at home, he would arrive bronzed and short and stout, with a half-dozen newly bought books in his briefcase. On the coffee table beside his armchair were two fresh packets of cigarettes, one of Camels, the other, Rameses II, from which he smoked alternately while he read, and the air above his bald head gradually turned blue. He read the books with concentration and dispatch, and as he finished each, he would toss it aside with a gesture of final dismissal, and open another. Among his weekend assortment of reading there were never less than two new books of poems—volumes by Rupert Brooke, John Masefield, Siegfried Sassoon, Robert Graves. He and my Uncle John were the only two men I knew with whom I could talk about modern poetry. His manner was totally different from that of my uncle. He was explosive, sharp, and emphatic in his convictions—with a cast in his left eye that made him look ferocious. In lighter moods, he could be as hearty and genial as a well-bred pirate. He was not at all like his two mild-tempered sons—Jack had a younger brother—who interested themselves in electrical gadgets, elaborate toy trains, and crystal radio sets. The boys seemed always to be teetering on the verge of very bad health; their initiative seemed to be sapped, their energy drained.

The entire household, islanded like mine from its neighbors, fascinated me, and I found it a welcome refuge from a not too friendly world. Jack, whose interests were far removed from poetry, regarded me with friendly tolerance. Whatever we had in common were the intangibles of taste and emotional response: we laughed at the same jokes; in respect to sex, our innocence and reticence in speech were closely matched; our social manners were formal, shy, and almost inarticulate. We took care to appear—and this with a touch of careful neglect, such as unpolished shoes—fashionably dressed; we wore low-cut starched collars, imported from London, and British-cut flannel blazers. These likenesses in taste distinguished us from our schoolfellows, and were enough to sustain a friendship that stopped short of personal intimacies. We never confided family secrets to one another. We respected one another's private grounds.

I amused Jack's mother by writing verses to her musical compositions. Of women I have met who toyed with the arts, rather than practiced them, Jack's mother was the most disarming. She took childlike joy in the writing of her compositions, and would strum them, in a parody of earnestness, on her grand piano, concluding her renditions with a soft self-deprecatory laugh. During these moments, her lightheartedness was contagious—her husband was caught up in it, so was I, and her two sons. I now suspect that fits of depression seized her whenever the house was empty of visitors—this would partly explain the nearly constant presence of the music teacher as well as my many invitations to her house. I was asked to make a six-week visit to their Bay Shore home on Long Island during the summer of 1918.

Even as I accepted the invitation, I had premonitions of finding a second home—without thought of responsibilities to my family—in New York. I felt somewhat like a boy who had decided to run away from home—but the invitation had, of course, made the running away seem proper, safe, and ultra-conventional—with no revolt involved.

Jack's father was to take me to New York. With him I took the luxury overnight express from Chicago to Pennsylvania Station, and perfect host that he was, he assumed that I knew well the amenities of the Pullman cars. On arrival at the Pennsylvania Station my gaze was filled with the cathedral-like arches of its thoroughfares, the streams of sunlight pouring down between the undulating fields of immense Allied flags, hung high overhead. The thoroughfares themselves were crowded with varicolored uniforms—uniforms of all nations —wheeling, gliding to all points of the compass. Jack's father steered me forward, through the flow of uniforms and up a flight of steps into the street where, waiting at the curb, was the maroon Pierce-Arrow. In the back seats were Jack and his young brother, and seated on either side of me, they soon broke into song. The two boys had just seen Irving Berlin's new musical show, and in an exuberant burst of mock patriotic fervor, the boys shouted out the refrains of "Oh! How I Hate to Get Up in the Morning" all the way from the west side of New York, across the Queensborough Bridge, and on into Bay Shore with its pebbled beaches, grayish-green waters, and neat little cruiser, where we were to spend most of the daylight hours of my visit.

By unspoken agreement, it was soon established that Jack's father and I held the same standards of literary taste in our reading—which included H. L. Mencken's *The Smart Set* as well as current books of poems—that was distinct from other reading in the household. But that summer my reading had been reduced to a very small minimum. The day was spent in shameless loafing on the cruiser, while the chauffeur, as captain, steered us in broad circles around the bay. At least four evenings a week, from eight to eleven, we sat in the Bay Shore movie house, where our appetite for movies of all kinds seemed insatiable—as though we could never see enough of them. Since Jack's father was known to be a dollar-a-year man, the manager of the theater and the boy who played the piano to accompany the pictures hugely indulged us: we dictated the pictures that were to be shown the following week as well as the musical scores that were to be thumped out as the film was shown. For the intermissions, we also chose the patriotic songs, directed from the stage by a plump Y.M.C.A. young man who had a pink face and a crew haircut, and sung by the audience. These performances were called "sings," and conducted with loudly shouted patriotic sentiments. The shouting seemed painfully awkward and strained.

All at once the Kaiser's War came closer to us than the images that cluttered the stage or flickering movie screen. One day, probably a Monday or a Tuesday—I had been so completely immersed in my leisurely routine that I lost count of the days of the week—Jack's mother and her music teacher companion decided to go shopping in New York, and by nine in the morning had departed towards Manhattan in the Pierce-Arrow. At eleven we had a phone call from the music teacher; she reported things gone fearfully wrong. As the car left the Queensborough Bridge to turn into the city, a soldier leaped on the running board, and announced himself as a military policeman and demanded to see the chauffeur's draft card. The chauffeur had none, but explained that he had a medical discharge from the army, having contracted tuberculosis while serving in Mexico during the Pancho Villa campaign. The M.P. refused to believe him, and placed him under arrest. Under the M.P.'s orders, the chauffeur drove the car with its passengers to the Brooklyn Armory where he was thrust, with hordes of other prisoners, into rooms without food, water, or toilet facilities, and without means of reaching friends and relatives by phone. The Pierce-Arrow was impounded. The two women were forced to hail a taxi so as to reach Jack's grandfather's mansion in Brooklyn Heights.

We were instructed to break into the chauffeur's room over the garage, find his discharge papers, and take them to Jack's grandfather's house. This was the kind of expedition we enjoyed. By six in the evening we had reached Manhattan by train, and a quarter of an hour later had crossed under the river into Brooklyn, where we found ourselves on an elevated train platform, completely lost. We scarcely knew how or why we got out of the train at this particular station. There was turmoil at the intersection of streets below us. Patrol wagons were lined up at the curbs, and as people strolled from stores, restaurants, and movie house lobbies, young men were torn from the arms of girls or swept off their feet and hustled into the waiting patrol wagons by an M.P.

Though we had no fear of the M.P. arresting us—we looked too young, and I, with my limping walk, too frail in health, to be mistaken for draft "slackers"—the spectacle in the street below us gave us queer sensations of alarm. Our descent to the street was wary and slow. I remember grasping the handrail at my side and the feel of the steps through my rubber-soled sneakers. Once we reached the pavement, we dodged into a cigar store to ask our way. A white-faced cigar clerk was huddled into a far corner behind a glass counter running the length of the store; he was gasping and speechless, raising his hands and elbows in a wing-like gesture, as if he wished, even at this distance, to wave us out of his sight.

We wheeled to the street again, straight into the arms of a tall M.P.—undoubtedly the figure behind us who had frightened the cigar clerk. The M.P. asked us if we needed help, and Jack showed him the small slip of paper that had his grandfather's address written across it, at which the M.P. whistled for a taxi, gave the driver our destination, and with a grave, mock smile, in parody of a footman, he hustled us into its rear seats. We were swiftly taxied into the presence of Jack's grandfather, an impressively tall and thin old Englishman with long, sweeping, white mustaches. A few hours later the chauffeur was freed.

The next morning, en route to Bay Shore from Brooklyn

Heights—and on a subway platform—I met a last, distracted straggler from "The Slacker Raid" of the day before. He was a boy about my size, dirty, and in wrinkled clothes that were too small for him. He edged up to me—too close, I thought—and showed me a ticket stamped "Far Rockaway." The fear in his face was pitiful. "I got to get out," he said, "out of the city, in a hurry, or they'll get me. Is 'Far Rockaway' far enough?" Without knowing where Far Rockaway was myself, I assured him that it was. "Is it beyond the Rockaways?" he went on. "That's very important—it has to be twice as far." I moved away. A subway door flashed open, and I stepped onto the train.

The next morning at our Bay Shore breakfast table, with a folded copy of *The New York Times* in his left hand, Jack's father talked of "The Slacker Raid": it had been a military crime, rising out of stupidity, fear, and a childish show of power; some multi-star general had panicked and imposed a curfew because he thought volunteering had tapered off; Wilson had acted quickly, the general had been relieved of his command, his prisoners released, the Armories emptied. Jack's father threw the paper aside, and we spent the rest of the day on the cruiser, where he sang London music hall songs while Jack accompanied him on his harmonica.

It was then time for me to return to Wisconsin, and I was permitted to make the trip by train alone. As the train entered the station at Chicago, where my father met me, I felt at least five years older than when I had left for my holiday, a piece of self-deception that showed me to be younger than my years indicated. Chicago no longer seemed exciting to me, and Milwaukee seemed sleepy and tame, shrunken in size. I felt restless, eager to go East again, and beyond New York, to join the war in Europe. I went to an Army recruiting office, and attempted to volunteer, where the medical officer re-

jected me so forcefully I felt crushed; the confidence in myself, so rapidly built up during my short stay in New York,
began to totter.

To stay at home seemed complete defeat of everything I
wished to come true. Gratefully I accepted an invitation from
my Aunt Martha to spend a month with her and her husband,
Arthur, on a visit to another one of Mother's sisters whose
husband ran a sawmill, up in the huge pine forests of northern
Wisconsin, near an Indian reservation. Though I was moving
in the opposite direction from my choice, away from the
cities into the wilderness, Aunt Martha's quiet understanding
of my difficulties, for she was still my confidante, soothed my
discontent. It was in the great pine woods that a whole new
spectrum of colors were opened before me in the bark of a
great pine tree that stood in front of the cottage we had
rented. There I discovered bright lavenders and serpent greens,
and livid reds that vanished into neutral grays at a distance of
ten feet away, and a hundred yards beyond the tree, was a
deep, icy, black and silver lake, round as a mammoth well.
It held the reflection of the moon in absolute stillness, and
dark, impenetrable waters spread around it as though they
mirrored the very depth of night.

As my uncle's Ford took us past the Indian reservation,
we saw miles of makeshift shacks, hills of manure, and broken
farm implements, scattered along an ill-paved highway.
Through ragged clearings between garbage heaps we saw a
few Indians slowly drifting into the far distance. It was as
though we had caught a glimpse of a medieval slum, long
abandoned to the disasters of unyielding poverty.

Scarcely more inviting was the poor-white settlement—
populated largely by migrant laborers from Kentucky and
their families—near the sawmill, where much of the same
blight of poverty ravaged the landscape: jerry-built, tarpaper
shacks reared tattered faces through the clearings. Yet through

these alleyways of rubble and tin-roofed squalor, there were signs of something bright and living. It could be discerned in the music of these people, the lilt and fall of their voices raised in song. Yet, as one came closer to these creatures and looked into their pale blue eyes, framed by the glint of sunlight that seemed to pour from their yellow hair, the faces looked mindless and scarcely human. In their unworldliness, they were trusting and childish: their work at the mill was paid in scrip to be honored only at "the company store," where they could never earn enough to pay their bills. During the winter months, their heatless tarpaper huts were death-traps; only the toughest survivors greeted new fugitives from Kentucky in the spring. Several years after my visit to their northern slum, I heard that following a week of subzero cold in February, the few Kentuckians who had not died had set fire to the mill, and its ashes had dissolved into the melted snow.

My retreat into Wisconsin's pine forests made me feel that I had retrogressed into the summers of my childhood, when my mother would take me with her on a two-week holiday at her Uncle George's farm in the rolling lake-and-dairy country of the state. Every morning I renewed a half-hated, half-desired acquaintanceship with Nature. This began with the freezing discomfort of washing myself at a pump rising out of a kitchen sink. After a few trials, I learned how to prime it, but I never went through this series of operations with the enjoyment that others spoke of them. From the kitchen I stepped out onto a stoop where a rough workhorse and wagon waited, and from which my unshaven, large-mustached, good-humored granduncle George lifted me high up to the driver's seat, and a second after, clambered up to seize the reins and sit beside me. From then onward, I drifted through a sensual haze of sweet-smelling hay and clover, rose-tinted dew and pastel yellow sunlight, crossed with pale blue shadows. It was as if my head was made of straw, and I had fallen asleep again. I sat up straight and took deep breaths of morning air.

On my return to school that fall, I felt at even greater distance from my fellow students than I had before. The school diminished, then receded into a new perspective. From this telescopic view, I began to see things I had left unnoticed.

At the school, scholarship students stood out very prominently indeed; their very lack of expensive carelessness in dress betrayed them; they were unstylishly clean and neat—which left them elaborately ignored. My sympathies turned in their direction, but my relationship, even to them, was tenuous, for my friendship with Jack and his family placed me on the unnamed "side" against them as though I were actually "hunting with the hounds." I did, however, form a casual acquaintanceship with one of the scholarship boys whom I shall call Waverley Jones. He was a small boy, dressed in gray checked cloth that his mother had carefully cut over patterns and sewed for him, so that at sixteen he still wore britches that fit snugly above the knee over his long, almost hip-length black-ribbed stockings. Like my friend Jack, he wore silver-rimmed eyeglasses, and whenever he lifted them off, he always looked naked and lost. His single approach to levity was to balance four or five books on the top of his head, and then trip gingerly to his seat in the classroom. The performance never provoked applause.

He had the manners of an exceedingly polite little old woman, with a way of placing one thin hand to the side of his mouth whenever he whispered pleasantries and arch observations. In profile his face had classical clarity and straightness of feature; his nose had the shape of the Goddess Athena's, and his mouth readily made, with a slight pouting of its thin lips, a cupid's bow. His grades always rose over ninety, yet he seemed to treat all his studies with equal indifference.

Because he seemed vaguely interested in fiction, and because he looked so lonely at school, I invited him over for an evening's visit to my house to show him our library. I introduced him briefly to my parents, and then I attempted to entertain him for an hour, a job more difficult than I anticipated, for though consistently polite, it was clear that he did not share my interests in reading. The next morning, and without explanation, my father forbade me ever to let the boy step foot in my house again. He advised me to break all contact with him, advice which I took readily enough, for my relationship to Waverley had an uneasy turn of "Do-Goodism" in it, a touch of patronage that seems to corrupt most humanitarian impulses. I sensed there was something wrong about Waverley, but could not name it. Nor could I clearly understand my father's vehement dislike of him—for, after all, he was the most intelligent boy I had ever brought around to the house, and one whose quiet poise was almost too well-sustained to be believed. But since I also felt there would be something priggish and Waverley-like in me if I attempted to defend him, I gave up the effort to gain his friendship.

Soon after his visit to my house, another aspect of Waverley came to light. He had a passion for acting, and a charming gift of wit in speaking his lines that impressed his English teachers. The Academy was preparing a production of *The Merchant of Venice*, and much to Waverley's happiness, he was assigned the role of Jessica. When he put on petticoats for dress rehearsal, he leaped up and spun on his toes like a ballet dancer. I had never seen him look so pink-cheeked, and radiant. Then he was handed Jessica's bodice and satin skirts which he fitted on with the greatest haste. Suddenly a pool of water flowed beneath his petticoats: he was incontinent with delight, and as suddenly in tears, deeply humiliated. He ran from the dressing room. The following evening, at the play's performance, he was a sad, determined, and restrained Jessica. Among themselves, the boys seldom mentioned the episode in the dressing room, and never to Waverley's face. Wherever he walked, in classroom or hall, he was given wide berth, and after his graduation from the school he dropped out of sight. I doubt if he ever saw any of his fellow classmates again.

But, of course, not all the scholarship students at the school had Waverley's temperament and fate. Some of the scholarship boys were of tougher fiber. Of these I remember two, both sons of Lydia Hanson, a Danish woman of tart and vigorous character, who taught French at the school, and was the first person I met who urged me to read Marcel Proust. I also remember seeing the early paperbacked volumes of his *A la Recherche du Temps Perdu* lying on her desk, and of her telling me firmly he was the greatest of modern writers. Her praise of him had an air of seriousness she seldom assumed; her usual tone was sardonic and crisp, and her eyes took fire from her wit.

Mrs. Hanson's history was anything but ordinary, for her father had been an Italian singer at the Danish Court, while her mother had been a lady-in-waiting. The Danish Court had been her finishing school and university, which gave her a command of Scandinavian languages as well as of French, German, and Italian. She fell romantically in love with a visitor to Copenhagen, an eccentric American scientist of Scandinavian origins, and after their marriage, she accompanied him back to Milwaukee. But her husband could seldom be persuaded to stay at home, and soon drifted out of sight completely. Mrs. Hanson, who now had four children of her own to support, became governess extraordinary to the children of the Milwaukee rich. Neither she nor her small family was overawed by the pretensions of Milwaukee wealth, and both recognized provincial snobbery as a futile and ridiculous imitation of grander snobs in the greater world. I suspect that, not without a trace of bitterness, she felt vastly superior to her husband's well-to-do relatives and their wealthier neighbors who had tried to snub her. Certainly her early years in Copenhagen were of a kind that would provide her with special understanding of social hierarchies unveiled by Proust. It was she who told me of the irony implicit in so many of Hans Christian Andersen's so-called "fairy tales," and made me aware of his contribution to psychological literature.

3

The Eastern (Gate 1)

As my terms at school approached their end, I grew increasingly unhappy—not because of leaving school behind me, but because I felt restless in my native city and wanted desperately to expand my horizons. In retrospect, my visit to New York had acquired all the glittering aspects of an interrupted dream. Yet, when I rather timidly advanced my hopes of going to college in the East, I ran into stiff opposition from my parents. I felt injured by their lack of understanding and sympathy.

What I did not know, and learned only much later, was that my father's business was in one of its periodic fluctuations downward, and that expenses in caring for his family had, for the moment, mounted very high. What made things even more difficult was that to his children he always pretended—and this in an offhand, modest manner—to be far richer than he was. The large house that he loved, with its retinue of three servants, plus a nurse who cared for his mother, as well as my mother's mother—who were both living with us at the time

—involved costs that were beginning to reach beyond his means; and to this was added the support of another household, that of my half brother, Johnny, his wife, and two children. Johnny's precarious venture into business had ended disastrously, and my father's pride was too great to allow him to wallow in bankruptcy.

No matter how far out of family favor Johnny slipped, I always delighted in his company. I never tired of his comic burlesques of big businessmen—Rotary Club members and civic leaders. Johnny's mimicry had an edge of daemonic frenzy: his flashing china blue eyes held unexpected resources in fantasy. At one moment he was a trembling, stupefied lamb, ready for slaughter on the Stock Exchange; at the next, he was a stock salesman whose bargains ranged from diamond mines to cocoanut oil, from roofing tiles to toothpaste and chewing gum—millions of shares—in the crackling baritone of a sideshow barker. These performances were all very well for the entertainment of a younger brother, and they probably amused a half-dozen fellow drinkers in the back room of a saloon, yet they did not seem to go over very well when acted out with slightly more serious gestures for the approval of bank managers. And whatever loans he was able to obtain were granted in my father's name.

Among my father's secret worries, Johnny's alcoholism must have found a prominent place. My father seldom spoke directly of Johnny's drinking, but on one occasion when he did, I had a brief glimpse of his deep anxiety over the fate of my half brother. During a summer holiday from school, I acted as general factotum and errand boy for my father. Early one morning, after our hasty six o'clock breakfast, we had driven over to Johnny's house, and on arrival, my father had sounded the horn. At the blast the sash flew up, and Johnny's face appeared at the window: "I'll be right down. Good morning, Father!" Then we waited for a long five minutes—at the end of which the front door shot open, and Johnny, breathless, leaped from the threshold into the car. There was a moment of snow-blanketed silence; then Johnny, smiling, his breath restored, opened his patter of the thousands of dollars he made and lost, the figures soaring into the morning sky, percentages added, subtracted, and compounded. I watched my father's frozen face, the profile sharp and pale. By that time—in another five minutes—we arrived in an empty street, for it was far too early for traffic, at Johnny's office door. On leaving the car, he lifted his straw boater and bowed solemnly to my father, then turned and with the keys jingling merrily in his right hand, plunged forward to unlock the front door of the battered brick building rented for him.

Three hours later my father strolled over to me. "Please run over to Johnny's office to see if he's still sober. Over the phone I can't get a single intelligible word out of him." Fifteen minutes later I reached Johnny's office: there he was, seated at a roll-top desk, a bottle of gin in one hand, and a whiskey glass in the other. He was weeping. "Your father is a wonderful man," he said over and over. "Always do what he tells you to do, my boy, he's a wonderful man." When I returned to my father I assured him that Johnny was himself, an ambiguity that seemed to relieve his mind, for as he lit a fresh cigar he looked more cheerful. As for myself, I was slightly angry at having been sent out to spy on my half brother, and at having been obliged to see him at his worst.

Within our immediate family circle, Johnny held the position of a naughty child who remained in constant need of forgiveness. Though he had married "the wrong woman," a rakish, "lace curtain" Irish girl, "out of nowhere," and though no one could lend him money with any hope of getting it back, and though he could not be trusted with any responsible task or errand (and perhaps because of all these reasons), he had won my mother's affection. It was she who defended him whenever he faced the silent, freezing censure of his father.

My father had greatly loved his first-born child, Henry, Johnny's elder brother, who, at fifteen, died of typhoid fever. Johnny was then fourteen, and had already become the half-neglected, wheedling, apologetic, "charming" younger son. Henry had received many small attentions and gifts from his father; Johnny stole things and was whipped for stealing and lying, or was pointedly ignored. He would have to beg his way back into the family circle by telling such a fantastic falsehood that everyone laughed and patted him on the head. Soon after he had learned to read, Johnny quit school, and with quick-witted ease glided from one briefly held job to another until he landed in the freight forwarding business—which, so it had been hoped, would make him self-supporting. To me he had been the good-natured half-innocent comedian, who, after frightening me by sawing the wooden Chinaman in two, made up for his crime by giving me an Edison phonograph and a dozen or so records. At the time I thought of going to college, I had no idea that Johnny's finances were in such treacherous disorder, and that they acted as a drain on my father's resources.

The standards of education advanced by Grace Lusk and Dr. Pratt at my preparatory school had their effect on my own conceptions of what was best for me—if I wished to be a writer—to learn. This meant that I looked down my nose at local standards for higher education, and that, so far as my future was concerned, my father's prejudices against colleges and schoolteachers were also against my convictions. I was too much my father's son to speak up openly against his prejudices, just as I had refused to quarrel with him when he called me a "mental cripple" because I wished to be taught Latin at school, instead of acquiring it at home as he had taught himself to do. Silently, my will was turned against his.

However silent I had become, I still made it clear that my intention was to go to college—while privately I still held to the hope that college would be so far away from home that it would open doors to the great world beyond it. My father proposed that I go to Marquette University a few blocks away from where we lived. He had already made an appointment for both of us to meet the director of admissions at Marquette. This action immediately seemed to sap my own initiative for revolt, and to leave me open and vulnerable to my father's will. To this I added my childish fears of Roman Catholics that had been awakened by my English grandmother's warnings against the "R.C.'s" who had invaded London in the ancient days of Bloody Mary, and had apparently provoked difficulties ever since. There was also a lurid, anti-Catholic weekly paper called the *Menace*, filled with crimes of the Popes, as well as of priests, that had fallen into my hands, and was my first encounter with this sort of "propaganda," a kind of reading matter as violent and as ill-informed as my uncle's domineering female employer who so many years ago had called me an "infidel."

Soon enough, and during a free noon hour, my father and I were invited out of the bright summer sunshine and ushered into the cool and darkened waiting room of the admissions office at Marquette. Quickly—his feet gliding beneath the skirts of a soutane, a face bland and smooth shaven—the director materialized before us, and dropped into a chair. With a transcript of my school record in his hand, he announced softly that though I had not yet graduated from preparatory school, I could enter Marquette at once—the university would consider it an honor to admit me. I was not flattered; instead I thought him deeply grained in hypocrisy. And, for a split second, I was more frightened than ever. Yet I had enough courage to thank him for his invitation, to rise from my seat to say that my father and I would think things over. At last, I had taken the initiative from my father. As we left the building I turned to him: "You wouldn't want me to go to an inferior college, would you?" In answer, he put his arm around my shoulder and assured me that he would not force me to go to Marquette.

Did my father share some of his mother's English distrust of Jesuits? If so, he would never admit it. A few months before dying at the age of ninety-six, his own father had become a convert to the Roman Catholic faith. In his youth my father attended Episcopal services, and had been christened in that faith, but after his second marriage he took the position of one who stood above all creeds, and insisted on the right of his children to make their own choices among them. His view was that of a tolerant agnostic—but whether this grew from his readings in his father's library of eighteenth-century philosophers, or from the successful preaching of Robert Ingersoll throughout the Middle West, I never knew. I do know that he was firm in his expressed belief that all forms of religious and racial prejudice were barbarous.

After the visit to Marquette, the deadlock over choice of colleges was partially broken: we compromised by my consent to register at the University of Wisconsin in Madison, not as far away from home as I desired, yet away from too many family attachments. My father felt the university was too "progressive," too "radical" in its influence on young people; therefore, in allowing me to go to Madison, he was taking a risk. He also feared my health was still too frail to permit me the liberty of making my way far from home. To both of us, the compromise was edged by uneasiness and dissatisfactions. I was to test my ground in Madison by starting my freshman year during the abbreviated summer session. This was to prove at once that I was fit to take care of myself, and I experienced a sudden sense of liberation—from paternal influence, and from my father's business, of which the little I knew, I did not like.

At the moment of graduating from my preparatory school I fell into day-dreaming of a golden-tinted past, of which my visit to Long Island was a crystal fragment, and receding behind it was a glimpse of Cathleen Nesbit's lips and eyes, and the shake of her head in its delightful toss of page-boy-cut black hair, and behind her a vision of Cousin Elizabeth who had grown into a tall, pink-cheeked, slightly withdrawing girl, who had dropped from my view into business college. When we entered the Kaiser's War in 1917, she left for Washington, where she became a secretary in one of the government offices near The White House. She seemed to have wandered off into obscurity—and I had no wish to emulate her fate. Even my compromise in going to Madison looked more attractive to me than her escape from family habits, tastes, and responsibilities. The spell that had held us together for a brief season in childhood (as though we had been lovers in *A Midsummer-Night's Dream*) had fallen away. Ten years after Elizabeth had left for Washington, I heard gossip of her unhappiness over a love affair, then rumors of an attempted suicide, and finally, news of her death.

I entered the university during the summer session. In the summer, Madison, dominated by its three centers of attraction, the state Capitol, with its brilliant dome, the university, set on a high hill, and a clustering of five small lakes nearby, had the air of being a resort town. Indeed, the greater number of its frame houses seemed to have been built for summer residence, as temporary shelter from the waves of heat that each summer flooded the shallow basin above which the town emerged. The lakes, and the tree-shaded walks around them, were the only areas of refuge from the hard sunlight, reflected from sides of houses and the pavement. Studies within the college walls moved at a weary pace: imagination clung to images of diving from a splintery run down a wet pier into one of the lakes. Work assignments were suitably undemanding. For my amusement I read the novels of H. G. Wells—in particular, *Ann Veronica*—and participated, at a safe distance, in the emotions roused by the suffragist movement. For several weeks, I was a committed partisan of Wellsian "free love."

But I had also won freedom of another sort: this was the freedom to lock the door of my room, and if I wished, to write till dawn turned the white curtains at my window to bluish-gray. I enjoyed my lonely excursions beyond Bascom Hall of the college to visit an Indian mound that had the shape of a monstrous bird in flight. I made no attempts at friendships and learned to loaf, for I had read somewhere in *Leaves of Grass* that "I loafe and invite my soul." With this I set myself the welcome task of writing at least one exercise in verse a day: parodies, light verse, and imitations of poets I admired. My great discovery in the university library was *Underwoods* of Ben Jonson. When the fall term opened, I felt refreshed.

In October of 1919, the new college year begun, the university was filled with ex-soldiers, returned from local training camps as well as from far places overseas. Of those I happened to meet, most were unstudious, skeptical, and vaguely embittered. The war had uprooted and bewildered them. Those who had been sent as far as Paris, were dazed by shock of contact with a civilization of deeper resonance than theirs— and their responses were expressed in heavy drinking and sexual promiscuity. During warm autumn evenings shrubbery and undergrowth along the paths surrounding Madison's five lakes sheltered many boys and girls, all in various stages of undress.

It was against this background of youthful excesses and adolescent disillusionment that the actual intellectual life of the university moved toward its accomplishments. Due to the initiative of Robert M. LaFollette, and the university's president, Van Hise, education at Madison had a liberal and opalescent halo; Moses S. Slaughter of its classics department was one of the founders of the American Academy at Rome. Students from foreign countries as well as from New York, Boston, and Philadelphia, were attracted to its campus where the air was bright with promise. Though I still regretted not traveling east to college, Madison was far less provincial than I feared, and I soon learned that its faculty had been recruited from the faculties at Yale, Harvard, and Columbia. As if to display its national appeal and interests, the Wisconsin undergraduate literary magazine imitated the format of *The New Republic*, and had newsstand distribution in New York.

In Madison, exhibitionism had its will in conversation, rather than in frenetic action. Talk of sex, "sex in the head," as D. H. Lawrence had called it, was of longer duration, and of greater frequency than campus love affairs. Though banned from undergraduate university courses in psychology, Krafft-Ebing, Havelock Ellis, and Freud were the authorities quoted at our midnight sessions. And among us, the books passed from hand to hand were *Fanny Hill*, *Women in Love*, and *The Satyricon*. I sometimes wonder if there had ever been a time when both students and faculty gossiped so freely about one another's private life—even the most innocent-looking of Madison front parlors and music rooms took on a conspiratorial-confessional air whenever a tea-trolley, loaded with cakes and watercress sandwiches, came into view.

Above the flow of gossip certain occasions at student-faculty teas had more lasting rewards: one was meeting Irving Babbitt of Harvard, who declaimed against his favorite antagonist, Rousseau, and who, because he wore a broad black silk stock with his dinner jacket, looked surprisingly like steel-engraved portraits of Sir Walter Scott. There was also a memorable disappointment in meeting G. K. Chesterton, who extended two thick fingers to my grasp, and mumbled something behind an untidy mustache. I had the impression of seeing a Falstaff manqué, the heartiness hollow, and the wit gone stale.

But far more enduring than student gossip and visits of lecturers from other universities and shores, was an all-pervading atmosphere of youthful Epicureanism, inspired less by Walter Pater than by a new translation of Lucretius, published in 1915. The author of this greatly refreshing and vigorous *De Rerum Natura*, with its unfamiliar Anglo-Saxon overtones was William Ellery Leonard, poet and philologist, Latinist, and professor of Anglo-Saxon in Wisconsin's English department. It would seem that Leonard's passionate agnosticism, expressed through the medium of the ancient Roman, struck deeper roots in student questionings than could be answered by further readings of *Marius the Epicurean*. In any case, Leonard's *De Rerum Natura* suited the mood of boys returned to the disillusionments of peace after the truce of the great war in Europe. How deeply Leonard's version of Lucretius affected young readers generally I cannot say, yet I was not surprised to read in Willa Cather's description of Midwestern campus life reference to Lucretius, which makes me suspect that Leonard aided a Lucretian revival that had begun during World War I. I sometimes fancy that it is probable that Lucretian philosophy, however slightly it may have been acquired, contributed its share toward post-war skepticism and sense of doom.

As I might have expected, my meeting with Leonard was certainly impressive. It was in the orchestra seating-area of a Madison theater about three minutes before curtain raising time at half past eight in the evening. Sounding through aisles to the left of me I heard my name, and as I turned, I saw a tall, prematurely white-haired man striding toward me, forcing

people seated on my left to struggle to their feet and to glare
at both of us. He wore a rough tweed suit and a loosely
knotted, lavender crepe bow tie. Although the necktie was
Byronic, its wearer had the appearance of a huge, cheerful,
ruddy-faced seraph, stepped out of a water-color by William
Blake. Because of the attention he had drawn by striding
toward me, I felt that he was shouting at me: he gave me his
name, and mentioned a sonnet I had contributed to the literary
magazine, and said he had made up his mind to be my adviser
at the university. I was rather more than flattered, for I had
heard that he took special care of unworldly, unconventional,
and promising students—he was guardian angel of the visionary and the shy.

From then onward, I was a frequent guest at Leonard's tea
parties where the talk was vigorous and the tea weak: Leonard
himself was less the host than the honored guest, while his
second wife, a pale, red-haired young woman, seated herself in
farthest corners of the room, knitting or mending, with an
overflowing wool or sewing basket at her side. It was said she
seldom if ever left the five room apartment where they lived,
or dared to step outside, for she was kept caged by Leonard's
fears of being left alone, and of the house being empty when
he returned from his lectures. Leonard's afternoon talks at the
tea table were continuations of his morning lectures, filled
with explosive quotations from Beowulf, or concluded with
rolling echoes of the sea from Homer.

Though I scarcely appreciated its value then, the great
worth of Leonard's conversation was in its candor—a violent
blaze and shedding of light. His opinions were forthright; his
puns erudite, grotesque, and his wit abrasive—all of which
served to make him unpopular with his less distinguished colleagues. In a provincial society, like that of Madison's, his
pleasantries were resented and misunderstood. He was not the

kind of New England native who could caress the vanities of his Midwestern neighbors.

His father had been an idealistic newspaper man and Unitarian minister—with a temperament not unlike that of Bronson Alcott—whose prospects were always noble, while the material facts of his daily life foreshadowed bankruptcy. His son's road was by no means easy: receiving scholarship grants, gained at the cost of long labor, allowed him to enter Boston University, then Harvard, and later Göttingen University in Germany where he found a homeland for his imagination. Later, his love of German culture and its scholarship held so great a fascination that, before he finally completed his doctor's dissertation at Columbia in New York, he felt compelled to return to Bonn for further months of study.

Leonard's autobiographical poem, *Two Lives*, telling of his marriage to a frail, precariously balanced girl who committed suicide, and *The Locomotive God*, his autobiography in prose, were confessions in the high Romantic spirit of Goethe's *The Sorrows of Young Werther* and Jean Jacques Rousseau's *Confessions*. In the writing of them, Leonard did not spare himself: he is their anti-hero as well as protagonist. In *Two Lives* Leonard sought out the causes of his young wife's suicide, and in *The Locomotive God* he attempted to unearth the origins of his phobias by reaching down to his childhood fears of death. He was well aware of the teachings of Dr. Freud, and was also conscious of James Joyce's *A Portrait of the Artist as a Young Man*. He was also aware, as he confessed in *The Locomotive God*, of a compromise he had made between his love of the classics and philology, with the result, so he wrote, that "I have a respectable name in two worlds of scholarship; a venerated name in neither."

Today, forty years after the writing of his confessions, his reputation as a philologist has fallen away into nothingness,

while his name is clearly identified as the translator of Lucretius into English verse. His Romantic affinities were also in
contrast to his love of the classics, and so were his divided
gifts as poet and teacher. Yet the Lucretian poet survives and
will probably endure, and one overhears strains of his music
in an elegy he wrote in memory of his first wife, soon after
completing the translation of Lucretius. The elegy also reflects
the landscape of the Madison both knew so well:

The corn-shocks westward on the stubble plain
Show like an Indian village of dead days;
The long smoke trails behind the crawling train,
And floats atop the distant woods ablaze
With orange, crimson, purple. The low haze
Dims the scarped bluffs above the inland sea,
Whose wide and slaty waters in cold glaze
Await yon full-moon of the night-to-be.
(. . . far . . . and far . . . and far . . .)
These are the solemn horizons of men's ways,
These the horizons of solemn thought to me.

(*O Earth and Autumn of the Setting Sun,*
She is not by, to know my task is done!)

It was through Leonard's advice that I resumed my studies
in Latin that I had left behind me at preparatory school, where
Cicero's *Letters* had caused me many half-hours of despair.
Leonard told me flatly he would not permit me to enter his
classes in Anglo-Saxon unless I renewed my studies in Latin
under his colleague, Moses Slaughter. Leonard was a discipli-
narian; I had no choice but to follow his rulings. Outside his
classes, Leonard was a critic of middle-class stolidity, a contributor to the *Nation*, a propagandist for Socialist causes, a
friend of the conscientious objector, and because of his Ro-

mantic attachment to Göttingen and Bonn, decidedly pro-German. Although I dissociated myself from Left Wing students on the campus—I did not like their self-conscious crudities, their noise, their lack of interest in everything except politics—Leonard's championship of Left causes was, so I believe, an active influence on my sympathies after I had left Wisconsin for New York.

While at college, I thought of Leonard as the exceptional Socialist, more of an anarchist, in his New England fashion, than a Communist: though his poetry had an inept Shelleyesque-Byronic diction, his gifts and insights were essentially poetic; and surely he was a man of broader experience and of greater stature than any of his colleagues.

His demand that I renew my acquaintanceship with Latin was seconded by the pleadings of a girl. In my eyes she was a more intimate, even lovelier Cathleen Nesbit, with quickly intelligent blue eyes and midnight-black hair. With a brief half-melancholy, half-childish grin, she could quote Catullus at me, and hint, that if I sat next to her in Latin class, she would play the part of Lesbia to my Catullus. But I would have to wait, for she was still in love with someone else who had just died. There was an air of lightness in her promises, but I fell deeply in love. As to my relearning Latin, that had become part of my destiny.

Among Leonard's colleagues, his two best friends were Moses Slaughter and O. J. Campbell, and each man acted as host for one of the two undergraduate clubs that met every fortnight of the college year. The clubs had, I think, a distant source of origin and a dim analogy to the Cambridge Apostles. I also think their members took themselves less seriously than their far-removed British ancestors, yet they were no less exclusive in choosing their membership and no less proud of their intellectual pretensions. The clubs were not debating societies, but informal discussion groups; in politics, they were vaguely liberal in character—and whenever well-known writers happened to be visiting Madison, they usually attended a meeting of one club or the other.

The more exclusive club of the two was a Sunday supper club in a private dining room of a hotel. Moses Slaughter was host: girl students were invited as well as men. Though the girls were listed among the university's "weighty intellectuals," there was nothing solemn about them. They usually prepared themselves for supper by a chaste Prohibition Martini, furtively mixed in their sorority kitchens, which added a cosmetic flush to their cheeks; their eager conversation and admiration was much relished by the purveyors of masculine wisdom.

In contour and manner Slaughter resembled photographs of Edward VII, even to the way he held his cigarette, and the cut of his beard. At a Sunday evening supper, he was the very nearly perfect chairman and chaperone. His presence would make certain that the talk around him was bright, yet decorous, and he was always at his best when encircled by attractive girls. When someone tossed a copy of Gertrude Stein's *Tender Buttons* on the table, he countered this gesture by apt quotation from Cocteau's "A Call to Order," and from there, he began to talk of Italian Futurism.

When talk at the supper turned, lightly enough, to the new novelists of the season, and the names of F. Scott Fitzgerald, John Dos Passos, and William Faulkner floated on the air, Slaughter would lean back, light a cigarette, and ask us what we thought of the latest recruits from Yale, Sinclair Lewis and Stephen Vincent Benét—how were they doing? Behind Slaughter's manner, which was more European than that achieved by the Europeans themselves, and beneath the air of authority he carried as one of the founders of the American Academy in Rome, was the brilliant, enthusiastic, loyal undergraduate at Yale, and behind the studious Yale undergraduate, the determined boy, born on a lonely farm in Iowa. In a different way from Leonard, Slaughter too held a likeness to Ezra Pound, in their common feeling of spiritual and geographical distance between themselves and their place of origin. Both Slaughter and Sinclair Lewis—two Middle Westerners—were fated to die in Rome.

Was there any logic at all behind this last coincidence ending in death? There is in it perhaps the interesting alchemy of historical and psychological incident. The closing of frontiers on the North American continent had slowed down the flow of populations moving west; the rapid growth of Middle Western cities produced a harvest of prosperous men and women, whose sons and daughters (of which Henry James had found a youthful model in his Daisy Miller) turned east to Europe. The economic determinist would probably say that the sons and daughters were following in the trail of their fathers' European investments, and he would be half right, half wrong. It is also half right to say that American heirs and heiresses were sent to Europe to seek out and to capture European titles (often by marriage) and things of virtue to store away in American museums. But this well-known cultural phenomenon which extended from the mid-1870s to the present day cannot be explained in material terms alone. There was a transcendental aspect of this *Völkerwanderung* that had little concern for worldly status or material gains. It was as Romantic and idealistic as you please. In its lighter moments, it carried with it a half-innocent air of educational tourism, yet beneath its surfaces, there was and still is a semi-religious impulse to seek out and rediscover cultural-ancestral origins.

Slaughter's death in Italy occurred while he was a resident at the American Academy. In Rome he was a familiar figure, as was his wife, who wrote historical studies of the Italian Renaissance; if anything, they were more at home in Europe than they were in Madison. It seems appropriate that Slaughter's grave is in the Protestant Cemetery at Rome, and that a bronze plaque bearing his name is to be found near Shelley's grave. Not that he cared much for Shelley's verse—he preferred Catullus—yet the placement of his remains was consistent with his taste and aspirations, for an essential quality in Slaughter's temperament was a brilliant regard for poetry.

The other club, sponsored by Professor Campbell, was strictly male in membership—a writing club at which a small group of undergraduates read aloud their papers, and subjected their readings to the alert, and usually destructive, commentary of their fellow members. Feelings were not spared, yet to serious writers in the group, this sometimes insensitive discipline had its rewards; at the very least, it showed the necessity for rewriting, and projected, however immature it may have been, an objective standard for verse and prose. At these meetings, usually held in the music room of Professor Campbell's house, the young author, faced by his critic, would often turn pale with injured vanity and anger. I remember one overgrown boy, with a large sallow face, who had come from an Illinois farm, and had fought in France, whose lips began to tremble every time a red-haired, red-faced ex-fellow-soldier would call one of his stories a goddam crashing bore. This was torture, and ugly to watch, yet the sallow boy's writing improved, and if it remained graceless and inept, it gained some semblance to liveliness.

Without any of us being aware of it, his red-faced critic was archetypical of his post-war generation, and his violence was another symptom of that day. After leaving college without a degree, this particular version of a Hemingway-like hero, born in a small Wisconsin town, eloped with the wife of one of his professors. In bed with her, and to their mutual horror, they discovered his impotence. The next morning, the professor's wife found him naked, his throat cut by a razor blade, on the tiled floor of their hotel bathroom.

Whatever shortcomings our writing club was heir to, the proximity of Chicago to Madison was not without importance. To young writers of the Middle West, Chicago was a step eastward in the direction of New York; it was also the home of Harriet Monroe's *Poetry*, and the temporary camping-ground of Margaret Anderson's *The Little Review*. Sherwood Anderson had made his presence felt there, and he had become the benign champion of young writers, a group that included Hemingway, Faulkner, and Hart Crane. Chicago journalism made its contribution by reprinting a weekly column on music and the imported arts from Europe by James Huneker. However superficial Huneker's observations were, however deeply stained by the colors of *fin de siècle*, he furnished youthful readers with a company of names seldom heard in the schools. His column provided a background for exploration of the real avant-garde. It was through Chicago's influence that the international flavor of magazines such as the *Dial* and *Vanity Fair* found approval at our Sunday night supper club— these, and *The Little Review* were the touchstones of all things dangerously new. Without quite knowing it, members of both fortnightly clubs were preparing themselves for the writings of the late 1920s, for a renewed appreciation of Gide, for Joyce and Proust, and that strange something that Eugene Jolas in his magazine, *transition*, was to call the "Revolution of the Word."

The search for a new aesthetic, however vaguely (and belatedly) felt and guided, stirred the curiosity of even those undergraduates who were least attracted to the arts. Among these was Philip LaFollette, the younger son of Wisconsin's senator, whose devotion was entirely given over to politics. He was one of the founders, with Leonard, Slaughter, and myself, of our Sunday night supper club. During the last quarter of my freshman year, I became acquainted with young LaFollette, at a students' restaurant that kept late hours, for both of us had formed the habit of studying between six and eleven o'clock in the evening and dining at midnight—when the place was almost empty, and the service better than usual. There we would talk until two or three in the morning. Philip's eloquence was no less forceful than his father's, but free of rhetoric. His enunciation was precise, his tone decisive, and as he warmed to the subject, his eyes flashed—usually with anger or indignation—behind his silver-rimmed eyeglasses. He was the first real intellectual of my own age that I had met, and because he looked so much older than I, and spoke with the authority of firmly held convictions, I soon fell under his spell. He introduced me to the doctrines of political liberalism (a far cry from my father's conservative Republicanism); and since he had been trained since birth in the pragmatic politics of the LaFollette machine, he had little difficulty in putting my own political innocence to rout. I found him alive to theories and interests that were outside the understanding and sympathies of most of my other acquaintances. He could talk knowingly of Bergson's *Creative Evolution* as well as of Nietzschean drives to power, and the very excitement in his voice made me aware of the practical application of philosophy to the raw fibers of daily life.

Beyond the circles of undergraduate clubs, of Philip's post-midnight discourses, there was Margery Latimer who kept herself well apart from fortnightly dinners and undergraduate intellectuals. She was enrolled at the university as a special student through the largess of Zona Gale, novelist, playwright, and philanthropist, trustee of the university and native of the small town, Portage, Wisconsin, where Margery was born.

Margery was indeed a special student in more than one meaning of the term. Her looks were those of a preternaturally healthy country girl, and at a time when it was fashionable for skirts to rise above the knee, her dresses were of high-waisted calico prints trailing down to an inch or two above her ankles—as though her home-sewn gowns had been tailored on patterns cut by Kate Greenaway. Her ruddy cheeks and her hair, cut shoulder-length, had the same country look; her lips seemed never to have known the touch of lipstick. And her wide blue eyes, now dreamy, now shrewd, now bright with malice, now gay, or very grave, were always startlingly clear. Behind this amazing façade there was a serious young woman who spent at least six hours of the day writing her novels and short stories. She ignored the literature courses in the university and read deeply in Willa Cather, Katherine Mansfield, and in the writings of that strange, precocious genius, Mary Butts, an English girl living in Paris, whose brief *romans à clef* sketched in verdigris portraits of the expatriate community. Like many promising Midwestern writers of her generation, Margery went far afield to find her affinities and "ancestors"—and in her choice of the widely unknown Mary Butts she had selected a guide whose mind had a sharper cutting edge than had Katherine Mansfield's—and whose prose had been stripped of all clichés.

There were days when Miss Gale would accompany Margery into a classroom, and then withdraw to a far corner, to look on with mouse-like sensitivity and alertness. At other times Miss Gale was almost ferocious in the pursuit of young admirers and disciples; there was no doubt of her need for them, just as there was no doubt of her generosity. She herself, when many years younger, had been, along with Ella Wheeler Wilcox and Edna Ferber, one of my uncle's protégés on the staff of the *Evening Wisconsin*. She had made an idealistic cult, as he at one time did, of youth. At the university she founded the Zona Gale Scholarship for the benefit of promising young writers. Like other critical Midwesterners of her generation, including Irving Babbitt and Paul Elmer More, Miss Gale sustained an interest in Far Eastern esoterica, and as

Babbitt turned toward the teachings of Confucius, and More to the Forest Philosophers of India and Japan, Miss Gale, through the influence of A. R. Orage, found her "world-view" in Gurdjieff's "Harmonious Development of Man."

As an early recipient of a Zona Gale Scholarship at Wisconsin, and a loyal friend of Miss Gale, Margery shuttled back and forth between Madison and Portage, a sleepy little river town, and after that, between Portage and New York. In 1922, Margery, after contributing a few sketches to the literary magazine, moved on to spend the next few years in rooming houses in New York. Though her country girl appearance was no less unusual, no less buxom on the streets of New York than it had been on a college campus, she looked more mature than the girls who emulated the dress and manners of F. Scott Fitzgerald heroines, the young ladies who dominated the fashions of the day. She felt herself to be more serious than they, and whenever she spoke of them, her Midwestern drawl took on a patronizing tone. *We Are Incredible* was the title of her first published novel, and incredible, rather than fashionable, or bohemian, she seemed determined to remain: through an era of Prohibition and "flaming youth," she was unconventional enough to refuse cocktails and cigarettes. Listening to Orage quote Gurdjieff was her dissipation.

By the time I came to New York in 1923, she had learned the art of imposing her personality on her environment. Whether in a Chelsea or Greenwich Village rooming house, the rooms she lived in seemed uniquely hers: the small portable typewriter, the studio couch, the glimpse of her copper hair and white bare arm in the dressing mirror on the wall, chintz curtains at a sunlit window, a fire at an open hearth offered proof that she had brought Portage, Wisconsin to New York. The cleanliness of the room with its fragile, gaily painted yellow wicker chairs and tables seemed to deny the presence of the cluttered, dirty street below from which one entered a battered door and mounted two flights of darkened stairs.

Her sunlit bedroom was less a proper bedroom than a well-scrubbed, well-ordered place to write. One then noted that near her typewriter was a quire of paper. Out of her window one half-expected to see an open field in spring where a calm river flowed and where blue-shirted farmer boys wandered with cattle. In rooms such as this, and during the years between 1922 and 1932, she wrote four books: *We Are Incredible, Nellie Bloom, Guardian Angel,* and *This Is My Body,* and of these, the two books of stories, with their themes of youth pitted against adult senility and blindness—*Nellie Bloom* and *Guardian Angel*—are the best testimonials of her youthful promise. She had made the short story her true form —she had yet to learn how to sustain at length the rhythm, the color, the immediacy of prose that echoed a speaking voice. In her stories, whomever she emulated, the pastoral imagery and accent were her own. Not unlike the early Sherwood Anderson's, her language had begun to acquire the authority of one who lived and wrote through instinctive needs and sensitivity. No wonder New York critics and editors at cocktail parties began to speak of her as a Midwestern Katherine Mansfield: they respected her rejection of the Prohibition martinis that they offered her; they were half-hypnotized by the straight blue stare of her wide eyes; they accepted her calico Kate Greenaway dresses as the rightful dairymaid costume of a prodigy from Portage, Wisconsin, and one of them, the current literary editor of the *Nation,* believed, mistakenly enough, that she wrote poetry after midnight in her chintz-curtained room. And in the dimly lit drawing rooms east of Park Avenue where Orage read aloud to his silent assistants from an early manuscript of Gurdjieff's *All and Everything: Beelzebub's Tales to his Grandson,* when

Margery stepped into their presence there was a fresh stirring in the air.

It was in New York that Margery reintroduced me to Kenneth Fearing, the future poet and novelist, who had entered the university at Madison shortly before I left it. She and Fearing were great friends; they shared at least one meal of the day, and when they walked out, arm-in-arm, they made an incongruous, if not uncharming pair. Fearing's dress was shabbily urban: he was thin, dark-haired, dark-skinned, and a cigarette hung from his lower lip; his brown eyes gazed at the world through horn-rimmed owlish eyeglasses. Though tall as she, beside her he looked like a bright, naughty, small boy being led away from a pool hall by a protective parent. It was she who had straightened the lapels of his unpressed jacket and knotted his tie; it was she who persuaded editors of magazines to print his poems, as she did for me, while the editors, not thinking of the poems they accepted, thought of the girl, and were certain that she wrote them, and that my name and Fearing's were her pseudonyms. This error became a joke between us three—our secret joke against the "Establishment" of that day—for Fearing's poems no more resembled mine than our poems resembled Margery's prose. We concluded that the literary editor of the *Nation* scarcely, if ever, read the verse he published—and in any case, he had been dazzled by Margery's blue-eyed stare.

Once a week, all three of us met in Margery's room for a cup of coffee at four in the afternoon. One cold April day Fearing had not shown up—a half-hour passed, and we grew worried. Margery and I hurried over to his rooming house to find him still in bed and unconscious, lying beside an unlit gas heater turned on full blast. Together, and with the aid of his landlady, we shook him back to life. Within the hour he was smiling back at us, with his sheepish, naughty boy expression. We threw an overcoat over his shoulders and walked him briskly out of his room to Margery's. We never referred to the incident again.

Fearing was the son of a prosperous Oak Park, Illinois corporation lawyer and a restless daughter of New York's well-known Flexner family, who deserted her husband and son while Kenneth was still quite young; in actuality he had been a much neglected child. In New York Fearing evolved three admirations: H. L. Mencken, Dashiell Hammett, and the Communist Party, for all three possessed, so he believed, the very quality of toughness toward which he aspired. In his verse, he carried one step further than Carl Sandburg the heritage of Whitman's realism; in form, at least, he anticipated the unrhymed verse of the New York-Black Mountain-San Francisco schools of the 1950s; and if William Carlos Williams became one of the acknowledged masters of the three schools, Fearing was a hidden ancestor. By 1940 the cutting edges of Fearing's verse had become dulled by repetition—his own, as well as that practiced by his imitators. Not unlike Hammett's "Thin Man" short novels, Fearing's verse has a bright metallic surface; it is swift and spare, and at its best, is a kind of un-rhymed light verse, topical and sharp, not without warnings of the dark world around it.

Margery Latimer's interest in Kenneth Fearing reminds one of Edith Wharton's maternal concerns for the welfare of Ernest Dowson, who caught and held her attention, when they crossed paths at an English colony in Dieppe. Mrs. Wharton had responded to the appeal of Dowson's middle-class raggedness, his boyish attempts at worldliness, his efforts to be French when he was ever so English in everything he said and did. Fearing's neglected-child helplessness, his boyish, daredevil Communism with its undertones of sentimentality —for Communism all over the world has its underside of sadism, sentimentality, and unconscious hypocrisy beneath a surface of toughness—were close indeed to Dowson's inability "to take care of himself," and his *fin de siècle* cynicism.

Margery Latimer's friendship with Fearing came to an end when she left New York to marry Jean Toomer, a promising Negro writer, who was also a member of the group surrounding Orage. She died in childbirth in 1932 at her parents' home at Portage, Wisconsin.

In writing from Portage to a recently married friend, Mrs. C. D. Haagensen (June 30, 1929), Margery's characteristic manner is shown, for she wrote as she talked, and as her feelings mounted, a note of hyperbole is overheard. Her relationship to Zona Gale had become strained, and she was probably thinking at this time of getting married herself. Was "I'm going to die soon" a premonition of her early death? Perhaps. It is more likely another one of her flights into hyperbole. In her last book of short stories, *Guardian Angel*, the story, "Daisy Turlock," has a more definite premonition of early death in it, yet its young heroine who dies, single and forlorn, was far more repressed and deathward-looking than Margery ever thought herself to be.

Dearest Alice . . . So why not stop off here instead of Madison. If I had a car I would take you over to Madison or meet you there. But we haven't and we probably won't now because my parents lost all their savings in the bank failure. Zona's husband took over the bank—isn't that strange to think of her connected with money and business? It is strange. I'm not mad at her any more or influenced by her or anything but just gleefully fond of her. Much better, isn't it? My griefs have been giving me a nice rest lately and I'm quite happy, enjoying existence so much that I am sure I'm going to die soon. Dear Alice, I love to think of you married and happy.

This is such a divine day and I have just come from a

picnic with my father. We went to the old Indian agency house. A divine place all falling down but so majestic and so like a mansion, a real one. The rooms are utterly empty and filled with bird's nests, the chairs are just one or two sticks, the windows are falling out, the fireplaces have been closed with cement. But nothing can change the form of the place. You breathe differently inside. You must see it. I have a darling old friend down there, the lock keeper. He made himself a set of false teeth out of pearls from the river. Usually he doesn't wear any at all.

Imagine I got a long telegram from Jonathan Cape and Harrison Smith who have started a publishing firm in America. They want to publish something of mine. [They published her last two books.] . . . Also an invitation to Harcourt Brace from Lewis Mumford. They all have rejected me at some time and I am really no different . . . so why should I accept them now? Kenneth [Fearing] says very bitterly that I'm not successful enough to be so high hat about it but I say I'd rather flop in the gutter than be taken up by people who once wouldn't risk me . . .

Love from
Margery

Looking back at the scene, the talk in the letter is a souvenir of the moment as well as a self-protrait. It was a day when Wisconsin grotesques, like the old lock keeper, were still at large, and also the day—1929 itself!—when bank failures foretold the collapse of stocks on Wall Street and the Great Depression.

In my freshman year I shared the amenities, including a very low rent, of a draughty, ramshackle, clapboard rooming house, whose landlady was so careless a housekeeper that she feared inspection from university authorities, and was therefore docile to the demands of her roomers—which included the privilege of holding sessions of talk, not always sober, over black coffee or raw red wine until the dawn-lit hours of the morning.

One of the roomers in the house was an ex-sailor, scarcely my age, who had been wounded in action during the first World War, and had received from the Navy a pension large enough to enroll him in the school of journalism at Wisconsin. Born in a suburb of Chicago, he had run away from home at seventeen to join the Navy, to join in the adventures of a first-class war as well as those of sailing all the seas. He had walnut-colored skin and was of Welsh ancestry, slender, wiry, short, with deep brown, slightly slanted Oriental eyes; his physique had the same look of antiquity that one finds surviving among Cornishmen and Welsh, and among those who live in the Hebrides. No one looked less Chicagoan than he. Like many another Welshman, famous or unknown, his surname was George, and since it was preceded by the initials W. L., one thought of him as Lloyd, rather than as William, the William being too English and too usual.

Beneath the surface, however, Chicago had left its mark upon him—in his clear dislike of the English and things English, in his love of things exotic and far away. His days at sea had given him plenty of time to read, and in a library aboard ship, long before the revival of reading Melville in American colleges, he discovered *Typee* and *Omoo* and *Moby-Dick*, and like myself, he was discontented with the university's offerings in American literature. Our championship of Melville was a sign of our protest against the narrowness of Wisconsin's American reading list. And again, like many Chicagoans of his generation, French literature—this probably through the influence of James Huneker's syndicated column in a Chicago Sunday paper—caught and held his imagination: the names of Stendhal, Balzac, and Flaubert seemed to open expanded vistas, uncharted sailings, and ports unknown. This was a generation that, as it circled Chicago's Loop on elevated tracks above the city, read *La Nouvelle revue française* to and from daily jobs in offices; and about whom it has been said: when good Chicagoans die, they go to Paris.

Post-war, isolationist Chicago was extraordinary, all the more so, because many Chicagoans fancied themselves to be violently anti-British. A candidate for mayor of Chicago called his opponents "redcoats," then put a group of his followers on horseback, dressed as Paul Reveres, and had them charge down Michigan Boulevard, shouting, "The redcoats— the redcoats are coming." Behind this turn of showmanship which everyone enjoyed, laughed at, and then dismissed, there was a vague Midwestern feeling that the British had tricked up into joining them in World War I. However deeply my friend Lloyd may have shared this feeling, his patriotism and his love of adventure remained unimpaired. After college his love of adventure sustained him in journalism, and when he was much older, and World War II had arrived, it carried him through reenlistment in the United States services on commissions that took him around the world. He was as staunch a loyalist to American causes—with the same heroic temper—as Rudyard Kipling was passionate in his defense of the British Empire.

At Madison, Lloyd and I formed a committee of two to reform readings in American literature. After reading generous portions of Melville, we turned to the far extremes of unlikeness—Henry James and Theodore Dreiser. When I was forced to remain three weeks in bed, ill with post-war flu, it was he who served me milk and crackers from a tray in my shabby room, the torn lace curtain streaked with soot at my bedside, the iron bedstead, an apparition out of a nightmare. After my supper, he read aloud to me through half the night, James's *The American,* and following it for the sake of contrast, *Sister Carrie*—a contrast great enough in style and subject to cut through the mazes of my illness, and to oblige us to confront our emerging preferences in literature. In discussing the two writers we were somewhat surprised to find ourselves on the side of the expatriate Henry James; it was the unthinking aspect of Dreiser's realism that turned us slightly away from him, his oversimplified solution to psychological problems.

Within the smaller circles of students through which I moved, extracurricular readings had become more alive than readings for classes. Among us, the publication of T. S. Eliot's "The Waste Land" in the *Dial* was an explosion even more devastating than the magazine's revelation of the work of Thomas Mann. Arguments over the poem were endless, and as I remember them, not enlightening. Yet one thing was made clear: students who argued over Eliot were certain that Swinburne's and Pater's "paganism" had dropped out of date—even "Satanism" at its 1890 naughtiest had suddenly acquired a hangdog, old-fashioned air. A few of us felt closer to Rupert Brooke's South Sea Island poems, with their hidden debt to G. E. Moore, than to anything that had evolved out of "The Mauve Decade."

Our ever-present, conscious protest was against the enforcement of Prohibition, and we went on drinking parties at roadhouses, or in fields, ten miles out of town: nauseous substitutes for gin were invented in college laboratories, and then distributed to us in zinc pails for us to transport farther into the country. For ballast, and to make the party seem outwardly respectable, we persuaded younger members of the English faculty in the university to accompany us. One of these was a young man with a recent Ph.D. from Harvard, whose features resembled (because of his heavy jaw, thick eyebrows, thick-lensed eyeglasses, black mustache, and underslung pipe hanging from his lips) those of Rudyard Kipling. Elder and conservative members of the English faculty disliked him; they thought him insubordinate, and far too dangerously modern in his taste—for he made no secret of his admiration for Henry James, and insisted that Hardy was a better poet than he was a novelist. When out on our drinking parties, he would talk for hours of his recent readings and rereadings in English poetry, and was among the first I knew to know and admire Wilfred Owen's poems. But he was at his best when he expanded on the subject of Thomas Hardy, and under his influence I began a series of poems in emulation of *Satires of Circumstance*. He also led me to the reading of D. H. Lawrence's *Sons and Lovers* and *Women in Love*. If some of us passed out cold soon after midnight, our drinking excursions were not without literary rewards—nor was all our time spent in the singing of drinking songs, some of them made up in the crystal heat of alcohol for the occasion.

Another stimulus to my writings was Witter Bynner's visit to Madison. Then at the height of his own career as a poet, he had heard of some light verse I had written, read it in an undergraduate magazine and praised it, and then, by a grape-vine route, invited me to meet him for tea at the house of a mutual friend. He was on his way, so I heard, back home from China, his head filled with adventures he had had there—and now he stood before me, a tall, balding man, with the gestures of a Boston Mandarin, smiling down at me, holding a steaming hot cup of tea in his right hand. With the grace of an ac-complished actor, he dropped, cross-legged, to a cushion at my feet, and looked up at me. He then began spinning a web of small talk, of a kind that seemed to charm everyone around us—and at that moment I thought of him as a citizen of the large world I hoped to enter after leaving the university. At this party, Bynner never seemed the guest, but throughout it, the welcoming and engaging host; even the intonations of his voice flattered everyone there; he had made an art of meeting people, and putting them at their unguarded ease. Years later, when I had read of his friendship with D. H. and Frieda

Lawrence in New Mexico, I understood why they found his attentions so flattering. He combined his social arts with those of portrait photography, and there was little surprise that the Lawrences posed for him willingly and successfully.

Among undergraduates in Madison, Bynner's praise of my writings and my meeting him at a tea party raised my social status considerably, for in the hermetic atmosphere of provincial academic society, any recognition from the larger world outside took on, if only briefly, exaggerated lights and shadows. For a short time I moved in the reflected glories of Bynner's charms, and I felt immensely grateful for the lift he had given my spirits, for his visit had come at a moment when ill health had left me feeling drained of hope.

In the years after leaving college I saw him at long-separated intervals—and only once when he seemed ill at ease. The occasion was unusual enough. It was in New York—and a small group of people, including Eliot's Midwestern relatives, came to hear recordings of T. S. Eliot reciting "The Hollow Men" at the apartment, if I remember correctly, of one of Eliot's New York publishers. I can see a chaste-looking, upright-sitting Eliot niece, serenely married and knitting garments for an expected baby, and an Eliot uncle telling someone how in St. Louis he had once been mistaken for Hugh Walpole. Witter Bynner had taken a seat in a chair directly behind my wife and me. He leaned forward to say a word or two to me; he looked fearfully old, flushed, and restless. He whispered at me, "I'm terribly jealous of Tom; I, too, went to Harvard." He leaped up and swiftly left the apartment, leaving me to wonder why Eliot, whose gifts were so obviously superior to Bynner's, should arouse such fury. Was this because of Eliot's frequently misunderstood humility? I suspect it was.

My last meeting with Bynner was twenty years later in the mid-1950s at a hotel dining table in Athens. He was deeply tanned, venerable, and bright, for he seemed to have drifted into one of the rare havens of extreme old age. He confessed to me that he was almost blind, but that Greek white light from Apollo overhead and the heat of mid-July had restored his senses—there now, he could see me clearly—the fog had dropped away. The last I saw of him was a wave of a long brown hand.

Back in Madison of the early 1920s, Bynner's kindness to me had also given me a small measure of authority with the girls I wished to know. With that small increase in authority came a rise in my self-confidence, and I acquired enough initiative to made advances to the blue-eyed, black-haired Dorothy who had lured me into Latin classes. It was not her fault that I had fallen deeply in love with her, for she had warned me that the image of her dead lover still haunted her, that his shadow still wavered between us whenever we met. And, of course, she did not know that I had superimposed upon her features the image of Cathleen Nesbit, a trick of self-deception on my part that was scarcely a compliment to her.

In retrospect it seems to me that this pretty, otherwise hardheaded, little girl from Philadelphia had been very indulgent to me, for I had a way of taking much for granted, of believing things I wished to believe—and of ignoring all things pointed in an opposite direction. I believed that by holding her in my arms I could win her to my side—which was boyish nonsense, as long as the shadow of her earlier lover haunted every street corner in the town of Madison.

One evening, and as if we were making an attempt to avoid the wraith-like presence of my rival, we strolled the paths surrounding Madison's five lakes. It was through a glorious June twilight. At last we watched, between the trees across the lake, the slow rising of the moon. A pale, translucent, reddish glow walked among the trees. It was as though the chaste Diana of the ancient poets had fallen in love, and was suddenly flushed with unfamiliar warmth and desire. We turned to each other, and then sat down on a small rise of grass and moss, and Dorothy, with a girlish grin put her arms around my neck, and I, my anxieties floating away to nothingness, was happy beyond anything I could say. Below us flowed the murmuring, unseen waters of the lake.

It seemed to me then that Dorothy had completely surrendered herself, if not to me, to the charms of poetry. A few days later she gave me, as though she were parting from a treasure, her coffee-stained and battered copy of Quiller-Couch's familiar, blue-bound *Oxford Book of English Verse.* I kept it as a souvenir of the June twilight and the walk with Diana, but I never dared tell her how much I disliked Quiller-Couch for his impertinent rewriting of Sir Thomas Wyatt. But then, Dorothy and I were always on easy terms whenever we talked of Horace and Catullus, and whenever Dorothy appealed to me most, I thought of Lesbia.

A day later she announced that she was soon leaving college, and I could do nothing to detain her; she had taken her bachelor's degree that June, and now she had decided to go back to Philadelphia; possibly, she would enter graduate school in the East, this coming fall. A week later, she was gone.

Try as I could, I could not shake her out of my imagination, my hopes, my mind. My only relief came in writing verse, poems inspired by ancient poets, Catullus, Horace, and Lucretius, and I began writing unrhymed verse in English— if Thomas Gray's *Elegy in a Country Churchyard* had been haunted by Lucretian melancholy, so was I. It was in the shadows of my wakeful nights, in the cold north winds that came whistling through loosely fitted wainscotting and windows, circling my brass bed and warped pine table where my typewriter rested, my cigarettes, my ash tray, my electric torch. My stick leaned against the back of a wooden chair.

In the autumn following my unhappy spring and empty summer, I must have gone through what was then called "a nervous breakdown." My solitude increased its hours; most of my friends and acquaintances at the university had left Madison; I glided into and out of classes, speaking only to a few. I set my face against the making of new friends. In my shabby room I wrote from eight in the evening until midnight. And after midnight, the electric torch and my stick became my intimate companions, my guides to take me walking through the woods surrounding the town. I alternated between feeling wholly miserable and gloriously enjoying my self-imposed solitudes, for the sessions of insomnia that kept me awake at night had increased the volume of my writings; in actuality, I had begun to find my "voice"—and this discovery prevented my dissolution into the darkness of self-pity.

My midnight journeyings gave me a refreshed nocturnal view of Madison, and it awakened my curiosity as to what took place in the by-streets of the city, in its pool halls, and all-night lunch rooms. I soon found that the underside of life in Madison was well under control; patrolmen and taxi-drivers did not yield up their secrets, but went on drinking endless cups of coffee, and the lightly clad waitresses who served them were too old, tough, raw-boned, and red-eyed to be seductive. Yet in one pool hall my search was partially rewarded by the arrival of a loudly dressed, hard-voiced boy from New York's Broadway, who claimed that he paid his tuition, room, and board at the university through his winnings at playing pool. His first step was to break down the morale of his opponent before the match began—and the opponent was usually a drunken barber or a red-faced farm hand. The boy would set his smart gray Trilby on one side of his head and shout at his fellow player across the table: "You're so dumb, you'd think Christ was killed by the Indians." The man would then make a lunge at him, restrain himself, and then, wild-eyed, begin to play—usually to lose. I soon learned that the boy was a drifter, moving from one university town to another, and whenever he found a suitably angry opponent, probably earned his way fairly well. As I then saw him, he was an urban, twentieth-century Huckleberry Finn, as adventurous and as footloose as I wished to be, and I dreamed of reversing his traveling westward by going to New York and learning to be as much at ease among all classes of New Yorkers as he was among small-town citizens of the Midwest. This, of course, was fancy. In the light of a serious moment after breakfast the next day, I knew the boy was headed toward oblivion: he could land nowhere but in an obscure country jail, where he would receive kindly treatment until his New York relations sent money enough to ship him back home.

I decided that my own adventurousness had deeper roots, had more serious motives than that of a boy who made a precarious living at the pool table—it was clear enough that he would never grow into being another Willie Hoppe. My restlessness had part of its origin in the feeling of estrangement my entire family felt, the estrangement I felt, when as a child I slowly walked into a bakery to buy a dozen Vienna rolls. The large German girl behind the counter handed me the bag of rolls, then said, "Why do you talk so funny: you come from far from here?" She did not believe me when I said I lived around the corner. "You come from the East," she said as she smiled down at me.

Another part of my feeling of estrangement was a conviction that few Midwesterners around me would understand my devotion to writing and poetry—and even if they did, they would be contemptuous. If I were to keep on writing, I knew I could not feel at home among neighbors who thought of nothing beyond business affairs, country clubs, and a new car every year. Even the revival of interest in the arts, led by Laura Sherry and The Wisconsin Players had begun to dwindle; and the Pabst Theater no longer subsidized repertory acting groups who excelled in producing little-known plays of Wilde and Shaw; wherever I turned, either in my native city, or in Madison, I felt the lights had gone out forever.

However dark, however lonely the view around me seemed by day, by midnight, after several hours of writing, my sense of adjustment to solitude would be restored. The fall of 1922 was a rather pleasant fall; it was less cold than usual, and on my walks around the lakes, my torch light uncovered paths of trodden leaves, not snow. Red and yellow fungus and pallid toadstools lined my way; deep green and thick fir and pine trees sheltered me from northern winds. One night, I wrote till two, and my walk was through the gray-blue mists of early morning. As swiftly melting fragments of light fog swirled around me, the air seemed to awake, and far above my head, there was a hint of dawn. Then, as I entered a small clearing where, on my left, I saw the silver waters of the lake, I heard a girl's voice reciting Latin poetry. The lines were from Lucretius: they were indeed his invocation to Venus, and goddess of all lovers, and of creation itself. It was the girl's voice that made the air seem marvelously alive, that gave it color in the slowly increasing light of dawn. Then on my right, at the far edge of the clearing, I saw the girl, seated on a fallen tree trunk, leaning against a tree behind her, and I recognized her as one of the members of my Latin class of a year ago—her voice had the floating clarity of unearthly music. If she saw me, she did not show it.

There had always been something unearthly, something Uranian, something of Tannhäuser and the Unicorn clinging to her image, and yet, if she were looked at in a glaring light, something of the grotesque. She was the nineteen-year-old daughter of a German professor of French at the university. He was a widower; she was his only child. He kept her dressed as though she were no older than twelve, her skirts above her knees, her legs in long black stockings; a black elastic cord beneath her chin held a large brimmed hat firmly on her head, and her yellow hair fell in two tightly braided pigtails down her back. Her figure was mature: she had broad hips and ripened breasts. She moved with great, conscious modesty and lowered eyes.

Safe in the woods and mercifully free of the embarrassment she seemed to feel while attending classes and walking the streets of Madison, she sat at ease. At last she was hidden from the curious gaze of her fellow students, who so often turned to look at her as she strolled the campus with her gray-bearded father. Here, in the half-light of early dawn, her unbecoming costume veiled, only the outlines of her figure visible, only the music of her voice reciting poetry overheard, she herself evoked the image of a northern Venus, strayed and alone, bringing back a touch of spring in the odd season of an Indian summer, to the very edge of a foreign wilderness.

Her image was my last clear view of Madison and its associations before I left it to journey to New York in early February of the new year. Before leaving I had first to make certain of my credits for a bachelor's degree, and by talking matters over with my dean, I discovered, to his surprise and mine—for my arithmetic was as bad as ever—that I had more than enough credits to receive it. What held me back from receiving honors were mediocre grades in analytical geometry and German. The near-failure in geometry had been very like school failures one encountered in nightmares, and so it was (with the exception of one student who did very well in a class of five sophomores) for the rest, most of whom fared worse than I. And because of another boy in it who failed so completely that he was obliged to drop out of the university, the class was memorable: for the boy, tall, awkward, silent, dressed in an ill-fitting R.O.T.C. uniform, was Charles A. Lindbergh.

Another boy who was "odd man out" at the university was Stanley Weinbaum, a rosy-cheeked, curly-haired, rather plump freshman, who introduced himself to me in the smoking car of a Madison-bound train out of Milwaukee. His good humor was instantly contagious, and as he sat down next to me and lit a cigarette, I found myself smiling back at him, fascinated by almost everything he said. On a charming easy level, he combined the merits of young Joseph with those of David and his harp.

Stanley had a number of "ruling passions": these included playing his guitar as though it were a lute, alliteration in writing verse and chanting it, mathematics, Turkish coffee, the invention of scientific gadgets, and cigarettes. In his speech, he had great purity of diction, and a love of entertaining everyone around him—this last with an artless air that seldom failed to please. His one hatred was military drill, and he exerted all the skills of his inventiveness against participating in it.

The offices of the R.O.T.C. were in a formidable Victorian Gothic red-brick Armory, where basketball games were played, setting-up exercises performed, and on the second floor, files of drill attendance stored. Unless one had a permanent medical excuse (which I possessed) non-attendance at drill meant expulsion from the university. It was the crime of crimes. Stanley had made up his mind to cut drill ninetenths of his stay at the university. He carefully noted how the drill sergeant marked attendance on a card—he then assembled a kit for picking locks, and thereafter, at midnight, once a month, the locked doors of the Armory would give way to Stanley's craftsmanship; trembling, he would mount dark stairs to the files, and mark himself "present" for each of his absences at drill. Both his courage and ingenuity were admirable—but the preparations for these excursions, and the excitements, fears, and sense of victory after them, were so tremendous that when he turned up at my room, at two in the morning, he would be in a state of near collapse. We would then rush out to an all-night lunch counter and order cups of the blackest and hottest coffee we could get. Within a few minutes, he would start singing verses he had composed in the manner of Omar, or of Swinburne, or his own latest version of a French villanelle. The more demanding a verse form was, the more it delighted him, and he played with it as though it were an intricate and prismed toy.

But the university and the town of Madison were not made for Stanley Weinbaum, not for a boy who would forget his classes from one week to the next, who would strum his guitar all day and made a habit of writing all night five or six days a week. It was, I think, near the end of his sophomore year that he left the campus not to return. His instructors were less displeased than baffled, for he belonged to a world that was other than theirs. He was like a cherub floating far above the campus. Distance and a thin rain of mist obscured him from view.

A few years later, I heard he had written a vast number of science fiction stories that appeared in pulp-paper magazines, and there he was highly respected as a forerunner in certain types of fantasy. Except for the writings of H. G. Wells and Arthur C. Clarke, science fiction has remained a genre far outside the range of my interests. Its thrills and speculations are too inhuman, too unrevealing of human motives and moral insights to hold my attention. Clarke's stories have disarmed me by their wit and well-informed ease in the telling; and Wells's *The Time Machine* is a social parable that has survived seventy years and two world wars. These are rare fish in science fiction waters. I trust, without having read Weinbaum's ventures in that ocean, that in writing science fiction, he fulfilled his own life pattern before his early death: certainly his pleasure at entertaining many was fulfilled, for the plotting of a science fiction fantasy is often a colorful and intricate affair, one that delights the creator as well as his readers.

During my last few weeks at Wisconsin, I was under pressure cramming for my examinations, and concluding, much to my own dissatisfaction and boredom, a B.A. thesis on the plays of Arthur Pinero. I felt I had been unjust to myself and to my subject—yet the feeling was not without its results in my far future, for my unhappy experiences in having to read and comment on Pinero's plays were portents of my later rejection of social realism in the theater, and were also among the reasons I came to admire the parables of Franz Kafka and the plays of Samuel Beckett, rather than the Leftist propaganda of the Soviet and American would-be proletarian drama and novel.

If my professors in Madison were dubious of my abilities to make my own way in New York, they were kind enough to disguise their doubts, and to write letters introducing me to their friends in the great city. Their willingness to sanction my immediate going to New York alarmed my parents. What my parents saw was not, of course, me as I saw myself, but a nervous, impractical, half-innocent child who could not walk without the aid of a stick. The possibility of my finding a job to support me was slight. My disposition, my mother told me, was far too amiable, too diffident, too yielding, too feminine to be another Charles Dickens. She would give me money to buy a bookstore, where I could sit down, my stick at my side, to welcome customers. That would be safe and pleasant and sensible. I would probably never marry, and a bookstore, even in Milwaukee where people seldom bought a book, would bring in enough to keep a single man in pin money. My father could always save me from bankruptcy. I quickly admitted all the half-truths in her argument. I agreed I was far too amiable—which was why I would ruin any business I stepped into; the bookstore would merely waste her savings—for I would be writing poems, not making money.

My father, pale with anger, told me I was a fool. He had read my poems, he said, and thought them good. But didn't I know, fool that I was, that in this country I would waste the rest of my life throwing pearls before swine? I needed care: he would care for me by giving me work in his own business. That would be sensible, that would be sane. I said that through neglect and absent-mindedness, I would ruin his business. I admitted that I was good for nothing, good for nothing except the writing of my poems. That was all I cared about; that was all I could do. But once I landed in New York, I would surely find a job.

I knew something of the risk I was taking, for the evidence I had of being able to write was very small. My typed manuscript of poems was so slender I feared to let anyone know how thin it was, for I wished to show my poems at their best. Some of the poems had been accepted by Harriet Monroe's *Poetry* in Chicago. These made me feel that my stake in the future was not entirely a dream. But for the moment, I would have to be taken on faith, or perhaps a turn of phrase whenever I talked about poetry. A year ago in Madison, I had lost two large manuscripts of verse, including fifty sonnets; I no longer regretted my loss. I enjoyed the prospect of traveling light, of being forced to make a fresh start. I was happy to leave my three and a half years at the university behind me, glad to be leaving Milwaukee for New York.

4

The Eastern Gate (2)

IN CONTRAST TO my holiday visit to New York in 1918, I
rode eastward this time without benefit of Pullman cars
and porters; the ride of some thirty hours was in sooty day-
coaches and smoking compartments, where floors were soon
cluttered with torn newspapers, and washing facilities were
meager and rare. I had fifty dollars in my breast pocket, a
portable typewriter, a bulky wardrobe trunk, and in my right
hand, a pale yellowish-green copy of Stendhal's *The Charter-
house of Parma*, translated into some of the most villainous
English that ever defaced the pages of a book. It speaks much
for the power of Beyle's mind and genius that somehow or
other, the irony, the Romantic magic of the book shone
through the confusions of crazy syntax and febrile rhetoric.
I had identified myself with Fabrizio, his boyish adventurousness, his charm, his lack of shrewdness. During the stretch of
the long ride east, he was excellent company. At last, the book
fell from my lap, and I waked to the noises of the train and
the city. The train was on elevated tracks, slowly winding its

way between rows of red-brick tenement buildings where half-naked, stolid men and women stared, like drunken animals, out of open windows. To me this came as a vision of Hell rather than the sordid everyday spectacle so commonly accepted as a part of urban existence. If my imagination was stirred by what I saw, it became, if anything, overactive: I imagined filth and despair behind the naked creatures I saw moving through their rooms; I imagined stench-filled hallways, piled wreckage behind bolted doors, of places where even the armed police scarcely dared to go. I began to feel faint, and it was not until after I had landed at Grand Central Station, checked my trunk and typewriter, tipped a station porter, and drank a cup of coffee at a station lunch counter, that I could face the city.

From the Grand Central Station I took a taxi across town to the west into Chelsea, where, so I had heard, I could rent a room cheaply, and in the same neighborhood, test the efficacy of one of my letters of introduction. The letter was to Dr. Horace Kallen who had bachelor quarters in a Chelsea brownstone front, near the brownstone offices of *The New Republic*, and not far from the equally dignified brownstone housing of The New School for Social Research where Kallen was an inspiring, if caustic lecturer, and one of the founders of the School's policy in providing graduate education for adult New Yorkers. At Harvard, Kallen had been a protégé, friend, and disciple of William James; with James, he shared a shining faith in Pragmatism, but in Kallen's case, the optimism behind Pragmatic thinking was cooled and shaded by overtones of Hebraic fatalism. He had already published *The Book of Job as a Greek Tragedy*.

Chelsea, so it seemed to me, was the perfect setting for the world of Dr. Kallen's making: the Gothic structures of a theological seminary were within hailing distance, and to the west and north, were the slums of Hell's Kitchen, named, I believe, by Romantic Irish-Americans, who lived in them. The environment was also colored by the presence of Herbert Croly's and Walter Lippmann's *The New Republic*, where liberalism was ever so slightly tempered by Harvard skepticism. All these, I thought, were elements in Kallen's view of the universe—certainly they contributed to the drift and play of his conversation.

I saw before me a huge-shouldered young man, in a broad-brimmed, half-gallon Stetson hat—there was levity in his touches of academic dandyism, the brightness of his bow tie, the set of a fawn-colored top coat. His complexion was deep brown-olive, lightly flushed, and he had the full-lipped, sharp-curved smile of a Pakistani Buddha. And generously, he offered himself as my shepherd through the urban pastures, caves, and wilderness of Greenwich Village. He was a kindly guide, for whenever he felt that my morale was running low, he invited me out to a round of visits in the Village, first to a restaurant, then to see his "young people," his many friends living in lofts and shabby studios, promising boys and girls who were among the contributors to *Vanity Fair*, *The Liberator*, and an "arty" large-leafed magazine, *The Playboy*. Most of them were of the Left Wing generation immediately following Mabel Dodge's *Movers and Shakers*, and to them John Reed was a hero of greater magnitude—enshrined, as he was, in the Kremlin—than any other figure in American history. All were waiting, so it seemed, for the revolution to catch fire in the streets below 14th Street. And as they waited for the conflagration they whiled away the time in making love.

In spite of my gratitude for Kallen's intervention, I soon felt that a slight haze of disappointment had risen between us. I felt that he felt I was not the kind of poet he hoped that I would be. I was much too diffident, perhaps also too proud, to talk to him in my own defense. I was then too young to know, as I know now, that philosophizing social scientists, from John Stuart Mill to the present, always wish that poets and poetry were more utilitarian—and less imaginative—than they prove to be. He begged me to emulate the "proletarian" verse and ballads of a young poet, just arrived in New York from Princeton, whose narrative poems echoed Masefield's "The Everlasting Mercy,"—and whose efforts had been praised by friends of Edmund Wilson. The sentimental blandness of the Princeton boy's verse deeply offended me. I felt the futility of trying to explain that I was interested in doing something harsher, newer, and, I hoped, something more original. I said nothing, and therefore felt misunderstood.

Yet during our acquaintanceship Kallen gave me two glimpses into the trials of experience I never forgot. One evening I met him hastening toward The New School to deliver a lecture. His face was gray, his hands were trembling, and before he spoke, he removed his Stetson to wipe his forehead with his white handkerchief. He looked about to faint. "No, I don't take drugs and I'm not ill," he said, "but this often happens just before I give a lecture. How can I face that crowd of people in a crowded room?" With a long intake of breath, he rushed away. And one day as we were walking toward the Village, he turned to me with, "There is no time in life when things become less difficult—from the cry at birth to the agonies we suffer in old age." It is probable that he had been thinking over—not only the trials of Job—but the warning of Sophocles: "Not to be born is the best for man."

When I went down from Chelsea (I had settled into a block called "Suicide's Row" on 23rd Street) to the Village, I often drifted into the parties given by Kallen's "young people." William Rose Benét was one of them; a number were reviewers of books on *The New Republic;* and some were simply boys and girls who were singing "Tut-ta-tut-Trotsky" to the tune of "K-K-K-Katy." Among the very attractive girls I saw at a party was Louise Bogan, half-reclining on a studio couch, a martini held glittering between the fingers of her right hand. In the noisy, ill-swept studio it was as if she had been dropped from the skies, as slender, as immaculate as the moon in its last quarter, her oval face in profile, clear and pale.

On East 10th Street, on one of those crisply clear, never-to-be-seen-again summer evenings in New York—for during the 1920s winds from both sides of Manhattan would effectively cleanse the air—I encountered Mrs. Elinor Wylie, and at her side, the straight-backed military figure of William Rose Benét. They were probably en route to or from a cocktail party; both looked radiant and larger than life. Caught up in the colors of the setting sun, Mrs. Wylie's hair and afternoon gown, even the slippers on her feet, were shimmered with red and gold. For a split second, one had the illusion of seeing a richly gilded unknown Botticelli spring to life.

My letters of introduction carried me to the staid offices of *The New York Evening Post* on Vesey Street—one in particular, to Christopher Morley, whose newspaper column, "The Bowling Green," was where I had first read John Crowe Ransom's poems. In that reception room, lined from floor to ceiling with black bound volumes of the *Post*, the hour I waited to meet Morley seemed centuries long. At last he arrived; his portly figure and round face seemed to light up the air around him. He assured me that though he could do nothing for me, I would succeed in finding work soon. His optimism was so contagious that I forgot my long wait and felt I had energy enough to ask for work at a half-dozen other places. Then Morley said he *could* perhaps do something; he could send out his colleague on the *Saturday Review*—William Rose Benét—to have a talk with me right there and then. Benét would probably give me a book of poems to review. He disappeared: five minutes later I was talking to the tall man who had been pointed out to me in East 10th Street as Benét. Benét now vanished for a second, then returned with a new anthology of recent British verse—I was to review it. The book was of small moment, and my pay for reviewing it scarcely paid my bill for dinner in a cheap restaurant, yet Morley's good-humored encouragement—which had warmed and flattered me—and Benét's politeness—with its flash of understanding—cheered me through many dark weeks ahead.

In the slippery arena of literary journalism where many souls are lost, and few reclaimed, Morley and Benét held places of especial character and trust. In the early 1920s, Morley was widely known as the champion and friend of Joseph Conrad—and of Sherlock Holmes. Benét was a discerning reader of verse and a generous critic; he erred only in his negligent attitude toward his own writing, his indulgence in a journalist's carelessness. His creative energies were spent in supporting, and often inspiring the writings of his brother, Stephen Vincent Benét, and those of Elinor Wylie. He had the reticence, the pride, the courtesy, the look, the manner of his Spanish ancestors—and these were far removed from the conventions of those who worked with him in newspaper offices.

Many years after I had first met him, I came to appreciate more fully how wide was the range of his readings in English poetry; how deep was his attachment to it. After his death in 1950, his widow showed me his marginalia in books of poems he had given his brother, Stephen, and to Elinor Wylie, before their marriage. This marginalia extended well beyond his poetry library. His readings in prose as well as in verse were indicated, and the range included Croce's discourses on tragedy along with the latest (circa 1948) disillusioned commentaries on the Soviet Union and Karl Marx. From such notations one could trace the path of his attractions to Communism during the late 1920s and early 30s, for then Benét, like many other liberal-minded newspaper men, "the lib-labs" of the era, was shocked by the poverty-haunted spectacle of the Great Depression. Benét had received his early journalistic training on the Pacific Coast: he shared the heritage of Populism with its "silver-tongued boy orator" William Jennings Bryan—and to this was added an environment conditioned by the writings of Ambrose ("Bitter") Bierce, Jack London, and the hardy, persistent Socialist, Upton Sinclair. Consistent with his California training in journalism was his still earlier friendship with Sinclair Lewis when both, with their talents unrecognized, were undergraduates at Yale. They were critics of the "Establishment." Both had more than a rational share of American idealism coursing through their veins. The great difference which distinguished one from the other was Lewis's histrionic shrewdness, his ability "to show off," as opposed to Benét's raised eyebrow in rejecting the vanities of showmanship.

In the days when I first met Benét, my need for finding enough work to keep myself alive was very real. Curiously, I had no lack of luxuries. My acquaintances gave me press tickets to the experimental productions of The Theatre Guild, which gave me lonely access to the stage, since I was too shy to speak to the theatrical critics around me. A revival of Ibsen's *The Wild Duck* caught my imagination, and in it I saw implied criticism of my own drift toward Left Wing sentiments and reform. Whenever I was in low spirits I thought of the play and identified myself with the young reformer who brings disaster with him wherever he walks. In bookstores, through tolerance of benign booksellers, I would sometimes spend an hour or two of quiet reading in books from their shelves. And to my delight I discovered art dealers on 57th Street had free afternoons for strolling visitors, and whenever I could spare a half dollar to have my trousers pressed, my shoes shined and my shirt laundered, I would celebrate by going to an art gallery, rather than eating lunch. The journey would take an entire afternoon, for I was a slow walker, guiding myself across town from Chelsea to Fifth Avenue, glancing at shop windows, resting on the steps of the New York Public Library at 42nd Street to witness battered, unshaven derelicts, scarcely awake from their binges of the night before, dipping brown fingers into grease-stained pockets and paper bags and scattering bread crumbs to flocks of quick-trooping, importunate pigeons. The brief rest over, what a relief it was to cross the street, and to enter a smartly appointed tobacco shop where a low-voiced, respectfully formal clerk would hand me a packet of Virginia cigarettes across a glittering plate glass counter. Through such indulgences I made myself fit to face the world—as change from my fifty dollar check sifted dollars through my fingers: the small fortune that they represented grew smaller every hour. This was a trial of my patience and morale. By the time I strolled into an art gallery, I may have been dizzy for want of something to eat, but my sense of well-being was restored. I could gaze at a Kandinsky or an early Chirico with lightheaded, yet well-poised self-detachment. Chattering young matrons from the Junior League surrounded me and fluttered in the wake of art dealers' assistants. Since I was in the same room for an hour or so I shared with them the unself-consciousness of unearned wealth. Like them I rode above mere thought of money. Beneath these surfaces, my early love of painting reasserted itself; it was as though I had never interrupted my visits to The Art Institute of Chicago where I felt secure and glad in my admirations. No wonder I felt refreshed and restored in courage.

One new acquaintance told me (and his advice still seems a little mad) that I could fend off starvation by feeding myself in the privacy of my room four apples and a loaf of bread a day—an excellent diet, he insisted—but the very thought of that solution to my troubles gave me nausea. He seemed officious—but actually, was he pulling my leg? Since I could not pay for three, I settled for two meals a day.

Romanticism as well as hunger drove me out to breakfast anytime between four and six in the morning. The discomforts of my room, the sagging bedsprings, the straw mattress, the naked, splintered, pinewood floor, the leaking gas heater, the smell of insecticide also contributed to my early wakefulness. With relief and expectation of adventure I stepped out into the thin blue mist of silent Chelsea and walked east and south to Sixth Avenue where I had found a German bakery that placed on a half-dozen damp, iron-legged, marble-topped tables a cut of coffee-cake, a bowl of oatmeal, and a cup of coffee. Instead of a waitress, a bus boy pushing a mop in one hand across the floor served the few sleepy patrons: a pair of policemen, a taxi-driver, a thinly-clad, shivering girl with a mannishly dressed, hoarse-whispering, heavily lipsticked woman at her side. These figures, so I thought, were potential dramatis personae for a play; yet as I watched them, nothing seemed to happen. Only once did I see the smallest fragment of action. Early one morning, a flashily dressed young man glided up behind the girl, bared her breasts by ripping open the front of her blouse, and attempted to pull her to her feet. The woman at her side leaped up and jammed a large, half-empty sugar bowl over the fellow's head. The policemen dragged him away while the woman began to caress the girl.

One evening a week, usually on Saturday, on Perry Street in a smoky, overheated cellar, I went to a place affectionately called "The 3 Ds—Dinner & Drunk for a Dollar." Since the country was still deep in the Prohibition era, special introductions to the place were needed, and as one was slowly shepherded through an iron gate to the dining room by the headwaiter, one was carefully cross-questioned by the stout Italian proprietor who paced the darkened corridor. This formality was probably more to impress uptown guests than to protect the restaurant from sporadic raids of the easygoing Greenwich Village police. At "The 3 Ds," the drink, served before one ordered food, was a large bottle of raw red wine spiked with alcohol. An equally crude and headache-making variety of beer was served at the bar. Since the food was dubious in taste and character, the bottle was emptied before dinner arrived in a rush of courses; within ten minutes plates with half-tasted salads and entrees were whisked away to make room for a small portion of a dessert that looked as though it had been made of isinglass. By the time coffee was served appetites as well as logical thinking were numbed; temperatures rose, faces flushed, hands gesticulated, voices roared: one seldom remembered one's exit from the place or how one landed in bed eight hours later. The clientele was made up of actors, writers, editors from publishing houses, homosexuals— a restless crowd, all teetering toward the fringes of bohemia. Of these Walpurgis-nights, I remember only two brightly lit details. The first is that of a pathetic, leering face of an elderly actress, her painted eyebrows and wide, brick-red lips, framed by metallic-looking peroxide curls. Or was she a "female impersonator"? The other memory is that of a great hooked nose with a black-ribboned pince-nez clamped on it, and below the nose, a red moist mouth, which was emitting denunciations of the poetry of Hart Crane. The mouth belonged, so it said, to Crane's editor, and the mouth was in grief over the foul manuscripts he had to edit. I remember that my defense of Crane was effectual enough to silence him, but after that angry effort, there is total blackness; whether or not I got back to Chelsea that night I do not know.

It was pride rather than strict necessity that demanded that I earn my living. When my mother, certain as ever that I could not make my own way, sent me checks in the mail, I refused to cash them. In the light of common sense, this was childish sulkiness. In the light of a deeper practical reality, my very stubbornness strengthened my will and forced me, however sheltered and immature I was, to face unlovely facts. In respect to getting a job, I made the worst possible first impression. My air of diffidence, for which my father had so often scolded me, was all too apparent. Though I was neatly dressed, my nervous tremor (it made others nervous to watch me light a cigarette) did not inspire confidence—nor did my habit of leaning on a stick. Though everyone I saw was polite enough, the best I could hope for toward earning a living were odd jobs of manuscript reading and book reviewing, and both were badly paid. I made up my mind to face these facts—and then promptly ignore them. I employed a kind of conscious self-deception to attain my ends. In this last—probably because I never knew the lack of money in my childhood—I was so successful I could not convince myself I was near starvation, and down to my last half dollar.

However often I counted the silver in my pocket on that particular morning, it never totaled more than fifty cents. I had one of my extremely rare blind fits of anger, anger at the world, anger at my own ineptness and failure to get a job. I would not cash my mother's check; I could not go home. I had with me a letter of introduction to Horace Liveright; I walked the twenty blocks or so uptown to his publishing house, and there, brushing past the office boys and secretaries, I stepped into a dimly lighted room—or was it because of my anger, it seemed so dark?—where Liveright sat at ease behind a desk. To me, the olive-skinned figure with its arched eyebrows looked like Lucifer, newly fallen into Hell. He glanced at me with skeptical, questioning eyes. Out of my anger came my voice; my usual manner had melted away, or gone up in flames; I must have talked, unchecked, for fifteen minutes, telling Liveright what was wrong with his current list, and when I stopped for breath, he picked up a manuscript on his desk, and threw it at me with, "Well, young man, if you know so much, take that home and read it; I'll send you a couple of manuscripts a week; return them with your reports—" and with this beginning, I began to earn my way. On Liveright's promises, I established credit at a restaurant run by two ex-vaudeville comedians, who by being stranded on burlesque show tours were sympathetic to my need to eat two meals a day. Though their bald-headed faces retained an off-stage gravity, they were like stock figures in a clownish act, for one was tall and thin, while the other was short and fat. The food in their restaurant was either overcooked or semi-raw, yet their kindness to me transcended any possible lack of appetite on my part. Forty years later when I saw the Broadway production of Samuel Beckett's *Waiting for Godot,* I thought of my two saviors—certainly Gogo's generous spirit was very like those of my restaurateurs.

Even with Liveright's help my means of keeping alive were precarious, for my "free-lance" reporting on manuscripts never earned me more than twenty dollars a week. My other odd jobs were writing movie reviews for the *Amalgamated Garment Makers Union Weekly* and writing reports on scenarios for the New York office of Paramount Pictures. I was dazzled and amused by the would-be sensuous display of Egypto-Roman luxury in the reception room of the Paramount offices: one was led to expect a bevy of naked dancing girls to come dropping at one's feet on the thick red carpet. These never appeared, but instead, a crew of fourteen-year-old boys, dressed in gold-braided uniforms, occasionally marched in and out to empty and clean a tall brass ash tray, shaped like a lily.

My survival then depended upon three tenuous sources of income. But my time was my own to distribute as I pleased, and I discovered New York on my own terms and at the hours of my own choosing. After midnight I would walk through the theatrical district near Times Square, and I re-

member that on one early morning, I had a glimpse of John
Barrymore waiting for someone in a corner of a windswept,
vacant theater lobby. He looked shrunken and cold, and he
was gnawing on his fingernails. His clothes looked as though
he had slept in them for over a week, yet over the line of his
upturned coat collar, the famous profile was intact. His blunt
fingers and bitten fingernails were to me an irrational disappointment; at the moment I failed to realize how much of
a hero I had made of him.

In New York I came to cherish my after-midnight solitudes, my wandering up and down between the red-brick
Victorian gingerbread clock tower of the Jefferson Market
in the Village and the naked glare of light pouring from Coney
Island shooting galleries and lunch counters on Broadway
above 42nd Street. The ugliness of Broadway was both frenetic and depressing. It seemed to be peopled by a sleepless,
drifting subway crowd that rose from and disappeared into
the iron stairway below the street: blind violinists, legless and
armless men with tin cups pinned to their coat lapels, an army
of derelicts, weaving through the crowd, and all those around
them were somehow deformed by their contact or proximity.
It was as though an ancient curse, caused by the touch of evil
or misfortune, filled the air; and yet the crowd, with its painted
smiles and garish jewelry, seemed in search of nothing more
than instant pleasure, two fingers of whiskey straight, or
clutching the pliant body of a dance-hall girl. The same
doomed atmosphere clung to the interiors of movie-houses
along the street, places where, as the heroine on the screen
begged for her life, the audience groaned in anticipation of
the beating she would get. These scenes would drive me
downtown to the serenities of streets below 14th, between
Sixth Avenue and Fifth, lined with brick-fronted narrow
houses, each with its iron-work grilled gate in front of its
kitchen cellar door, and its wisteria or ivy vine creeping up-

ward to its roof and chimney. A Washington Irving early-nineteenth-century charm seemed to contain these streets and buildings. I remember the gray-blue light of early morning rising around them, and in one street, on its south side, an air of mystery hovering over the remains of a crowded Jewish burying-ground. These walks were my adventures through the contrasts that Manhattan had to give me: they were not unlike the tensions set up between my superabundant energy and my frail health, between my transcendental sense of great well-being and Romantic lassitude.

My return to Chelsea and "Suicide's Row" soon became a torture. On my way upstairs to my attic room I passed the open door of one of my fellow lodgers. She was in a rocking chair. Beneath her uncombed yellow hair, she had a sweet, not very clean, blue-eyed, idiotic face; her lips pouted slightly —she was probably not more than eighteen years old. She was dressed in a transparent voile nightgown, cut low and slipping from her thin, white shoulders. As she rocked herself, backward and forward, like an old woman, she stretched out her pretty naked feet. To the rhythm of the rocking she sang a low-pitched little song which she interrupted to explain to me, as I paused outside her door, that she could never leave the room because she was waiting for her husband to come home. And at another open door stood a red-cheeked, broad-shouldered boy of twenty, who told me he had run away from home on the farm to join a circus; he had wanted to be an animal trainer, but had lost his job too soon, and hitchhiked his way into the city, looking as best he could to find another circus. I would then slowly wind back to my room. These encounters, however, were not too frequent, for my pale-eyed, slatternly, yet vigorous Boston-Irish landlady with a flick of her ragged broom had appointed herself my protec-tress. I was a special guest, with awesome objects in his train like a typewriter and a large, actorish-looking wardrobe trunk.

Other lodgers, mounting to my room, were shooed away. As I worked through half the day at my typewriter, she stood guard. And when my fellow lodgers complained of the pounding of my typewriter, she came to my defense. She never pressed me for my rent, and even encouraged me to ask for credit at restaurants; she marveled that my words, typed out on paper, brought me the checks she cashed for me several times a month.

Instead of settling down in "Suicide's Row," I became more restless, more distracted; my dreams flowed into nightmares, and there were times when I scarcely noted the change of night to day. I thought of moving down from Chelsea to a rooming house run by a homosexual dentist in Greenwich Village, a benevolent creature whose large blue jaw always seemed in need of a closer shave. I had met him at "The 3 Ds," and he offered me a room with a front view in his house for six dollars a week. I was assured by one of his tenants that neither he nor his friends would attempt to draw me into his circle, and that beneath his ungainly features, his benevolence was genuine. Curiously enough, the man was photogenic; after his office hours, he posed as a model for men's clothes, a pipe between his teeth, his blue jaw jutting out with exaggerated masculine firmness, in advertisements in *The New York Times*. From his house, his dental practice, and his rugged features, he earned a tidy income. He could well afford to rent me a choice room in his house at a cut rate.

It was a nightmare that forced my decision to move there. I can still remember fragments of the scene it brought before me. It was as though I were standing in the center of 23rd Street, looking upward at "Suicide's Row." The brick façades of the houses had taken on a livid purplish color, and above them, the sky had turned from bright to fading apple green. Moving toward me, naked to the waist, her white skin gleaming, came a sweet, idiotic face between strands of yellow hair fallen to her shoulders. Her pouted lips drooped mournfully, and from them came a long drawn-out moan, increasing in volume until it seemed to fill the dream. The sound was OOOM, OOOM, and OOOM again. OOOM haunted me for weeks. Though the meaning of the nightmare seemed obvious enough, its sound had frightened me, and seemed to warn me —as though I had been commanded to leave the gutters of Chelsea streets behind me. To exorcise the dream I began writing a new cycle of poems which six years later assumed the title of *Chelsea Rooming House*.

The room in Greenwich Village cost me more than I could actually afford to pay, and this meant I had to cut down the number of my meals in restaurants. This, I thought, could be beautifully contrived, for I had discovered a Spanish restaurant on 14th Street that served an eight-course dinner for fifty cents, and if I could teach myself to live on one generous meal a day, five days a week, I need not worry. The Spanish dinner was served in lavish portions, swimming in olive oil. The place, like "The 3 Ds," was an iron-grilled, cellar restaurant, filled with a steady patronage of elusive, pasty-faced, dark-clothed, bright-eyed men and women, who seemed to come from nowhere, and then dissolve in cigarette smoke in the corridors beyond the dining room. The faces were always the same, and I felt oppressed by their vague, expectant smiles and long silences. The waiters glided past me as though they were funeral mutes, black-coated-and-tailed images in a dream. I began to suspect that the place was a dive for cocaine and heroin addicts—and if one made the proper signs, drugs could be bought on the premises. When I had eaten my meal and rose to leave, one of the mutes would step to my side and politely usher me to the door—which was an extraordinary gesture in a restaurant where the dinner cost only fifty cents.

Soon the dream-like atmosphere of the restaurant followed me back to my room where I would try to work at the typewriter so as not to fall asleep. My legs felt cold and heavy as iron. Events seemed to take on a dream-like sequence. One evening I looked up from my typewriter to see a huge smiling Village cop with a half-filled bottle of gin in one hand and a thick empty tumbler in the other. He filled the tumbler and offered it to me, and I gratefully accepted. "That'll wake you up," he said. "It's on the house. There's a party going on, and I'm helping out." And surely enough, the whole house shook with explosions of high-pitched voices.

On another evening, I was awakened at my typewriter by my landlord who was in a confidential mood. He told me he had spent the early half of the evening calming down his boy friend who had come to the house at half past six, frantic and trembling. The boy was a highly strung young man, over-correctly dressed—with his bowler hat, Chesterfield topcoat, and tightly rolled umbrella. He had a serious round baby face that looked as though it were about to crinkle up and wet it-self with tears. His dignity seemed always near the vanishing point. He was a teller in a bank, watchful and meticulous in all his movements, his eyes sliding to the right and left. Today had been a very trying day; he had had trouble balancing his accounts, and yet, the routine had become a bore. When he entered the subway at its rush hour, it was impossible to get a seat: people pushed and climbed ahead of him, triumphant, seating themselves like kings and queens, while his right hand clung to the strap above his head, his body swaying with the lurching of the train. As he hung there, it seemed that every-one in the car had turned a face up to stare at him, perhaps to ridicule the way he wore his hat and gloves. Were they point-ing at him? Had they begun to smile? Would they crowd him off the train? He could feel blood flushing his face, bringing heat to his eyes, his forehead, his hair. He began to scream, "I'm *not* a homosexual," louder and louder, over and over again, until he reached 14th Street where at the car stop he ran from the train, up the stairs into Union Square, hailed a taxi, leaped into it, and arrived, exhausted and weeping, at his Greenwich Avenue address.

My peculiar lassitude following my visits to the Spanish restaurant extended its hold over me. When I woke in the morning, I closed my eyes and fell asleep again, usually sleeping until two in the afternoon. My assignments of work soon went undone; my reviews of current films were postponed; my passes to the theaters were unclaimed. I could not write letters, for I was ashamed to confess my mysterious laziness to anyone. Hunger did not trouble me greatly, and since I did not enjoy my diet at the Spanish restaurant, my normal appetite had disappeared. Giving up breakfast was no longer a sacrifice. I could wait for dinner. My difficulty came in the effort to get out of bed at all; it took me at least an hour to dress. It became extremely pleasant not to think of food—and very luxurious to lie in bed looking out of the window, to watch the sky change its colors and clouds their shapes over the roofs of the buildings across the street. Every time I opened my eyes, a new picture filled the window. As afternoons drifted by, sunlight would slant over the battered brick façades across the street in miraculous variations of red and gold, and I would seem to float above the roofs into the sky. This was very like the exalted feeling I read about several years later in books on psychic phenomena and spiritualism. Was this sensation of floating a kind of levitation? Was it caused by fasting? These questions could not be answered then. The effort for me to think of anything at all was then too great. I could merely drift as though I had entered the pastures of the sky; were they the Elysian Fields? Not quite. For those green meadows, near the stream of Oceanus, were in the distant west, beyond the sunset with suns and stars and twilights of their own, where small birds sang, where in quiet nakedness lovers met each other, Eros triumphant in the green shadows. And yet, perhaps the sky was their true home; Lucian had found them, the very Islands of the Blest, wandering in higher regions, near the moon. I was too tired to care where I had traveled. As evening gathered in the corners of my room, I struggled out of bed, dressed myself carefully, and by exercise of strenuous will power, dragged myself down the stairs, into the street and through the gate-like iron door of the restaurant. Even the walk of six blocks north had become unreal; the shop windows on Sixth Avenue had taken on an uncertain, unearthly glow, with deepening shadows at their corners, out of which emerged from a taxidermist's shop, the moth-eaten chest and belly of a standing bear. I half expected the bear to step out of his window and walk the street with me.

One cold fair morning, the month was November, will power overcame my growing tiredness. I got up to look at my face in the mirror; it was as golden-yellow as an Oriental's, and so was the rest of my body which seemed to burn softly, throwing off a dim yellow light. My landlord dropped in; I had not paid rent for a month. He gave one glance at me, then smiled. "You've got a fine case of jaundice," he said. "You need a doctor, not tomorrow, but today." I went back to bed. I remember a few of my Village acquaintances crowding around me, offering me a bowl of soup which I could not drink. I also remember a gray-faced, gray-haired ex-army doctor X-raying me, and his giving orders that I be shipped to the New York Hospital, where I landed in a ward in which all the patients, including myself, were wrapped in a depressing color of dark blood-red blankets. I opened my lips and no sounds came: I felt that I was the only one in the ward who could not get the attention of a busy, cold-faced, straight-featured nurse. That is, I seemed neglected till Dr. Kallen dropped in for a visit, then suddenly I had the services of the chief surgeon in the hospital as well as a battery of interns and nurses. But I was not that easily satisfied; I fancied other patients in the ward were being deprived of the attention I now received—and in my half-conscious state I went into silent rages against the injustice of the world, its brutalities, its terror. In a bed not far from me, an old man had died, screaming for his mother. I was horrified at the poor creature's cowardice in the face of death, and infuriated at the calm, deaf lack of response his cries brought from the nurses. Certainly, there was no catharsis here. Men were treated like brutes and died like brutes.

Within a few days my mother arrived from the Middle West, and since excellent care had revived me, she was allowed to carry me off to a suite of rooms she had reserved at the Brevoort Hotel, then well-known for its gifted chef. During the past six months, I had often longed for a dinner there, and now, I was on a strict diet of skimmed milk, grapefruit, oatmeal or boiled rice. My mother made up for my austerities by being particularly charming: I was proud of her voice which had always enchanted me, and the ease with which she impressed my New York acquaintances, including Dr. Kallen. There was a touch of magic in her personality that rose to occasions, that graced her manner, and was the light behind her quiet blue eyes. I admired the way she seemed less provincial in New York than in Milwaukee. And I quickly learned that I had underrated her ability to adjust herself to new surroundings. Away from home she seemed years younger, more alive to everything she saw and heard, and I then began to understand how it was that she, a young girl from a poorly tended farm in Wisconsin's dairy country, made her way with so much success in the newly prospering city of Milwaukee. Coming to New York gave lightness to her step and reawakened her youthful enthusiasm, it was as though she were on vacation from all daily cares.

Although from time to time she would daydream over

the beauties of the richly pastured lake country where she had been born, her nostalgia for rural places had a Winslow Homerish, picture-book quality. She saw them as lands where maple trees grew into slopes of shade, where uncut grasses flowered, where placid lake waters were so still and clear that one could lean over a rowboat's stern to watch whole schools of perch and bass go wavering through green and silver shadows down below. Yet I noticed that her fancies of lost summers never lured her into buying—when my father could well afford it—a small summer house in the vicinity of her early home. I suspect that memories of uneasy poverty, of grinding household chores in a clapboard farmhouse, cut across her images of pastoral serenity and brought her brief intervals of nostalgia to an end. Therefore, when she had left the farm behind her, she had also taught herself to be most at home away from home.

In our suite at the Brevoort it did not take much argument on my mother's part to persuade me—I was still too weak to work—to go back to Milwaukee with her for two weeks. This was with the understanding that I return to New York to start again. Though I had little to show for all my efforts— a poem published in *Vanity Fair*, and a villanelle in a Greenwich Village magazine, both of which attracted favorable notice from critics—I had gained confidence and the gain impressed my mother. Through the drifting waves of violence and despair I witnessed in New York, all the way from the garish crowds on Broadway to the tenements of Chelsea, I felt I had discovered my setting for city poems. I felt I had "found something to say," something beyond mere personal expression, something beyond the usual and expected. My dramatis personae were taking shape; I felt that they, my characters, were almost ready to speak.

By the time I came back to New York, I had about two-thirds of a manuscript of new poems. I believed that an "imitation of life" was an imitation of life's dramatic action, and that its rhythm and its music were timed to the rise and fall of a character's feelings and intuitions. I believed that an entire poem should stand as a metaphor of human destiny. My hope was to accomplish this end in the poetry I wrote. And I also thought that the best proof of my convictions was to write the poems, rather than to theorize too much about them—that a poem's meaning was implicit, composed of the right (often the fewest) words in the best order.

5

Gray-Prismed Morning

WHEN I RETURNED to the city, I kept myself alive—but scarcely more than that—by writing "copy" for a public relations firm whose clients were New York real estate agents. My theme was the glory of living in New York. There we were, a crew of a half-dozen young men behind typewriters. The eldest among my colleagues were alcoholics, fired from *The New York Times*, the *New York World*, or the *Evening Sun*, the feverish ghosts of their profession; the others boys from C.C.N.Y. We were in the office loft, high above Columbus Circle. Below us stood Columbus, stone-blind and motionless, on his pillar. Behind him rose the trees of Central Park, a web of interlacing twigs and boughs in winter, and in summer a waving forest of green leaves. Below Columbus, the traffic steered in an unending crescent; to his right, at an angle of forty-five degrees, was a famous, white-tiled, open-all-night dairy lunch room with its white-capped chef making flapjacks in the front window which David Belasco in his production of an urban melodrama had reset, life-size, on a

Broadway stage. The place had gathered an aura of rumor around itself: it was there, so it was said, that F. Scott Fitzgerald used to turn up, roaring tight, at three in the morning. It was there I had my rather grim noon meal, for twenty-five cents, of boiled rice, hot milk, and a cup of tea. I had graduated from the shreds of a bohemia that still existed below 14th Street; I had rented a room in the low seventies between Central Park and Broadway. It was a back garden room, gravely furnished in deep reds and browns, in an imposing brownstone house, sedately run by a sweetly smiling, rose-cheeked spinster who was devoted to Christian Science and the reviews of books she would like to have read. I remember her showing me with wistful excitement and approval a long review of Marianne Moore's *Observations*, illustrated by a large photograph of the poet in the Sunday Book Review of *The New York Times*.

Yet even in this retreat where I could not invite a friend to come up and have a drink with me, there was a far glimpse of the life I had seen in Chelsea. Across the back garden on the second floor of a house facing the next street north of me, a window would open, and out of it a completely naked girl leaned, like Rapunzel, who had been ordered to let down her hair. This girl cheerfully waved her long white arms toward anyone who chanced to look up at her.

Even on holidays, I seldom traveled below 40th Street and east of Fifth Avenue. I had decided that during my last year at Wisconsin, I had cheated myself of gaining all that I should have learned. I set up a fresh reading course for myself at the 42nd Street Library: this was largely in prose, in American history, and in fiction, principally German, to make up for not following through after my studies in freshman German at the university. This led me to reading Thomas Mann's *Buddenbrooks* which gave me another view of my own middle-class origins in the most German of American cities, Milwaukee. At the 42nd Street Library, I began to fill in large gaps in my reading, even in Latin, which reinspired me to continue my English versions of Catullus. All this was enough to keep me busy, so busy that I would plead ill-health to my employers at the Columbus Circle job, to spend more time at the library, which by self-directed means I had converted into my private institute of higher learing in graduate studies. As during the years before I went to school and college I was my own instructor, reading in greater depth than my school and college schedules permitted. I also had the advantage of forming my own opinions of all I read, rather than adapting them from the lips of an eloquent lecturer.

It was in the summer of 1925 I met and married Marya Zaturenska, who had returned to New York after spending two years on a Zona Gale scholarship in the library school at the University of Wisconsin; her adviser there had been William Ellery Leonard, from whom she learned scattered legends of my erratic behavior, and the varied charts of my collapses and revivals—my despairs quickly followed by waves of my Micawber-like optimism. I was a predictable risk: only the most romantic and courageous of young women would have taken the chance of marrying me. At that time, of course, I was far too deeply in love myself to see myself in such rational terms: all I saw was a slight, dark-haired, beautiful girl in a fluttering lilac-tinted organdy dress, who was as passionately devoted to poetry as I was. We had been introduced to each other by Kenneth Fearing, who looked more determinedly bohemian than before, clothes unpressed and flapping in the wind: he was then wearing larger, rounder, and blacker tortoise-shell-rimmed eyeglasses, which instead of aging his face, made him look more the abandoned child of absent-minded parents than ever.

I soon found that Marya used the 42nd Street Library for the same purposes I did, as a fortress against the pressure and noise of New York, as a graduate school, and as a source for books beyond any we could afford to buy. It was where she, at fifteen, had written some of her first poems; poems that had caught the attention, when they appeared in print, of John Jay Chapman, Vachel Lindsay, Willa Cather—and among English writers, Alice Meynell and Siegfried Sassoon. Her poems had also brought her offers of scholarships from colleges and universities. Of these she chose Wisconsin's library school, and she hoped by becoming a librarian, she could find shelter for writing poetry, for poetry was part of her sense of being alive, part of her awareness of religious faith and its meaning. Her poems haunted the imagination and the soul, and her lyricism was that of music sounding through a dream.

Although we were not as wholly impractical as we may have seemed to more than a few of our acquaintances, we could not resist renting a one and a half-room apartment on the south side of Washington Square. One of its disadvantages (which we did our best to ignore) was its location at the rear of the house, at the end of a long dark hall. Another was its single, tall and narrow, soot-stained window that looked down into a dank areaway. The main room's attractions were in its high, barn-like dimensions. Our few sticks of furniture —a studio couch, a few odd chairs, a bookcase, and a table— plus ourselves, looked abandoned in space. In that sense we had plenty of room; but we could not open the tall window hovering over us. The advantages we had lay outside the room. After we had walked through the unlit hall, opened the front door, and paused for a breath of air at the top of a short flight of stone steps, we confronted Fifth Avenue. And the Square had charms few could deny.

On a fair autumn day the Square itself compensated for many discomforts and lack of money. There was sunlight pouring down from an open, far blue sky; there were nurses pacing with their carriages through the park; there were pink and olive, half-naked Italian children splashing in the fountain; there was a curving line of double-decked green buses, waiting for passengers to ride up Fifth Avenue—all were there, the best of New York, I thought in New York's best weather. To the right was the house, marked by a brass plaque, where Alan Seeger of "I have a rendezvous with death" once rented an attic room, and to our left was the Judson Tower, planted as though it had been a Giottoesque afterthought by Stanford White; in the park, hidden by tall bushes and on a pedestal, rose the bronze head and shoulders of a forgotten poet, who judging from his precisely trimmed beard and empty eyes, had been both respectable and harmless. The moral to be drawn from his oblivion was clear enough. In America, over-refinement in the arts is a bid for extinction; for better and, sometimes, for the very worst, rough edges and violence are among our enduring merits. These are saviors from the curse of mediocrity.

In one of the red-brick houses across the way lived the painter Edward Hopper. One afternoon at the Whitney Museum, when its quarters were on nearby 8th Street, a few steps west of Fifth Avenue, I saw Hopper's spare figure buttoned up in a Chesterfield topcoat, bending forward, hands clasped behind his back, to examine a canvas painted by a young contemporary. I heard him sigh, scarcely above his breath, "At last they're all beginning to paint like me."

Soon after we became accustomed to our room and a half in Washington Square, a two-week siege of illness brought an end to my job of writing on New York real estate. Once that drudgery of writing three thousand words a day was well behind me, I welcomed the adventure of trying to support both of us by book reviewing—in those days, as we approached the years of the Depression, a clearly hazardous one. We were never sure of what would happen tomorrow— much less the day after next. This was a precariousness I half enjoyed; nor could I fully believe we would actually starve. With a day of fair luck, there would be a lamb chop and fig-pudding for dinner—and extraordinary luck would give us dinner with wine at an Italian restaurant a few blocks south of Washington Square. On Friday evening, after dining frugally at a small restaurant, we found that the whole of our wealth was a silver quarter, shining brightly on the green burlap tablecloth. The quarter was so small a sum as to appear frivolous; we hastened to spend most of it on a packet of cigarettes. That night we slept peacefully.

The next morning, I glided softly, rather than walked, in my slippers through the dark hallway to the mailbox near the front door. There was a long envelope waiting for me. It was from *The New Yorker*. I had almost forgotten that a few weeks before, and under a pseudonym, I had sent off some light verse to its editors; here, on acceptance of the verse, was a check. If I remember correctly, the check was for thirty-five dollars. We slipped on our best clothes, and a half-hour later, we were ordering an elaborate Saturday-noon breakfast-lunch at Charles' Restaurant, over on Sixth Avenue. We felt very reckless and happy. I remember Marya smiling at me across the table.

It was in this touch-and-go, up-and-down fashion, we made our way, and by strenuous efforts, paid the rent. "Free-lance" writing, so it seemed, left little time free for anything else. Holidays disappeared from our calendar: even Sundays were reserved for half-days at the typewriter. On Sunday evenings, however, we accepted invitations to a large open house gathering off Riverside Drive, above 100th Street at the apartment of Luis Muñoz Marín, afterwards Governor of Puerto Rico, and his wife, Muna Lee. Both were poets, and bilingual, and wrote with equal ease in English and Spanish: Luis was a contributor to H. L. Mencken's *The American Mercury*, and to the

Nation. Their guests were an extraordinary combination of Arctic explorers, European journalists, young New York writers, Spanish-American military men, and soldiers of fortune: talk was of revolution, the wisdom of the Eskimos, reindeer meat, the novels of D. H. Lawrence and James Joyce, the poetry of Robinson Jeffers. Political, military, and literary arguments ran their continuous course throughout the apartment in whispered manifestoes of political discontent; with them flowed the names of Marx and Unamuno, Bertrand Russell and Croce, Freud and Veblen, and over these warring factions weaved the host, handsome, witty, a delightful mimic, and ineffably tactful, a forefinger vertical at his lips, silencing a raised voice by giving its owner a fresh tumbler of bathtub gin.

No less successful at keeping order among their social fauna was his matronly young wife, who wore a Spanish shawl in swirling reds and blacks and orange tossed over her shoulders and a dove-gray evening dress. Her large brown eyes dispelled all rudenesses, and the lightest touch of her tapered fingers on the sleeve of a guest's jacket would be sufficient warning to lower voices.

To sustain arguments, slogans would be quoted, phrases and sentences trembling in air: then perhaps, the recital of a few lines of verse, usually that of Robert Bridges, or of E. A. Robinson, or with a great sense of daring, that of newly discovered Gerard Manley Hopkins. By the time Marya and I returned by subway to Washington Square, the dawn light of Monday morning guided us up the white stone steps to our front door.

On those Sunday nights above 100th Street, we felt ourselves to be of a more recent, more "serious," somehow more *responsible* generation than that which drifted off to Paris soon after World War I. Though we had read Veblen thoroughly and only skimmed through *Das Kapital,* we felt certain that the revolution in Russia had freed "the prisoners of starvation." Though I thought of myself as a "fellow traveler," I also thought of myself as an American, and I refused to think of Russian politics, to note the differences between a Trotskyite and a Stalinist. I felt the Communists would do more to help the victims of capitalism in this country than the Socialists or the International Workers of the World would ever do. I was an enthusiastic reader of the revived *Masses*, formerly *The Liberator* and now *New Masses*.

Since my feelings toward Communism are today the reverse of what they were in 1925, I find it difficult to say why I read the *New Masses* with such eagerness. Today I would say, "What foolishness most of the writing was; what transparent lies were told, how amateurish its approach to art and letters was, how blatantly political it showed itself to be." Like others who were then young, I believed the *New Masses* to be the place where new writers could be found, and for a brief time this was partially true. Robinson Jeffers's "Shine, Perishing Republic" appeared there, a poem as new today as it was then; so did parts of Dos Passos's novels, so did a few charming observations of things in nature by Whittaker Chambers, so did a group of poems by Kenneth Fearing. Of Fearing's friends, I was one of the few who knew that his readings were never as wildly Left as some supposed them to be; he read far more of H. L. Mencken's editorial counterblasts in *The American Mercury* than he listened to all-night back-room talk of Marx. A significant choice, I think, for Mencken's editorial eye (however far to the Right it veered) welcomed much of the writing the *New Masses* fostered; while the *New Masses* sought out potential "proletarian" novelists, Mencken searched the prisons for inmates who could write of their experiences. Today it is well known that the extremes of literary Left and Right have strong temperamental affinities—it reminds one that the brown-shirted Nazis of the mid-1930s compared themselves (repulsively, I think) to minute steaks: "Brown outside, but Red inside."

But likenesses of extreme Left and Right were unthought of in the middle 1920s, at least unthought of by young people who read Leftist publications and found them stimulating and worth discussing. In that sense, the "fellow travelers" of Communism in the United States were living in a state of innocence, far removed from the bloodstained policies of Lenin's Russia. This was a period when the benign and naive journalist of Socialism, Upton Sinclair, drifted further toward the Russian camp than he had intended.

Among my acquaintances was Joseph Freeman, who had been one of Max Eastman's students at Columbia when Eastman lectured on philosophy; Freeman worshiped him, and followed his lead into Left Wing journalism. Eastman was a handsome, charming, indolently poised intellectual, straight out of the American muckraking tradition. His influence permeated whatever literary policies the *New Masses* still held, over which Freeman, in his turn, exerted control. If I remember correctly, it was through my acquaintanceship with Freeman, that my wife and I were invited to lunch at Rose Pastor Stokes's pretty little house in downtown New York. Rose Stokes had long been known as "Rose of the Ghetto," the Jewish ghetto of New York's East Side; through that garish clutter of filth and poverty, the girl moved as though she were the reincarnation of the Rose of Sharon, and when she married Stokes, a figure in New York society, the newspapers made much of the event; the marriage was applauded as a triumph of the American "Melting Pot," and as the latest version of the Cinderella story. By this time, however, even this retelling with its glorious wedding, had receded into the past, its hero and heroine divorced; and Rose, now well into middle age and gray-haired, had grown flighty, rather flushed of face, like many another Grande Dame in New York society, and like them, she had become susceptible to the attentions of young men who raised funds for Leftist causes.

Her many years of living in prosperity had given her naturally gracious manners a nervous, girlish flutter, as though indeed she had been imprisoned like "a bird in a gilded cage." One of her accomplishments, so she told us, was composing new words for old songs, and with this she seated herself at her grand piano and sang to the tune of "Bonnie Prince Charlie":

> O Lenin is my darling,
> My darling, my darling,
> O Lenin is my darling,
> That bold chevalier.

> 'Twas on a Monday morning,
> Quite early in the year,
> When Trotsky came to our town—
> That yellow chevalier . . .

For a split second she looked like the naughty child who must have charmed Stokes—but no—she was deadly serious; there was a touch of violence in her shouts of "Lenin is my darling," and in the vigorous shaking of her head when she came to "yellow chevalier."

We were, of course, embarrassed by our own efforts not to laugh and by the vehemence and childish vanity of her performance. But if she noted our uneasiness, she did not show it, and still glowing from her exertions at the piano, she followed us out of her music room to her front hallway where we thanked her and said goodbye. We wondered if she had gone a trifle insane—yet she seemed respected as a generous patroness of "fellow-traveling" activities. We had been half-frightened by her fanaticism, while she looked vastly pleased with herself.

As the summer of 1926 reached its meridian, we decided to leave Washington Square. Since Marya was expecting a baby to arrive sometime during the following January, we would have to move into larger quarters than our one and a half room. But where could we afford to live? Not on the Square. Elsewhere in the Village there were a few cold-water flats that fitted my pocketbook, but we were certain that these would not fit the needs of a newborn baby, surely not on a cold winter night. We were advised to look abroad as far as Brooklyn, and through Brooklyn we searched as far as President Street. Had we been more experienced in finding suitable apartments, we would, I think, have done far better. When we came to President Street, with its two long rows of grayish buildings facing each other, we could no longer endure the torture of tramping streets and interviewing superintendents who looked like gargoyles, transplanted intact from the towers of Notre Dame. Here we found three rooms which, once we had climbed three flights of stairs, and closed the door behind us, were not impossible: there was plenty of heat. The great hazard was its ground floor lobby, which with its dusty, stunted palm trees, planted in brassbound tubs, looked like the entrance to a "cut-rate" funeral home. Crossing the floor of that desert, to and from the front door to the stairway, one imagined murdered women hidden upended in wardrobe trunks, stored in far corners. We tried to forget the existence of the lobby.

To counterbalance the Brooklyn misfortune—and through the good nature of an acquaintance from prep school and college—I was handed a job. The placement was precarious enough: I was hired as "production man" in the book-publishing division of a large, top-heavy organization that published several trade journals. The organization regarded its newly formed book division as an experiment, and my employer, chosen as its editor-in-chief, was looked down upon as a very "low" man in the organization's hierarchy. I was untrained for the job and my employer knew it—but so was he. He was a stout, wordless man, with a close-cut mustache and crew-cut hair, who smoked an underslung pipe with great solemnity, and had light blue protuberant eyes. He held a B.S. degree and flourished an engineering fraternity key on the watchchain across his vest. We got along by never questioning the authority of the other, both of us waiting for the final catastrophe of being fired. In the meantime, we drew our pay, and every two weeks or so, he invited me out to lunch in a nearby chop house—where needled beer was served, and soup was hot, and steaks and chops were cut so very thick that after lunch, I could barely stay awake for the rest of the afternoon. Generous as he tried to be, his luncheons left me feeling groggy and stupefied for the next twenty-four hours.

And yet, without admitting it fully to myself, I grew to love my job. I acquired a craftsman's devotion for making books to be read by engineers that were not ugly objects. My office was in Church Street, not far from Trinity Churchyard, and some twenty-one floors above the city. To my right, and through a large window, I saw the Hudson River with its miles of port and river traffic pouring out to sea. As each liner passed, I thought of Europe and envied happy travelers on board ship to London and Ireland. The view from my "crow's nest" window in the office gave me an irrational sense of security, as though being so high had placed me above all material worries, my barely sufficient pay, the anxieties preceding the birth of a baby, the stuffiness of my respectable Brooklyn apartment. The view never lost its freshness, and at this height, the movements of great ships, battleships as well as liners, took on patterns of living grace and serenity. The sunset skyscapes in green and umber over leagues of Atlantic waters inspired longings beyond the horizon. In my imagination New York had become the Eastern gate leading out into the world.

I had begun to treasure the few lunch hours of the week that were not devoted to further business with paper salesmen and printers and the subeditors in my office. I spent the liberated noon hours wandering through and around lower Manhattan, past the heroic statue of Nathan Hale, his arms bound behind him, and a bronze rope round his bare neck, looking every inch the glorified Yale boy he chose to be. And from Hale I drifted toward Trinity Churchyard. At these times, the spires of Trinity would remind me of my boyhood at St. James's in Milwaukee, its hymns and Anglican prayer book, its slender tower and stained glass windows with slanted winged sunlight pouring through them, as though the shafts of light were Jacob's ladder. Trinity itself was, of course, greatly different from St. James's—this church had an aura of mystery that no church of my boyhood had possessed, and was probably due to the historical associations gathered around it, the weathered appearance of the churchyard's brownstone slabs, the soot-blackened tombs that seemed to preserve images of a historical continuity rather than those of death. Grief over human fate and the mortality of flesh had taken flight and had been gathered into the rays of the sun above Trinity's spire. What had been left behind were names engraved on monuments.

When the days were warm, thick-muscled and squat Greek bootblacks commandeered sidewalk quarters beneath the stone-banked iron railings of the churchyard. With conspicuous vigor, they knelt to the pavement and polished the shoes of all who yielded to the tireless, wordless gestures of their salesmanship. And many did: under their waving, beckoning arms and hands, patrons seemed to advance in endless lines; as long as the prosperous, the suave, the fashionable stepped out into the streets, there would be shoes to polish, and money would fill the pockets of the bootblacks. That was the simple life, I fancied, free of trouble, an urban pastoral. I envied the tremendous good health of the Greeks; they looked impervious to the changes of season, of wind, and of weather. Their gestures lacked the slightest resemblance to servility; waving arms and pointed forefingers were commands, not supplications, indicative of violent pride and independence. The Greeks were, no doubt, descendants of the shepherds Theocritus had named, and today enjoyed a greater liberty than their ancestors knew. Disguised as bootblacks, they had warded off the evil eye, and were free of hubris—for what Greek would brag of being a bootblack?

One day my walk wearied me, and my fancies took the path they did in my childhood, when unable to walk from the house because of my unsteadiness, I watched with admiration street-menders from a second-floor window. Actually as I meandered back to my office, my fancies were portents of approaching illness. My face felt flushed and hot, and surely enough, I had caught a child's disease: scarlet fever.

My heroic wife, looking very frail herself, and not at all accustomed to nursing a two-month-old daughter and a feverish husband, was placed under quarantine with me in our three room flat where the only colorful pieces of furnishing were bits of china set out on a Welsh cupboard I had painted bright blue. This was a fearful time for her, for both baby and husband were in need of frequent and separate attention.

So many days and weeks of the year 1927 are blotted from my memory that the time must have been one of great unhappiness. Only the presence of the baby kept us sane. Our attempts to accept the anonymities of living in lower-middle-class President Street were a failure. Whether we realized it or not, Marya and I were "sinning against the light": she, in trying to carry all the deadly burdens of housework while neglecting her writing, and I by trying to be a third-rate "production man" instead of the poet I wished to be. We were defeating our own gifts and hopes; I like to think that beneath our efforts to conform to the dreary pattern of lives around us, we were struggling to escape it. Meanwhile our move to President Street had cut us off from our acquaintances in New York; we lacked money for amusements, and to spend a couple of dollars for a book meant a show of recklessness that we would pay for by eating less for a day or two. Certainly, my salary was so small, and my job so precarious, that portents of coming disasters on Wall Street had no meaning for me. So far as reading was concerned (I had begun to leave newspapers behind me on subway trains as I rode home at evening), the only bright moment I remember was carrying back to President Street a copy of Ezra Pound's *Personae*. It had taken me a long time to scrape up the money to buy it.

After my illness, and on return to the office, I found that my work had melted away to the lightest of duties. The book division of the firm was about to be dissolved, and I was the first to go. My editor-in-chief invited me to one of his luncheons. I remember the ugly yellow, light maple paneling on the walls of the restaurant, the hot soup I pushed to one side, his handing me a month's pay in advance, my descending the stairs into a subway back to Brooklyn, my wordless sense of guilt, my wife's straight, slender figure, her warm lips, her very great courage in telling me that I could keep all three of us alive by "free-lance" writing—a noble lie—and that the loss of my job had been a stroke of good fortune. I was near an abyss: I could feel the darkness of it mounting around me.

A few weeks later I accepted the offer of a job writing "promotion" articles for *Women's Wear*. My office was in a building where the floors were worn and sloping, and noises seemed to shake the walls. At least, these premonitions of things falling apart reflected my state of mind. How could I write copy on the subject of a daily called *Women's Wear*? Even the merest hope of my doing so was a kind of madness. My employer, the head of the firm's promotion department, of which he and I were sole members, was an admirer of the many-times-distilled wisdom contained in the tiny pages of Haldeman-Julius's *Little Blue Books* which were sold on book stalls at five cents a volume. He had gray hair that looked as if it had been carved rather than grown above his neck and shoulders. He had a voice that with ringing clarity recited whole editorials written by Arthur Brisbane for *The New York Evening Journal*. When he saw a cigarette between my fingers, he reminded me, more than once, that the building we were in was a firetrap—the walls and floors were tinder— and I was forbidden to smoke. Without a cigarette I felt stunned. The blank sheet of paper in my typewriter seemed to grow larger and larger with emptiness: not to light a cigarette was torture in itself, and the empty page before me made my plight worse. My mind had gone completely blank of the need to sell young women nylon underwear; if I could not smoke, it was better for them to walk naked. But these thoughts, I knew, would never have met the approval of Arthur Brisbane.

I had the impression that the man who was trying so hard to teach me how to write for *his* employers was not unkind. In his youth, he confessed, he had followed Brisbane into Socialism, and later, like Brisbane, he had experienced a change of heart. He now had little use for Upton Sinclair. He also confessed his admiration for Edwin Markham who wrote "The Man with the Hoe." After a month of patient counseling, my employer sadly handed me two months' severance pay and said he could not understand modern poetry: he had heard I wrote it well; he wished me good luck, walked to the door with me, and bowed me out of the office.

My second failure to hold a job stirred me to writing poetry again. And for the second time in my life (the first being the time I argued with my parents about my need to leave home and to live in New York) I was sure I was good for nothing but giving myself up entirely to poetry—all else was trivia, all else was failure, or worse than failure, mediocre efforts with mediocre results. Yet to do my writing and support my small household, I was forced to bend my pride enough to accept twenty-five dollars a week from my father. These new plans effected an escape from President Street.

In those days, I had become a faithful, if not regular, reader of the *Nation* and *The New Republic*. I believed that most of their contributors were sincere in what they thought and wrote. I respected them, and within a year or two I was contributing poems and book reviews to both. In *The New Republic*, I happened to notice articles by Lewis Mumford on Sunnyside, the model housing development on the outskirts of Long Island City for people in low income brackets, and if I remember correctly, in these he mentioned the Scottish community planner, Sir Patrick Geddes. Mumford and Geddes deeply impressed me, for both were, as my Aunt Victoria had regarded Emerson, men of plain living and high thinking. Behind Geddes's ideas stood the examples of John Ruskin and William Morris; and Mumford, in some of his writings, had some of the same social passion that inspired Ruskin's *Fors Clavigera*.

Through a Mrs. Grace White, a patroness of poets and a friend of E. A. Robinson, I learned further particulars of the Sunnyside plan, for she was also one of its sponsors. Mrs. White was the sister-in-law of the notorious and richly gifted Stanford White, the architect who had been shot and killed by Harry K. Thaw. She was a widow, thoroughly respectable, yet one of the last survivors of New York's "Mauve Decade," who might have stepped out of the pages of a novel written by Edith Wharton. Her abundant white hair, pure blue eyes, pink cheeks, and plumpness were signs of the pretty (often petted) child she had once been, a missionary's daughter who had spent her girlhood in green and darkest Africa, where she had been known because of her fair hair as the golden lily. On her honeymoon in Scandinavia, as she was always fond of retelling, she was pursued by the great Ibsen who offered to steal her away from her bridegroom and shut her up, like a Hans Christian Andersen princess, in a northern palace. Behind the ravages of rumor and family scandals, there were stories of the tragic loss of her own daughter and husband—all of which was far too terrifying to face bravely and left her sustained only by a kind of virginal, sometimes petulant idealism. To Marya and me she was unfailingly kind, and since she knew of our unhappy situation in Brooklyn she stood sponsor for our entering the Sunnyside community, while my father made the initial down payments. In my parents' eyes my becoming a householder was a move in the direction of "settling down." Indeed, the little two-story section of a row looked very clean, fresh, and not unattractive: three very plain rectangular rooms were on the ground floor, a large cellar room was my study, and upstairs were three small bedrooms and a bath. But these attractions, all too Spartan, did not attract model workmen: they were lured to another Long Island development, called "Little Venice," that had swimming pools lightly disguised as miniature lagoons, and houses that looked like blocks of Neapolitan ice cream. Sunnyside's inhabitants were taxi-drivers, artists, writers, actors waiting to be booked, as well as members of every political minority group in the United States, all the way from disciples of Huey Long and Single Tax devotees to ardent Communists. Viewed superficially, Sunnyside, with its youthful trees and bright green gardens and lawns, seemed an extraordinary hothouse and breeding ground for cranks. This was not bohemia but several stations away from it, for the red-brick rows of villas gave the place an air of quiet industry and virtuous calm.

I remember stepping into our villa before the moving men arrived, Marya preceding me to unlock the door while I carried Joanna in my arms. I seated her on the floor in the far corner of our living room, her back supported by the joining of two walls, her good nature unimpaired. She was a Rubenesque baby with golden curls which were a heritage of the sun, for she had been out on the roof of our apartment house every day the sun shone down on Brooklyn. Her approval of the empty room around us seemed all important. The house was blessed.

With a minimum of furnishings, our living room was not unpleasant: in these small quarters, our old-fashioned cane-backed chaise-longue had the air of being a huge, deeply upholstered sofa. In our dining room a bright inverted angel food cake baking-tin attached to the ceiling served as a light reflector over the table. Out of packing boxes I had painted blue and red, I devised bookcases, stacked against the walls of the living and dining rooms; and if not beautiful, the rooms looked unsuburban, as if those who lived in them were there on holiday.

Except for Joanna (and our deep relief at having escaped from Brooklyn), we were less assured of doing well than we appeared to be. My twenty-five dollars a week from my parents pressed hard against my conscience and my pride. To keep three of us alive, the income was really too small to give me freedom from anxieties; it was essential that I write criticism as well as poetry to add a few dollars to the allowance; and Marya was kept from her writing by the household routines of serving meals and caring for Joanna. We tried our best to create the impression of rather enjoying the rounds of light housekeeping.

Before long I came to dread those days of the week I ventured into New York to collect books for book reviews. I hated to ask literary editors on newspapers and weeklies for books. To put off, if only for a half-hour, the ordeal of walking into an editor's office, I would drink two or three cups of black coffee at neighborhood lunch counters, then mount stairs or ascend in elevators for a brief talk, prearranged by phone. At the end of four or five encounters of this sort, I would return home by subway, utterly exhausted—not through actual "work" but through the psychic strain of the humiliation I felt.

We were not hopelessly given over to all these worries. To Marya and me, the Lewis Mumfords, who lived three or four garden rows down the street, were among the rewarding aspects of Sunnyside. Mumford would invite us over for tea with Van Wyck Brooks, and Brooks, prematurely gray, slightly corpulent, extremely sensitive in manner, and a bit oracular, would talk softly of early New York writers. He was in contrast to the splendid brilliance of his host who showed us an early landscape by Thomas Hart Benton, a charming canvas of a Far Western prairie, the scene very different from that of Benton's grotesque murals. When Mumford was enthusiastic his joy was contagious. One understood at once why his influence on the staff of *The New Republic* had been so invigorating.

Mumford had an athletic spring to his walk, clear and amused brown eyes, red cheeks, and a swing to his shoulders, as though he enjoyed the pleasure of wearing his handsome Inverness cape. His wife, slender and graceful, reminded me of portraits I had seen of Mrs. William Morris. It was easy to see why Mumford was liked by elder liberals, for he represented the best, and most enduring elements in William

Morris's Socialism; with Van Wyck Brooks, he entered into the spirit of America's "Coming-of-Age"—and he was among the first, in a widely ranging literary revival, to stress the importance of Herman Melville.

The Mumfords also belonged to the visible world of my Sunnyside house at its most attractive moments, when and where the plot of grass three feet from our front door seemed always freshly cut and green, and where thin, youthful trees above it swayed in the wind, or were bent almost double in a gush of rain.

After the famous Wall Street crash of 1929, the political splinter groups and minority cults in Sunnyside began to grow restive. Talk of violent changes was in the air. There were rumors, and some of the rumors were not false, that Sunnysiders who had been dutifully paying monthly installments on their mortgages had also been overcharged, for the jerry-built plumbing and drainage in and from their houses had been proved defective, and some of the houses looked as if they were falling apart. As usual in cases of this kind, the politically active people, those who had no investment in the houses beyond monthly rent to a mortgage-payer who had moved away, were loudest in protest. They had something to gain and nothing to lose: they organized "rent strike" meetings. Committees were formed. Mothers pushing baby carriages marched round the streets shouting "rent strike" slogans. Baby sitters, to curry favor with their striking employers, disguised their reading of the want-ad section of *The New York Times* by wrapping it in the latest edition of *The Daily Worker*. Elderly people, whose life savings had gone into the buying of their houses, and who had everything to lose, were far less noisy and attempted to repair their homes. White-haired men, more agile than I could hope to be, were seen on ladders with mortarboard and trowel, replacing bricks pushed out by frost, which had dropped into their front garden plots from the second story of a cracked façade.

At this time (circa 1929–1931) I was moving closer to the Communist orbit, contributing to the *New Masses* as well as other little magazines—*Pagany*, *Blues*, and *Hound & Horn*. Although I was not a "joiner" I agreed to join The John Reed Club, which was composed of artists and writers who were avowed "fellow travelers," and affiliated with the *New Masses* —it was formed with the purpose of modifying the political domination of the magazine. The members of the Club, young, often naive, and certainly idealistic, lived for the most part in Greenwich Village; some were also members of The Liberal Club and ate their dinners at Romany Marie's. Though few would have admitted it, many members of the Club imitated the semi-bohemian manners of John Reed himself; the Club was well-named.

The buildings and rooms below 14th Street where the Club held its meetings were, as I remember them, unswept, cold, gray, and relentlessly uncomfortable. But my view of them was probably colored by the fact that I lived so far away and that it took more than a hour for me to travel by subway from Union Square to an elevated exit in Queens at Sunnyside. An evening meeting at the Club meant I couldn't get home till after one in the morning. I had to confess to myself that long subway rides to and from the Club dampened my ardor. And I soon discovered that I could not take seriously the literary opinions advanced by some naive members who in this respect followed the teachings of Upton Sinclair in *Mammonart*, heartily admired Jack London's novels, and regarded Shakespeare as an old-fashioned English bourgeois writer, who had the nerve to think that kings were more important than "down to earth" proletarian heroes. In this company, I felt that I was "odd man out," yet for the moment, I did not entirely relinquish the hope that a new, refreshing generation of writers would arrive from "away down under"—I was all for the broadest possible range of literary expression. Contributors to *The Masses, The Liberator,* and the *New Masses* now extended from Hemingway to Robinson Jeffers and John Dos Passos, all coming from differing levels of American society—call them middle-class, or what you will—the range was close to being classless. I also felt that time would separate the sheep from the goats, the gifted writers from those who were unimaginative.

Although my attendance at the Club's meetings became increasingly infrequent, my belief that time would dissolve the differences in point of view between me and a few of its members kept me silent. When the editor of the *New Masses* lightly scolded me for translating a "dead" poet like Catullus, I held my temper, while others in the Club assured me that the man was a kindly fellow who meant no harm. For the moment, I dropped my pride: I did not wish to seem smug, priggish, or fatuously "superior"—after all, I felt that time *was* on my side. What I did not know then was that I had a deeper understanding of Catullus than I had of motives behind the actions of Communist editors.

At meetings of the Club, the tongue-tied diffidence of my adolescence would return, and my relationship to it reached a climax when Joseph Freeman invited me to join the Communist Party. Freeman and I, and two or three others, as I now see the picture, made up a less fanatical group within the Club. And I was furthest away from political activity; I liked Freeman and felt I could take his advice. He understood that the best of my abilities went into the writing of poems; he also wished to attract more actual writers to contribute their best to the *New Masses.*

With Freeman at my side, I attended a small caucus met to welcome me to the Party. The group was warm and encouraging—but aside from Freeman, they seemed unimagina-

tive and ordinary, more like small storekeepers than the workers they talked about. I felt out of my element, very far out
indeed. I felt an immense distaste at being welcomed by them,
and at the same time, misunderstood. I had the vague feeling
that I was supposed to be grateful for their interest in me.
Suddenly, I balked. I thanked them. I said I could not stay up
all night talking politics, as they could. That was all right
for them, but not for me. And I walked out.

If I was to continue writing what I felt and thought, I
could not take orders from anyone—and certainly not from
people whose looks and pretensions I distrusted. I was glad of
my escape. I knew myself well enough to know that I was
unimpressed by writers who talked incessantly of their political beliefs; I was skeptical of "truths" in political dogmatism.

These few conclusions made me happy to stay away from
the protest meetings of "rent-striking" Sunnysiders, for it had
become all too clear that many were more interested in fur-
thering political action than in helping unfortunate house-
holders. And because I stayed away, they had grown distrustful of me. This last I soon discovered by the revival of an
old acquaintance.

As I look back upon that lonely figure, that thin young
man who wore a pale red beard—grown, I believe, in imitation of D. H. Lawrence—he becomes typical of strayed, unworldly Middle Westerners who had joined Left Wing or-
ganizations in New York. I shall call him William Beers.
In Madison, I had met him in the company of Leonard, with
whom he frequently played tennis. My acquaintanceship with
Beers had been very slight, for he had been enrolled in the
school of engineering, and we had little in common. His fair
skin always seemed to be peeling from sunburn; he seemed
forever dressed in wrinkled white tennis shorts—with his right
arm swinging a freshly mended racquet. Yet gossip I had

heard about him fascinated me: rumor had it that he had been born and brought up in an obscure Wisconsin farming village where he had been regarded as an infant genius at the piano, that his parents attempted to place him on tour as another Mozart, that they met with failure, and the child collapsed. All that remained of his promise was a strong bent toward mathematics and a ghostly counter-tenor voice that intoned quartets and symphonies.

One Friday evening in Sunnyside I heard Beers's voice over the phone. He told me he had taken a job with the New York Bell Telephone Company; he had recently married, was living in Sunnyside, was chairman of the "rent-striking" committee —and could he visit me next Sunday morning at eleven o'clock? He wanted to talk about "old times" in Wisconsin. I agreed to see him, but was completely mystified: what "old times" could we talk about? I scarcely knew the man.

Eleven o'clock arrived next Sunday morning, and so did he. I led him down to my improvised study in the basement and seated him on a battered old sofa facing the back door and a window over our heads, the sofa at right angle to my typewriter table; I then swung my kitchen chair that I used at the typewriter around to face him. Beers talked in an over-flowing stream, as if he had not heard the sound of his own voice for the past six months. He spoke of his loneliness in New York, of his homesickness for Wisconsin countryside, its lakes, its fields of yellowing wheat, its maple and catalpa trees, its vast, midnight skies above the plains, its clapboard farm houses, red barns, and silos—all these were haunting him: could I understand? Could I understand his love of symphonies that he had heard in the quiet of night at home—the deathless music that reached upward to Orion and the sun? In the city all this had stilled, was given over to disquiet and noise; he could not make friends; he was afraid to drink with strangers —all he could do was to add to his record collection, while his wife was in the hands of an analyst. What, if he had children, would his children be like?

Being chairman of the "strike" committee gave him something to do. Obviously he had chosen me, if only for the moment, as his father confessor; back in Madison, he had probably chosen Leonard for the same role. I found myself moved by his utter loneliness, his sense of being abandoned, stripped of his precocious promise, that had undoubtedly belonged largely to his parents' imagination. In coming to me, he had bared his chest to a comparative stranger. I did not share his nostalgia for Wisconsin; my feeling for its countryside was elegaic, devoid of any longing to return. I felt then, as I have felt so often, that I had just *begun* to write—and that the abrasions of living in and near New York were reinspiring me. Yet because Beers was neither mean nor (at present, anyway) grasping for power, and because he seemed so impractical and helpless, I also felt I owed him human sympathy—and then I heard curious, muffled noises behind me, behind the window, behind the closed basement door.

I turned about, and for a fraction of a second I saw faces crowded against the window pane, and heard the shuffling of feet on the other side of the door. I looked at Beers, who appeared flustered, and a little frightened. "Without my knowing it, they must have followed me," he said. "I'm the new chairman; maybe they won't trust me if I visit you." I did not see him again while I lived in Sunnyside. And after this incident, the Sunnyside strikers pointedly avoided me. They probably felt that if I was not "for" them, I was against them, and possibly, since I still contributed to the *New Masses*, "dangerous," perhaps a "clerk" who could be lured (in Julien Benda's terms) into "treason."

It was about this time that Marya and I visited the apartment of a handsome young couple, the wife a public school teacher, who had just been converted to Communism. The young man earned an erratic living by ghostwriting for very rich men letters of civic and national complaint to the "Letters to the Times" columns on the editorial page of *The New York Times.* Since complaint was in his heart, the young man had become an extremely skillful artisan; almost every letter he wrote was published and commented on—and his illiterate clients were greatly pleased. On the afternoon of the evening we visited them he had bought a copy of T. S. Eliot's *For Lancelot Andrewes,* with its famous preface in which the poet described himself as "classicist in literature, royalist in politics, and Anglo-Catholic in religion." My host was angry, and threw the book on the table, saying he wouldn't keep such trash in his house. I told him that I'd take it off his hands; without agreeing with Eliot's statement as a public gesture, I admired his verse deeply and wished to read his latest essays. Marya and I carried the book back with us, grateful for the gift. To Marya and me those pages were far more exciting fare, and immeasurably more profound, more humane, more human in their findings than the heavy, anti-intellectual, "proletarian" fiction our host and hostess felt they had to read. We were not trying to avoid the seriousness of "Depression literature," but we regretted its lack of human insight, and resented its childish melodrama, its effort to "write down to the masses." At the very least, Eliot put one's intelligence to work, and in his essays, since he had made an art of quoting poetry with startling effects, one was almost certain to discover new aspects of verse itself.

Yet Marya and I had made a few highly valued friends among our neighbors. One couple were Dr. Theodore Shedlovsky of the Rockefeller Institute for Medical Research and his wife. Shedlovsky was a young physical chemist, mathematician, and biologist, who had settled in a Sunnyside "villa" not far from mine: from him I learned of Willard Gibbs whose speculations on the laws of thermodynamics gave life and direction to scientific thinking of the twentieth century.

Viewed superficially, Shedlovsky was a "tough-minded" product of the 1920s and of Boston's M.I.T., one who hated loose thinking and cant. His alertness kept him slender and light on his feet. I admired his blue-eyed coolness, his gaiety, his sense of balance. Yet behind his skepticism shone a quickening spirit. When my son, Patrick, was scarcely four weeks old—while pediatricians failed to diagnose his illness—it was Shedlovsky's advice, gained at the Rockefeller Institute, that saved the boy's life. Shedlovsky was not, of course, a physician, nor did he ever pretend to be—but he did delight in clearing away wrong-headed medical practices and cutting through professional red tape. His gaiety had a way of breaking through my reticence and shyness. We also shared a liking for Irish whiskey.

It was at Shedlovsky's house I met Norbert Wiener, whose wit had the speed of light, and whose appearance was that of a cross between a mountain bear and portraits of England's James I. Wiener, his broad body rolling in a chair, warned us of the genie who, in the not-too-distant future, would walk from the womb of a computer. He said the genie would do all he could to rule the earth, and after it, the universe; that the actual revolutions of our time were in technology, and if we were wise, we'd better forget the less important political revolutions.

Our years in Sunnyside had aspects other than those of our immediate surroundings, and one of the brightest of these was a visit from Marya's friend, Harriet Monroe of *Poetry*, Chicago. Marya's verse had appeared in *Poetry* before mine had, and when she had entered the University of Wisconsin, Miss Monroe invited her down to Chicago for a visit to *Poetry*'s offices, to read manuscripts with her and to drink *Poetry's* tea. To meet Miss Monroe was a pleasure of an astringent, quince-like sort: she was gray-haired, thin, with a thin-lipped smile: then suddenly, with a flash of girlish charm, her eyes would light up, completely given over to enthusiasm and amusement.

Whenever I think of Miss Monroe, a montage of the city of Chicago takes form behind her. I remember the jungle-like panorama of slums and tenements I used to see from the elevated tracks of an electric-powered train. Behind the ragged sumac trees that brushed the windows of the train were dingy brothels. Not far from these were the Negro hot spots, where gin was served in coffee cups to the accompaniment of jazz, at crowded tables in semi-darkness, no one sober, no one sane. East and north of the jungle were sights of the black and silver river with fragmentary pieces of the moon reflected in it, the sides of the river hedged about by steel-edged skyscrapers. North and east of the river were the narrow beaches along the lakefront, where the lake, stretching far to the east, looked like the ocean itself, a great moonlit rippling surface spreading beyond New York, beyond Dieppe, beyond Paris, beyond the Continent, beyond the lesser seas, across wide Asiatic deserts to the Wall of China—this was the illusion, carried in my mind since childhood, of Lake Michigan, the endless ocean to the east.

Miss Monroe's Chicago was of other elements, other times, and these were associated with memories of growing wealth and power, of North Shore mansions that opened doors to receive Joaquin Miller and Oscar Wilde, and early in our century, William Vaughn Moody and his wife. That part of Chicago was proud of its patronage of the arts, proud of its worship of things new, proud of its lack of sources in a British heritage, proud of its creators of the skyscraper, John Root (who was a brother-in-law of Miss Monroe) and Louis Sullivan—and of course tremendously proud of the success of the World's Columbian Exposition of 1893, and the present Art Institute that housed so many modern French paintings. In the Chicago where Miss Monroe was both hostess and patroness, some few of its mansions had their walls lined with images of the Far East—wallpaper from distant China. The world of her imagination was never small.

Though Miss Monroe's *Poetry* was financed and sponsored by her friends among Chicago's well-to-do, her magazine skillfully sustained an international air. Tagore, the East Indian poet who had impressed and fascinated W. B. Yeats, had been one of *Poetry*'s early contributors, and Ezra Pound was its European editor. Indeed, Miss Monroe's internationalism was as much a part of her personality as her loyalty to and enthusiasm over the virtues of Chicago. She had reconciled these two halves of her nature so completely that no signs of possible conflict came into view. I suspect she needed both to keep her interests fresh and to ward off boredom. Miss Monroe was as restless and as virginal as one of Henry James's heroines; though the recklessness with which she ordered exotic cocktails at luncheon with us one afternoon marked her out as belonging to quite another time and place.

Miss Monroe, in other words, had temperament. Her Chicago accent disguised, while her firm will asserted, her romantic tendencies. Her view of my nervous manner—the slight tremor and unsteady walk—allowed her fancies to run astray. She insisted I had served in the U.S. Army and been shell-shocked during World War I—and however often I reminded her that this was not the case, she held to her own interpretation of my physical disabilities.

Her fits of anger were infrequent, but effective. When a ragged, unwashed Chicago poet walked into her office and attempted to bully her into accepting one of his poems, she hurled an ink bottle at him—in emulation, no doubt, of Luther exorcising the Devil. Yet a few months later, when she heard that the overbearing poet was near starvation, she saw to it that a sum of money came into his hands. She could also be as abrupt and witty as the Chicago debutante she was before she took up the arts, before she wrote glowing notices of the Armory Show for a Chicago newspaper. She was fiercely loyal to those who gave money toward the support of her magazine—even to Samuel Insull, the embezzler and key figure in the crash of Chicago's utility companies, which incidentally had wiped out Miss Monroe's personal fortune. Because of his generous gifts to *Poetry*, she invited him to her seventieth birthday party and instructed her guests, including me, to go up and shake hands with the tremulous old man who stood in a corner of the room, his thin white hair in relief against the gold-bronze tones of the Chinese wallpaper.

In the same spirit as that of her devotion to the magazine and its sponsors, she held faith in her own eclectic taste in verse. Though she remained cool to the writings of Eliot, Robert Frost, and Hart Crane, she was the candid champion of widely diverse poets: Ezra Pound, Carl Sandburg, Vachel Lindsay, and Wallace Stevens. Their poems were the touchstones by which she weighed the merits of younger contributors to her magazine. When one submitted a poem to Miss Monroe, one had to prepare oneself for a lively exchange of letters—in which she showed herself an argumentative and inspiring editor. Her arguments forced one to speak up for oneself. I remember her rejection of my "O Metaphysical Head—," my defense of it, and her demand that I return it to her for reconsideration. (After it appeared in *Poetry*, she informed me that she had sent it to Wallace Stevens who urged her to publish it.)

There was, I believe, a rather special affinity of temperament between herself, Stevens, and Pound. In 1910 she had carried the two small volumes of Pound's *Personae* and *Exulta-tions* from London all the way to China. "I . . . beguiled the long Siberian journey with the strange and beautiful rhythms of this new poet, my self-exiled compatriot," so she wrote in her autobiography. Travel to far places, and occasional meetings with fellow Americans in London, where in her youth she had called on Henry James and Whistler, was her way of testing experience and renewing life.

In retrospect, my memory of Miss Monroe carries with it an image of her associate editor—Morton Dauwen Zabel, another native Chicagoan, many years her junior. Not unlike hers, his devotion to *Poetry* was of a chivalrous spirit, and like hers, too, was his combined love of travel and loyalty to Chicago. At the time she introduced him to us, he could not have been much more than twenty-five, an extremely blond young man, obviously shy. Although no single feature of his face resembled those of Gerard Manley Hopkins (as seen in photographs), his nervous sensibility gave the illusion that he recreated the looks and manner of the Victorian poet: he had the same radical depth of feeling, the same passionate concern for ethical values in poetry, and was contemptuous of shoddy, merely liberal opinions. It was appropriate that among his finest essays written for *Poetry* were those on Hopkins and E. A. Robinson.

Zabel's conservatism acted as a balance wheel to Miss Monroe's delight in novelty, for in her weakest moments, she was inclined to believe with Carl Sandburg that "the past is a bucket of ashes." Zabel, when he felt called upon to do so, never failed to speak with vigor, and since his fair skin flushed easily, with pleasure, anger, or benign good humor, his manner would become that of a youthful parish priest's. One of my clearest memories of him is at a Chicago cocktail party, given at the apartment of one of Miss Monroe's well-to-do maidenly patronesses. The chatter in the room had become unbearably silly and provincial—when I saw him step to the piano, seat himself straightly (his preparatory school had been a military academy), and without prelude, burst into Bach's coffee cantata. His rudeness was precise and just.

New York was decidedly out of his milieu; on Fifth Avenue, even his military erectness took on a slightly hesitant, umbrella-clutching, Henry Jamesian air. Only in one place other than Chicago did I see him fully at his ease. That was in Paris, strolling between the white Queens of France in the Luxembourg Gardens. His rimless spectacles gleamed with light: he was all courtliness, playing host to the golden twilight of a European August evening.

But to return to our Midwestern excursions away from Sunnyside. These were, for the most part, holiday visits to my family in Milwaukee, and since one changed trains at Chicago, overnight stops at Chicago were frequent before going on to my native city. In Chicago, Zabel was often our host, splendid and sharp, showing us his newly purchased edition of Edward Fitzgerald's letters, or Wilfred Blunt's diaries, or bound volumes of Margaret Anderson's and Jane Heap's *The Little Review*. I remember one evening walking with him toward a restaurant near Michigan Boulevard. Suddenly the side street reminded me of a scene out of the ancient world— or rather, something out of the apocalyptic fantasies of John Martin—for wherever I turned, millions of mayflies seemed to swarm, their bodies and corpses swept by the wind over walks and shop windows, a storm of wings, frail limbs, and torsos, crowding space before me, falling at my feet.

No less strange was my experience at eleven at night, walking along, striking my stick against the pavement, in a prosperous quarter of Milwaukee near my parents' home. All around me was a peculiar denseness of quiet I had forgotten while living in New York, even in Sunnyside. The night seemed curiously dark. Then, from an angle behind me flashed a policeman's torch. What was I doing here? "Walking home," I replied. I became fearfully self-conscious of the way I was dressed. Did I look like a tramp?

My self-consciousness of dress has a long history behind it, starting before I can remember dates at all, and probably has a beginning in the first stirrings of puberty. Because my mother arranged my hair in very long curls, and tailored me in Lord Fauntleroy costumes, one day I had a shock of fear: could I be mistaken for a girl? I ran to my half sister, Florence, to ask the question. I forget her reply, but it was probably ambiguous enough for me to insist upon having "a boy's haircut." I remember my uneasiness until that operation was performed. Perhaps the surface of my concern for dress was merely middle-class priggishness and conformity, but I think not. At a deeper level there was a touch of dandyism in it, a touch handed down from my grandfather, with his Regency effort at style (shades of Beau Brummell!), through my father to myself: it was the preparation of a façade against enemies, even against the world. The first philosopher of dandyism was, of course, Narcissus, but this is almost a commonplace of psychological theory. Deeper than that was my need to counteract the impression made by my physical instability, my unstable walk.

Of course, I did not look like a tramp, or anyone dangerous at all: I wore a soft black hat and a well-pressed suit of dark gray flannel; I carried a gray, cheap, ashplant. Meanwhile, I walked the path to the doorway of my father's house—with the policeman close behind me. He waited till my father opened the door to admit me; then he vanished into darkness.

No doubt Milwaukee was beginning to suffer from the Depression that had been making itself felt throughout the country, yet to my eyes, its blandly cushioned middle-class surfaces remained remarkably untouched. I was aware only that usury was flourishing, that the underside of the banking world was in control, and working overtime. This I learned from a friend of my college years who was in banking, and who told me confidently that he was going to make a million dollars before he was thirty. His incentives were no more extraordinary than the hope of acquiring a better-looking and more expensive girls for weekends and a fine stable of horses. When the New York stock market finally crashed, I wondered what became of him—and six months later in New York I heard that several of my prep school acquaintances had committed suicide. I concluded it was not the crash itself that killed them, but loss of power through loss of money, loss of faith in oneself, and the subsequent encounter with nothingness. My visits west were, in any case, too brief to renew old acquaintances—but I soon came to think of the lives of the children and boys I had known long ago as being related to the short lives of the mayflies I had seen heaped up against storefront windows on Michigan Boulevard in Chicago.

Our returns to Sunnyside meant an immediate return to my writing book-reviews for a half-dozen different publications, and these were newspapers as well as weeklies, with deadlines to be met. My effort was to lift my reviews to the level of essays—and this was not always an easy task. It meant a great deal of supplementary reading, usually at the 42nd Street Library, an hour away from my front door. This also meant, in nine cases out of ten, much rewriting. It looked as though I were wasting time on trivia—as I paced the floor like Flaubert, in search of the right word. The right word for what? A brief review, that would be forgotten tomorrow. Yet my labors were not entirely misspent. Through moments of inspiration, I did manage to make clear, to myself at least, the essential seriousness of my critical opinions. I had one central belief:

I believed that living elements of both the past and the future could be perceived within the changing present—and at rarest intervals, one had a vision, if only for the briefest instant, of things as they really are. This belief informed my poetry as well as my prose. Therefore, I did not choose to be didactic, or content with an easy formula for discerning truth.

As for Marya and me, the coming Depression held fewer fears than for many around us. My own savings were non-existent. Our small balances in the bank were scarcely enough to sustain a checking account. I remember Marya saying that no matter what happened on Wall Street, we had nothing to lose, nothing to fear. I had been so far removed from money-making in my childhood, I seldom realized that I had less money to spend than most of the frightened, Depression-conscious people I saw around me. In this, I may also have shared in my family's curious legacy of Trinity Irish gentility—which ignored its own lack of money in its effort to better the condition of the wretched and the poor. Added to this, the pride of the Trinity Irish placed them in their role of alms-giver, rather than that of those who received gifts and doles. Yet the misery of the Depression poor gave me a sense of human waste and loss, and my poems telling of uprooted creatures in Chelsea and downtown Manhattan had begun to take on a prophetic character. Poems I had written five years before 1929 and earlier, had acquired a patina of timeliness. Even publishers were beginning to take an interest in them.

In the offices of Covici-Friede, then a new and avant-garde house, publishing Wyndham Lewis, Richard Aldington, and Ezra Pound's magazine, *The Exile*, my manuscript fell into the hands of the poet, Louis Grudin, who read poetry for the firm and advised Pascal Covici on the selection of new writers. My book was accepted, and the following year, Covici also agreed to publish my new version of Catullus's poems, which I had written in whatever time I could spare from the days and nights I wrote *Chelsea Rooming House.* The two books represented six years' inspiration, work, and pleasure, and in them, I had found my vocation. It was my hope that both books would transcend the urgencies of the passing moment.

As for theorizing about poetry, I had come far enough into the writing of my own poems to appreciate Robinson Jeffers's remarks on distinctions between poetry and prose: ". . . poetry is bound to concern itself chiefly with permanent things and permanent aspects of life . . . Prose can discuss matters of the moment; poetry must deal with things a reader two thousand years away could understand and be moved by. . . ." With these reflections in the back of my mind I went on writing.

Through the intervention of Malcolm Cowley, who was the literary editor of *The New Republic,* Marya and I received an invitation to a three months' stay at Yaddo, an artists' colony near Saratoga Springs, New York, subsidized by a Wall Street millionaire, and administered by Mrs. Elizabeth Ames, a shy, low-voiced hostess who received her strange young guests with questioning eyes. The main building on the estate was designed (circa 1900) in imitation of Carmen Sylva's Royal Palace at Bucharest. In the reception hall a fountain played, tinkling through day and night. An air of fantasy prevailed throughout the mansion, and was extended over its lawns, gardens, and terraces, where, at surprising intervals, marble nymphs chastely sported, fixed in air above the shrubbery and grasses. There were paths leading into pine groves that simulated forests: these led to the various guest houses. I inhabited one constructed to look like a ruined tower. At the far end of the estate could be heard the distant echo of galloping horses and hoarse cries of acclamation— signs that the Saratoga Racetrack was not far away.

Most of the guests were extremely young and from Depression-haunted cities; almost all, as they arrived, were bewildered by their sudden lift upward from urban poverty to the luxury of living on a benevolently endowed manorial estate. Mrs. Ames's task was not unlike that of a housemother in a girls' school, and it was complicated by the fact that her charges displayed more imaginative resourcefulness than most adolescents, while some seemed determined to make Yaddo their shelter for the rest of their days.

At that time—the early 1930s—unconscious fantasy took hold of several of Yaddo's guests—and their arguments over the privileges they enjoyed became warnings to me of what went on in the minds of those committed to Left Wing writing. Some felt guilty at having their breakfast served in bed, and tried to voice their complaints in Marxian rhetoric; others suggested that certain of their fellow guests be put on kitchen-duty and made to mow the lawns of the estate. Mrs. Ames had much to do to keep her charges in hand and to reassure the servants that they would keep their jobs.

Except for the fact that Mrs. Ames's guests did not pay for their keep, Yaddo, in being a haven from the world outside its borders, held a resemblance to Gurdjieff's estate at Fontainebleau. Yaddo's central mansion was very like (as Marya wrote, in her "House of Chimeras") that place where,

Through the long drawing room the summer seemed to fall
With a quick shimmer on the ground

And stained the wine-gold carpets, colored our fear
With chimeras and delusions; in that world
Only the life-sized portraits on the wall
Glowed in fantastic life forever clutching roses.

Outside the mansion at night a Gothic atmosphere seemed to possess the sky and terraced landscapes: the moon, throwing the blackest of her shadows through the pine groves, glided across the cloudless reaches of the zodiac. I half-believed the rumors that Poe, a hundred years ago, had been inspired by Saratoga's landscape to write his "Ulalume" with its image of "Astarte's bediamonded crescent" in the sky.

At Yaddo it was easy enough to be distracted by the tensions vibrating between its guests and the highly romantic atmosphere of its surroundings. Marya and I were fortunate: generously, Mrs. Ames sought out a lodging house in Saratoga where our two children could be cared for, and we could visit them every afternoon; we also had books to complete, Marya, her first book of poems, and I, a study of D. H. Lawrence's writings, and a group of new poems. We were happy to devote most of our time to writing—and freed from household worries, this was a luxury. In retrospect, I find reflections of Saratoga's nightscapes in the lines I wrote that summer; they were in "Stanzas for My Daughter" written when she was a child of six:

> Tell her I love
>   to make these words a song
> with her careful lips,
>   O bride.
> Spring and bridegroom at your side,
> save them for the deep and long
> silences when northstar light
> perishes down quicksilver steep
> walls of flesh where love and death
> make a counterfeit of sleep.

And there is a daytime moment of the Saratoga Racetrack in a later poem:

> Invisible sweepstake, but somewhere on earth real,
> the little horse on a white circle trotting
> clean limbs to victory
>   and spent,

the eyes still bright, insensible, lighting
the darkness of a stall.
Here is no dream, but happiness leans over
like the sight of God
to Broadway Jones or Harlem John
waiting for hope (like love) here for an hour
invisible, then gone.

The lines also recreated the atmosphere of the urban Depression in New York, as well as the permanent condition of those unfortunates, like my characters in Chelsea, who had strayed from the sight of God.

At Yaddo, Marya and I suggested to Mrs. Ames and her advisory committee that Morton Zabel of *Poetry* be invited —which they did at once—and the place had three Middle Western visitants, Zabel, James T. Farrell, and myself, each, I like to think, of very different temperament. At that moment, Farrell had just returned from a honeymoon in Paris with his young wife, Dorothy.

A year before, I had welcomed Farrell to an evening in Sunnyside: we were acquainted because we enjoyed reading each other's writings in the same little "advanced" magazines. On impulse, and on his way through New York to Paris with his bride, he rushed out to Queens by subway, and within ten minutes of his crossing the threshold of our small house, he had broken through my air of reticence, and we were talking as though we had known each other half our lives. He was earnest, voluble, hilarious, full of plans and lively anecdotes. We had a drink to his future success. His thick-lensed eyeglasses flashed; his wild black hair tumbled over his brow. And now he had leapt out of his chair, punctuating his Chicago-Irish accented phrases with generous sweeping gestures of his arms. We had another drink to the future success of all four of us. Farrell was entertaining himself as well as his host, hostess, and his young bride, yet beyond the hilarity, the warmth, the drinks, was a serious plan, and the plan, as I heard it that night, contained the synopsis of his future trilogy, *Studs Lonigan.*

Against the backdrops of Yaddo's fanciful interiors, Farrell seemed an archetypical Irish-American primitive. He was unique, and he knew it. His tremendous industry in turning out several thousands of words a day set him well apart from the other guests. He had made of his many hours of writing, a way of life: wherever he could find room to shelter a brass bed, a chair, a table to hold a cup of coffee and a typewriter—this last with a quire of paper—he was at the center of his universe. Whether the room was in a hotel in Paris, or on the East Side of New York, his surroundings were essentially the same. It was the center that mattered, and from it came the creations of the many novels and short stories, including "Reverend Father Gilholley," and *The Face of Time* as well as *Studs Lonigan.* Farrell's neo-naturalism was the most effective of its kind in American fiction, and like Dreiser's, Farrell's concerns were beyond the provinces of art. In the best of his writings, Farrell seldom fails to recreate the illusion of life, and in this his disenchanted Irish-Catholic men and women seem destined for an immortality. As for himself, he was the last major figure to emerge from Chicago's literary "Renaissance"—the last intellectual of his generation to rely on the tenets of tough-minded Pragmatism.

When we returned from Yaddo, even modestly featured Sunnyside seemed to be drifting to the lowest spirals of the Depression. I began to feel that everything looked worn-down, and that everyone looked less secure, less fortunate. Some of this feeling may have been caused by an illusion—for there was so much talk of the Depression, one began to see and feel it everywhere. In our household, we lived on lentil soup

four days out of seven—which was no great hardship because the meat sold in our neighborhood markets was scarcely
fit to eat.

I remember our Sunday dinners. By a freak of Depression
economics, it was cheaper for us to eat our largest meal of
the week at a Chinese restaurant than to prepare it at home.
The excursion to the restaurant was also an escape from household chores which gave a holiday air to the occasion. Yet
our holiday was not achieved without a gray Depression
prelude. To reach the restaurant, we had to walk westward,
carrying and wheeling the two children across a dreary
Queens Boulevard. Overhead was a gloomy, criss-crossed
superstructure of iron girders supporting the tracks and
station of a subway. At intervals, when a train swept by,
there was a shaking groan and tremor in the air. On our level
a half-mile of empty, broken storefronts, and crippled neon
lights, lined the broad, half-darkened street. We made our way
through a windswept litter of torn newspapers and sodden
shreds of cardboard boxes.

We crossed this desert, then mounted to our Chinese
refuge on the second floor, over an abandoned shop. In contrast to the street below, the large, loft-like room, sunny
though austere, seemed to welcome us. As I remember it, the
room was always more than three-quarters empty—other
diners sat at tables far removed from us, couples mostly,
dressed in colorless clothes, staring dumbly at one another. It
always seemed that we were the only happy occupants of
the place, and the two children, catching the mood of our
holiday spirit, were exceptionally good-tempered. One other
feature of the restaurant was memorable: it was the kind
of place where Christmas tinsel is stretched from wall to
wall a week after Thanksgiving, and remains, long past its
glitter, into the first week of August. We were young enough
not to allow the ungainliness of the place to ruin our Sundays:
it was certainly less desolate than the street below it, and on

our return to the streets of Sunnyside, east of the boulevard, the little brick villas somehow seemed enhanced by our journey.

The arrival of Franklin D. Roosevelt in The White House seemed to bring with it a change of atmosphere. At the very least, it brought about a shift in the Roosevelt legend, and a fresh turn to the character of American heroics. Roosevelt's overcoming of his injuries from polio gave hope to the many victims of the American Depression—yet his image rode so far above them that it was one of god-like splendor: stories (aided by his wife's writings) of Rooseveltian dynasty and destiny filled the air.

Roosevelt was the first major political figure in this country to make his presence felt everywhere by his voice on radio: it had the ease, the glamour of a professional actor's; it also had something in it that was closely allied to wit—without being witty—and its accents were those of authority. The evening he was to announce his cure for the Depression by radio, Marya and I were invited to hear the broadcast at the Park Avenue apartment of a handsomely dressed, promising young poet, who had inherited money and enjoyed giving large cocktail parties, at which he was usually overshadowed by tall, aggressive, and not too courteous guests. The young poet's political interests rivaled those of his writing verse, which meant that neither his politics nor his verse fulfilled his promises. On that particular evening the conduct of his guests was no exception to their rule. My impression of the poet's apartment, inherited, I believe, from a wealthy grandmother or aunt, was of a place where large sofas, chairs, and tables stood in the way of crowds of people, all trying to move past one another without spilling their drinks. A few tried, without success, to leap over sofas, or to climb on tables, and all seemed to take pride in ignoring their host, who in the butler's pantry assisted a manservant, handing out tall glasses, half-filled with bootlegged Scotch.

Then Roosevelt's voice was heard proclaiming a bank holiday, a shutting of the doors of all the banks, midnight that very evening. As the new President's voice sounded through the rooms, the guests were silent, stilled in various postures: it became clear that no money could be drawn from the banks for several days. Drinks were transferred from the right hand to the left, while fingers searched for change in vest and trouser pockets, or plunged inside their owner's jacket in search of a wallet. Enthusiasm for Roosevelt had undergone a chill. Some faces showed bewilderment: without money, real money, and lots of it, what could anyone do? And on such short notice of no money in hand, where could one go? One would have to stay home; having no money was like being under house arrest. How many taxi-drivers in the city would accept a check? I heard someone say he had only two dollars in his clothes.

Then I heard the breaking of glass, the smashing of glasses against the walls, against the mantelpiece, against the iron firedogs. There was the sound of glass breaking underfoot. The turn to violence broke the tension in the room. Someone shouted, "This is the end of an era!" Marya and I, though we wished to go home, were still wedged in the center of the room. With the help of a tall, rosy-cheeked young man who was willing to rescue us by elbowing his way through the crowd and dragging us after him, an avenue was made for our escape. His manner was vigorous and engaging, and with heaving shoulders, he steered us out of the apartment to the elevator shaft, and two or three minutes later we were making our way to the Lexington Avenue subway. The stars were high in the sky, the streets unusually empty and quiet. It was likely that Roosevelt's pronouncement had sobered the city. It was also possible that many were actually frightened at the thought of not being able to enter a bank the following morning. The idea of "business as usual" had been blacked out. If only for an imaginary second or two, everyone in New

York felt as poor as everyone else—that was my interpretation of the quiet around us—though the quiet may have been no more than a lull that had fallen over a well-to-do neighborhood.

The few days of the bank holiday were of no inconvenience to us: my father had sent me postal money orders that could be cashed within walking distance of my house. Since we were used to living on next to nothing, these small sums sufficed. And since we felt we had already slipped to the lowest rung of the Depression, for us any way out of it was up.

Which indeed it was. We had begun to get good news of my book of poems. T. S. Eliot had accepted it for British publication by Faber and Faber, under the title of *Rooming House,* and now Eliot had been invited to deliver a series of lectures in the States. I was invited to a small dinner given for him that preceded a reading at The New School for Social Research. The dinner was at a restaurant near The New School, recently moved downtown to 12th Street; the host was Horace Kallen, and the guests, beside myself, were Eliot, his elder brother Henry, and Henry's wife. Eliot arrived, in white-tie evening dress, ten minutes late: he was flushed and bright, and looked supremely exhilarated: he bowed to all of us and said, "Forgive me, if I seem a bit post-war, but I'm rather tight. I have to prepare myself to face all those people. I always drink before reading poetry." "To prepare a face to meet the faces . . ." went through my mind, while he leaned forward over us and slipped into a chair. He smiled at his brother, who looked so much like him that the resemblance gave me a small shock. Even the intonation of their voices was much the same, and there was a touch of deep affection in the formal courtesies they exchanged between them. As they glanced at each other, it seemed that both were looking into a mirror. This was to be, so Henry at my left side informed me, a real celebration, marking the first time he had had the chance to hear Tom read his poetry aloud. Their mother, so he informed me, did not quite approve of some of Tom's more "dangerous" poems, his Sweeney poems; they made her wonder what kind of company he kept. As for himself, he liked the poems immensely, he even liked the poems written by Tom's strange friend, Pound—what a very strange, extraordinary man!

Soon we were strolling into the large ground floor auditorium of The New School: with a bow, Eliot strode away from us, up toward the stage, his personality transformed into that of a public figure, and for a split second, seeing his face in profile, I seemed to perceive a resemblance to the features of a youthful Ralph Waldo Emerson. Now Eliot had mounted the stage and stood behind a lectern; he had begun to read a poem—and one was caught up at once in a stage personality that spoke with a pronounced British accent. To me, the reading was a *tour de force*, quickened, I thought, by the presence of Henry in the audience. And when Eliot preceded his reading of "Sweeney Among the Nightingales" by saying that the poem was like a modern painting, abstract and impersonal, I felt that he was addressing his remarks to Henry directly— in mock reassurance that he was only half as wicked as his family supposed him to be. I thought I saw him turn a bright flicker of a smile in Henry's direction. Henry leaned toward me and whispered, "I never knew that Tom could read so beautifully; he's a very fine poet." He looked as though the deepest wells of his affection had been stirred.

I believe that Eliot actually dreaded mounting to the stage, but once he was there, he lived up to the occasion, and seemed to enjoy himself—moreover, he overwhelmed the crowd that heard him. Some few had come with the intention of heckling him, but he met the occasion with such well-poised levity that his enjoyment of the moment became contagious. I have attended no poetry reading since that was so impressive, or brought at its close such well-deserved applause.

In contrast to the pleasure I shared at the Eliot reading was my distress in traveling by subway through Manhattan during the early years of the 1930s. Often enough, which was several times too often, I would be swept off my feet by crowds behind me onto a train. As the Depression deepened, the derelicts of the subways grew in number: they marched the length of trains, plunging from side to side, swaying with the motion of the cars, extending through their gray rags a shining tin cup or butcher-red-chapped fingers grasping a half-dozen yellow pencils. Some slept crouched embryo-fashion in corners of the trains' coaches; others sat at subway exits and entrances, grimacing upward at legs, torsos, and faces rushing by; some parked themselves on subway platform benches. Some were black, some were dirty gray-white, and some were yellow-tan-colored, small-boned, with delicate gestures and large dark eyes. Except for the few who balanced a bow across the strings of a violin, or attempted to sing, this company of underground travelers was mute—the tearing, metallic noises and explosions came from the brakes and swaying cars of the train.

I took certain pride in being able to ride past the litter, past the ragged threats of violence on the unshaven faces of men around me—without closing my eyes. I remember a re-current dream of that period: I was on a train, winding on a high elevated structure through the city—the city a combined Chicago-New York. The sky between buildings was the color of lead, the crowded train swayed in the air, and a dreadful odor arose from the streets: then as the elevated structure began to fall, a voice proclaimed, "That smell is the smell of death!"

One evening on my return home from the center of Man-hattan, the crowd behind me almost thrust me down the small gap between the subway platform and the train. My trip downward under the wheels of the train was a very near thing, but I righted my balance; hands, elbows, and knees behind me vaulted me across the gap. I reeled onto a seat, and was quite unhurt. Yet the experience, trivial and brief as it was, reawakened my phobias of subway travel, and though I managed to keep them under control for many years following my loss of balance in the evening rush-hour crowd, whenever I passed through a subway turnstile I felt uneasy. I tried to avoid crowds by walking to the far ends of the platform, seeking out the half-empty first and last coaches of the train.

In 1933, soon after my second book of poems, *No Retreat*, was published, I received a letter from Vevey, in Switzerland, signed "Bryher." Bryher is the pseudonym of Winifred Ellerman, and in the letter she introduced herself by saying she was a friend of Harriet Monroe, that she had picked up *No Retreat* in a Swiss bookshop and had a question to ask. Did my elegy, in the book, "A Wreath for Margery," refer to Margery Latimer? She, too, had admired her short stories and novels, and felt their affinity with the writings of Katherine Mansfield and Mary Butts. She had heard that she had died, leaving an infant daughter; she had also heard Margery's parents were poor—and could she do something to help—for the sake of Margery and the baby? I sent her the Latimers' address.

Through Harriet Monroe, Bryher again got in touch with Marya and me, and arranged for a meeting with us in New York, for she made periodic trips to the city, visiting the theater—she was fond of O'Neill's plays—and venturing into Brooklyn to see Marianne Moore. The setting for our meeting was Rumpelmayer's tearoom on the ground floor of the St. Moritz Hotel on Central Park South. I remember that the day was in late winter, that cold dark winds whirled through the streets, and that the leafless boughs of the trees in Central Park looked wet and purplish-black against gray skies. There was a smell of snow in the air. Stepping into the tearoom was like crossing the threshold of a winter palace. Inside, everything seemed to glitter quietly: the tea-trolleys, the silver sugar tongs, spoons, and forks, the teapots and canisters; and the white damask tablecloths, covered with tea cakes topped with white icing, and thin, white sandwiches, gave off a snowy gleam, with the occasional icy glint of a silver cake knife.

And from amidst this semi-brightness, Bryher moved toward us, a compact, small-boned figure in navy blue: navy blue beret, navy blue topcoat. As she approached, her right hand shyly extended in welcome, one remarked her amazingly clear blue eyes. Since, within a second or two, her shyness seemed to vanish, we could not have been too formidable, Marya and I and the two children, Joanna, large-eyed and seven, Patrick, almost two—who, at the sight of the tea things, broke into a half-dance, while his cherubic smile, red hair, and blue eyes made him look unusually gay.

What did we talk of that afternoon? I am fairly certain that we talked of poets and of poetry. If I remember correctly, I asked many questions about London, for to me, Bryher's modesty and quietness seemed supremely English—yet her manner did not entirely conceal her enthusiasms: she liked the Imagist poets, as well as the candor of economical, unvarnished prose; she thought H. D. excellent, Pound a shade inhuman; she liked the passionate concerns of Eugene O'Neill, though she held no sentimental brief at all for the Irish. She doubted that the Maginot Line was a tenable defense against the Nazis. She said I would certainly like London, and as for herself, she enjoyed the excitement of visiting New York; New York was a wonderful change of air. When we rose to go, Bryher, smiling, handed me a sealed envelope to be opened on my return to Sunnyside.

At home I drew Bryher's envelope from my pocket, and

since it was slightly crumpled, I tore it open gently. It contained an invitation to visit her in London during the approaching summer and with it a check to pay our passage across the Atlantic. The good news made us a trifle dizzy. We knew how rare such strokes of good fortune were. What pleased us most was that the gift came from someone we could respect, someone who had an artist's temperament and insight —and we also felt that she understood us. (Her own novels, published a dozen years or so later, brought recognition of her accomplishment, the re-creation of the historical novel as a work of art.) Her own reticence made me feel she would understand my pride and shyness in meeting people.

The prospect of a trip to the British Isles came at a moment when I saw the end of my road in book-reviewing. I was to write a highly featured notice of *The Forty Days of Musa Dagh;* I had made a fearful mistake in accepting the assignment, for the book was one of those long-winded prefabricated-for-Hollywood affairs. It was, I thought, shamelessly mediocre, but probably the best its author could do. The book's glossy paper and gray type strained my patience as well as my eyes; as I turned its pages, acres of boredom unrolled before me—to read *The Forty Days* was a chore for which I was temperamentally unfit. I wrote the notice, but I decided never again to do drudgery of the same kind.

"Why do you always say," said an angry editor to me after I had mildly dispraised one of his authors, "that one writer is better than another?" I replied that I hated mediocrity instinctively. And I might well have quoted (with greater logic) Ezra Pound's remark, "There's no democracy in the arts."

From then onward, I accepted my assignments in literary journalism with growing wariness. I looked for books that were likely to be ignored by the new social critics as well as by those who were elderly captains of established order. This gave me a chance to rediscover for the second time the poetry of W. B. Yeats: his earlier books were sold on "remainder counters" in cut-rate drug stores for under a dollar; his current books received only the briefest mention in literary journals. Left Wing critics gave out warnings that Yeats was a Fascist, and was therefore an "untouchable"—and I was beginning to note that almost every poet of stature was being dismissed as politically "wrong." (For the moment, the poets of "promise" were Auden, Day Lewis, Spender.) I was rather more than glad to write at length on Yeats wherever I could, and my researches into Yeats's writings led me to F. W. H. Myers's case histories in *Human Personality and Its Survival of Bodily Death,* which had left their impress on his thinking. I found that Myers was a man of extraordinary insights and that his writings haunted the imaginations of Henry James and his brother, William. Without my being conscious of the change, I had begun to lose interest in Left Wing literary opinions, and like the time Marya and I read Eliot's *For Lancelot Andrewes,* I saw a wide gap between transient Left Wing sentiments and works of art. Left Wing critics talked loudly of "humanity" and yet, for the sake of the proletariat, were ready to tolerate prison camps and murders. Talk and logic of this sort were repeated throughout the ranges of liberal journalism.

I was happy whenever I thought of leaving New York for this extended holiday in England. As we neared the day of leaving home for our transatlantic trip, our sense of pleasure quickened. Through Thomas Cook's, we chose an old-fashioned, small, one-class boat of the Cunard Lines. As we stepped aboard, I noted she was newly painted, scrubbed, and varnished, and though of uncertain age, looked smart and shapely. On that fine June evening, I shall never forget the roseate light of the western sun glancing through the portholes of the dining hall.

6

The Green-Rilled Islands

As our boat edged out of New York harbor, I had the feeling of "going home" to the British Isles, and I was also conscious of following the same route that my Aunt Victoria's mentor, Emerson, had taken a hundred years before. I wished to share something of Emerson's backward look at America from English soil, and at that time, I deeply felt, as a patriotic conviction, that Emerson's writings were a living source of American poetry. I also felt the need to see my legendary native continent at transatlantic distance, to place my relationship to it in perspective.

I was now "free" to explore—and this without fear of mere ancestor-worship—the regions of London my father's mother knew in 1820, even to High Holborn where *her* strange and feared Welsh grandmother took charge of the household when her mother died.

Did I, when a child visiting at my grandmother's, see a picture of this dark-skinned, mysterious Welshwoman? She wore a tall, conical, broad-brimmed black hat, like those worn by witches on Hallowe'en. Or was this a picture out of a childish dream, pieced together from my grandmother's confessions of how she dreaded the woman, who would rise out of nowhere to confront her, and haunt her sleep? Even now, I cannot explain why it is I have such a strong impression of her. The time was of a date before camera portraits were made. Could the picture have been a wash drawing? Was this strange Welshwoman, who had become so firmly fixed on the retina of my memory, a creature seen in a vision?

In asking these questions, I find myself approaching an uncharted field between Coleridge's psycho-physical "science of Opticks" and extrasensory perception. It is an area of which we know very little. Charlatans, as well as honest, questioning men, have entered it. It impinges on what we are thinking of when we speak of the "creative process." That was why Coleridge, with his sense of grief at having lost his creative powers, was so deeply concerned with "Opticks" and psychology. It was also why Yeats, feeling his need for a deeper understanding of human motives and of the universe than he thought he possessed, turned his face halfway toward theosophy, and then wrote *A Vision*. For his own reasons, which were not Coleridge's, he came close to the same uncharted field, and re-created, in his own image, the poet as seer.

On board ship, I also felt myself detached from day-to-day responsibilities, from futile worries over the Depression, the threats of violence in the streets, the lack of money. The children, my wife, and I, actually enjoyed the pitch, the roll of the ocean. We watched the colors of the sea turn from green to gray, from lead to blue—the uprush of foam and its dissipation into shreds of lace between the waves. At night, leaning over the rail, I fancied I saw shafts of light flashing through the moving darkness under us. Were these signs of flying fish and dolphins? As I gazed, I felt myself slipping into a childhood reverie. I was back in my uncle's library on Jefferson Street, and before me, open on my knees, was a large-page edition of *The Ancient Mariner*, illustrated by Dore engravings; was I witnessing the progress of Dore's sea-serpents across the waters? Of course, I wasn't, but the presence of the sea had restored me to the world of imagination and adventure. To me, as I drew near them, England and Ireland were the green-rilled islands of my boyhood vision.

One of the reasons I felt freed of immediate worries was contained in my being appointed, shortly before I left home, to the English faculty of a new college for girls, Sarah Lawrence College, in Bronxville, New York. My place would be waiting for me at the end of the coming September, now conveniently far forward in my calendar.

Our trip was blessed by good weather and we landed at Southampton in a calm, pantheistic Constable sunset. On the boat train to London, we hugely enjoyed our English tea and biscuits, which was just as well—for we were riding into a night of bewilderment and discomfort. It was Sunday evening, and I was completely unaware of London's "blue" Sunday closing laws that in those days strictly regulated the service hours of its public houses and hotels. Moreover, I had recklessly neglected to reserve rooms in a London hotel before sailing from New York harbor. I had assumed, irrationally enough, that London, like New York, would allow me to book rooms in a hotel by phone call from the Waterloo Station at eleven o'clock of a Sunday night: nothing was further from the truth. I had placed my family, myself, and my luggage at the mercy of a large, ragged, unshaven station porter, who swiftly installed us in a wretched-looking warren for sailors, called "The Waterloo Hotel," and then extended a dirty paw, demanding a half-crown. We were led to a dreary room, containing two brass beds, and infested by "creeping things." As we prepared ourselves for a sleepless night, we were still unsteady from the week-long rolling of the boat. Those parts of the unswept room that did not—again—resemble deckscapes in Dore's illustrations for *The Ancient Mariner* looked remarkably like Fagin's ragged quarters in Cruikshank's drawings. Six o'clock in the morning was announced by the entry of an unwashed girl in a dirty apron serving us hot tea and buttered toast. Through the submarine glow of a tall window at my side, I heard and caught glimpses of London's pacing multitudes setting off for work.

We made up our minds to explore the neighborhood of St. James's in search of another hotel. Loss of sleep had made me stubborn in my conviction that one of the many hotels in that region would give us shelter. A taxi let us down where we could see the guards at their paces outside the gates of St. James's Palace. For what seemed hours, we trudged from one hotel to another, getting hotter, more weary, and soot-covered at every step, and the children looking less and less respectable as each doorman turned us aside. The day was cloudy, yet unbearably hot, while the dimly seen, bronze cauldron of a sun seemed to throb over our heads in the gray air. We marched on past the noon hour. At last we stepped into Jermyn Street —where, as I remembered from my Grandmother Gregory's memories, Byron had once lived in furnished lodgings, and from where he used to walk to one of Samuel Rogers's famous literary breakfasts. As we trudged by the plate glass window of a haberdashery shop, I fancied I saw Byron's limping shadow glide across the street: I had grown lightheaded with fatigue. With greater clarity I saw black lettering above the fanlight of a doorway: CAVENDISH HOTEL. The building looked quiet and cool; I crossed the street to pull the front door bell.

The door swung open and there stood a tall old woman, with a piece of bread and butter held in her right hand. Her dark dress was carelessly hitched across her shoulders; her

brick-red face was set off by a shock of brilliant white hair.
I told her I was an American looking for inexpensive lodgings,
that my wife and two children were utterly exhausted—and
that she must take us in. She took a bite out of her buttered
bread and said: "You'll do. You look exactly like Paul
Draper, who wasn't a bad sort. I helped *him* out. I'm Rosa
Lewis!" Then she stepped back, clearly expecting me to react
to the revelation. I, who had never heard of her, looked bewildered, but this did not seem to offend her, for she went
on, "I had leaders written about me in *The Saturday Evening
Post*, and I'm known all over the United States. Come in. I'll
get a girl to show you rooms."

She guided me into a small dark foyer, where pinned on a
notice board near a freshly gilded birdcage lift was a slip of
paper on which was written: "Major Blake is to receive no
more drinks on credit." A buxom, red-headed girl, her face
fearfully mottled with flame-colored pimples, pushed me into
the cage. At the fourth floor she marched me out of the lift
and into a suite of rooms, the walls covered in red plush and
gilt, and the furniture of bird's-eye maple. "You can't take
these; they're too expensive," she said. "*They* belonged to
King Edward, and he slept here." Then she motioned me back
into the lift with "You can't afford them; I'll have to show
you something cheaper." I found her impertinence annoying,
but her pride in the establishment beguiling. She lowered me
slowly to the ground floor, and led me through a darkened
hallway, hung with seventeenth-century tapestries and eighteenth-century prints, which had the air of being an annex
to an auction room. At the end of the passageway was a large
square room, with an alcove and bathroom at its sides. A soot-
streaked window overlooked a parking lot. "A guinea a day,"
she said, and we closed the bargain. Though I knew I was
being overcharged, my mind was on my family waiting in
the foyer.

I returned to the foyer and gave orders to a young woman who vaguely resembled a chambermaid, for lunch to be served in our room to Marya and the children. As the girl turned away, I found Rosa Lewis at my side. "Now that that's settled, we'll have a drink," she said, and then invited us into her office. Marya had the children on her hands and felt obliged to refuse the offer, but I gladly accepted a champagne cocktail, with a strawberry floating in it, from the hands of a gnome-like, dirt-encrusted charwoman. Rosa Lewis lifted her glass, tasted her drink knowingly, nodded to the charwoman, and ushered me into her office.

As she sat down behind her desk, I saw a large, full-length portrait of a young woman, straight as a birch tree, obviously Rosa herself, painted in Sargent's manner, and certainly a typical example of Edwardian "society" portraiture. On the wall, at right angles to it, were a few portrait-photographs, shining under glass; among them one of King Edward VII, signed, "Affectionately, Albert," and another of Emperor Wilhelm, helmeted, with mustache erect, signed, "To Rosa, with love, Willie." Her conquests, so it seemed, had been of the first order. She had, I soon learned, been Edward's cook, then mistress, and the unofficial hostess of many a royal dinner party. Her reward had been this hotel, a gift from him, made shortly before he died; it would go, she assured me, to her relatives, who were now her servants—living in "expectation" of the valuables they would inherit at her death. The porter, who had been sent to Waterloo Station to fetch my luggage, would have a generous share of her belongings.

Her confessions, probably rehearsed and embellished many times before, to interviewers, or anyone willing to listen, threatened to hold me at her side forever. With some difficulty I managed at last to free myself from the circling web of her romances. As soon as I was free, I phoned Bryher to tell her of our arrival, and when I told her we had landed, rather precariously, at the Cavendish Hotel in Jermyn Street, I heard laughter over the phone. "How in the world did you find that place?" she said. "I'll send you a governess for the children in the morning."

I awoke next morning at five-thirty, noiselessly dressed so as not to disturb my wife and children, and set out for a stroll, along Jermyn Street that so filled my mind with Byronic associations. On my return, an ancient Rolls-Royce came to a halt in front of the Cavendish with Rosa Lewis's porter at the wheel, and I saw her step from the hotel's entrance toward the car. An oyster-colored macintosh had been thrown across her shoulders over a long nightgown. From a side pocket she drew out a pint bottle of Scotch, waved it in my direction, and helped herself to a drink. She was, she informed me, off to do her day's marketing; she would be back shortly, never fear.

With her assurance that our breakfast would wait on her return, I extended my walks through the neighborhood, and by the time I got back to the hotel I found my family at breakfast in a dining room that had witnessed better days; the large rococo mirrors were tarnished, their quicksilver backs moldy and worn, their gilt frames turning black, the brocaded hangings at the French windows faded and dusty. Yet a generous breakfast had been prepared, and was now being served, with radiant silver and china and a white damask cloth, Rosa Lewis herself in attendance. Seated on the edge of a chair and eyeing Miss Lewis with deliberate coolness was Miss Stevens, the governess sent by Bryher. As she confronted our hostess, she was lofty, and in her gray-haired, gray-suited, neat little way, formidable. In her presence, and overwarmed by whiskey, Rosa Lewis lost much of her poise; she had been informed by Miss Stevens that we had been invited to London by Lady Ellerman's daughter. Rosa Lewis drew me out of the room, and nervously, in a low voice, said that she would be glad to find me another governess, one that would be marvelous for my dear children—not an amateur like that person, perched on the edge of a chair. Miss Stevens briskly collected my son and daughter to trot them off to the zoo in Regent's Park.

Mention of Lady Ellerman had evidently stirred our hostess's imagination. As soon as the governess had departed with her charges, Miss Lewis broached the subject of selling me a farm in Dorset, as well as her ancient Rolls-Royce. Also, she had found the perfect gift for that wonderful child, my daughter: a gramophone, one with a horn big as a great, overgrown purple morning glory! The child would be enchanted! And I could have it cheap.

In the eyes of the children Maud Stevens was a creator of miracles; she not only introduced them to the joys of tea at Lyons Corner House, but within twenty-four hours had successfully transported us out of the colorful but cramped confines of the Cavendish Hotel to more spacious and comfortable quarters in King Henry's Road, near Primrose Hill. The lodging house was run by Miss Stevens's friend, Miss Hawkins, heir and daughter of "a military gentleman" who had served the Queen in India. Overnight, the extravagances of King Edward and Jermyn Street were far behind us, and we were buttressed by the somber virtues of lower-middle-class respectability.

I was soon to learn from Maud Stevens herself that Bryher had been *her* savior. Miss Stevens had been a salesclerk in a London bookshop for thirty years, where Bryher had brought books from her, and just as she was about to retire, the firm went bankrupt, and the pension, that had been promised her, promptly vanished. Bryher employed her as a secretary extraordinary, and her first assignment was the care of my two children, and she greatly enjoyed playing the role of a bookish governess, shepherding Joanna and Patrick through the paths

of the zoo as well as treating them to toast, tea, and cakes at
Lyons. She had the art of transforming the slightest of pleasures
into grand, almost Oriental, luxuries. The lighting of a cork-
tipped cigarette was always performed with an air of triumph
—it was, indeed, a sign that she had left the Victorian Age
behind her. She was then certain she had made her escape into
the new, if dangerous, twentieth century.

Though of Miss Stevens' generation, Miss Hawkins looked
much older. Miss Hawkins was sandy-haired, pale, and stately,
one who would never be caught sharing the frivolities of tea
at Lyons Corner House. And I felt certain that Miss Hawkins's
cat would never approve of such light conduct in his mistress,
for he was the most substantial and solemn Tabby I had ever
seen—perched like a sultan on a cushion, next to her chair
in her warm basement kitchen. Miss Stevens's moments of
sprightliness never failed to distress Miss Hawkins. One day
she let fall a shred of gossip concerning Mrs. Simpson and
"Davy." Miss Hawkins was upset, and paler than usual; she
confided to me that Maud Stevens was an old and treasured
friend—but think of her mentioning that woman's name! It's
disrespectful to the Royal Family. There were times she was
sure Maud had a strain of *French* blood in her, possibly from
her mother's side.

A little less than five years later, on the day Neville Cham-
berlain's lugubrious voice sounded a declaration of war over
Miss Hawkins's wireless, and I had returned for a brief summer holiday to London, she turned to me: "O how I wish I
had that Mr. Hitler here! *I'd* give him a piece of my mind."

Peaceful as Primrose Hill looked in the summer of 1934, it
had vague war-like associations in my mind. I recalled the name
from my reading of H. G. Wells's *War of the Worlds*, which
I had discovered in one of my childhood's attics: Primrose
Hill had then been a landing point for an invasion of London
from the air. Miss Hawkins informed me that during the

Kaiser's War, Zeppelin raiders dropped bombs there. Now, in 1934, the tall grasses on the hill afforded shelter to young soldiers and their girls, indulging in unmilitary pastimes.

The little pub around the corner was positively dreary, and I failed to teach myself the joys of drinking porter. Moreover, Marya and I had books to write, and with that in view, I resumed my reading of Emerson's *Journals* in the reading room of The British Museum. The well-like room, with its deepening circles of quiet, gave me the illusion of Time hanging, suspended, in the air; was it a faceless clock? It was invisible. In this hiatus, the perspective I sought came within my range of vision. As though guided by a Muse or daemon I wrote of Emerson, his presence rising from the aged and yellowed pages of the *Journals* on my desk:

And I have seen the world, heard the lark climbing
His golden sinuous music in dark air,
That speech unknown but to the subtlest ear
Echo through morning over St. Paul's dome,
Wing following through April's hemisphere,
Not less familiar now than earth at home:
England, the Colosseum of great minds.

Under deep trees, the bright-eyed mariner,
Coleridge, speaking and the music gone:
Miraculous white hair, the oracle
Voice descending, flowing on,

Knowing, perhaps, that I would understand . . .

This was Emerson speaking of his visit to Coleridge a hundred years ago.

The reading room, with its gift of quiet, inspired me to set books aside so as to further my own writing: the hours I spent there, freed from "noises of the world" that had seemed to pursue me in New York, restored my confidence. My desk became my writing table.

After spending a few hours in the Museum, I sought out another kind of haven in Charing Cross Road, the pacing-ground of second-hand bookshops, where I searched (and not without success) for early editions of Henry James's short stories and novellas. Marya and I decided that whatever touring we would do of London, James's fiction would be our Baedeker—by that means, we would avoid the tourists' routes. This we tempered by hints from Aldous Huxley's edition of D. H. Lawrence's *Letters*. In our way, we were aiming toward creating a London of our own. But Charing Cross Road yielded other discoveries. Among them was a pocket edition of Campion's *A Book of Airs*, as easy for me to carry about as an inexpensive Ben Jonson's *Underwoods* and a very compact edition of Landor's *Love Lyrics*—which had been earlier companions of my walks at home.

In Piccadilly we chose D. H. Lawrence's much praised Abendrodts for tea. We liked the shining spotlessness of the place, its mirrored walls, dazzling silverware, and white tablecloths—and its tea and scones at comfortably low prices. We thought it evidence of Lawrence's taste for scrubbed and clean surroundings and scrupulous thrift.

What we did not know then, but learned on our return to London in 1939, was that Abendrodts had been a front for Hitler's spies—which was why the place was such a model of Germanic cleanliness, and why the smoked salmon and white bread were both so excellent and cheap. In 1939 it had been replaced by a carelessly tended, "American-style" restaurant. Only once did we venture into it. It was on a Sunday. I had just bought and finished glancing through *News of the World*, because I had seen "H. G. Wells" over a front-page article predicting a second world war. A woman, seated at a table next to mine, seemed to show an interest in the paper. I handed it over to her. With a single glance at Wells's prediction, she began to weep. As I left the restaurant—and not without a feeling of guilt for spreading evil news—I saw the woman's shoulders still shaking with the effort to control her tears. Or did her weeping rise from another source? Was she a warning of coming disaster? In a fashion I could not explain, the woman, through her raining tears, had taken on the mask of an ancient sibyl.

Superficially, the London I saw during the summer of 1934 was not only more self-assured than it was five years later, but to Americans (most of whom now regard it as a weekend stopover by jet plane) it was a stolid city, still at rest in its long twilight of Edwardian grandeur; although The Great War had wiped out a generation of young men, and the reign of a middle-aged George V seemed to gather shadows, the World Depression seemed to be receding from British shores. One could still imagine that lines of contact with the past had remained unbroken. It was a moment when Americanisms in speech—usually fragments of outmoded slang— sounded "chic" and Hollywood gangster films were popular.

T. S. Eliot invited Marya and me to lunch; we met in his office at Faber and Faber in tree-shaded Russell Square. There, with a wave of his hand, he introduced us to Herbert Read. Read, though gray-haired, looked youthful and quick, and his boyish grin, though permanent, and perhaps professional, was ingratiating, apparently ready for anything that proved itself amusing. For the moment, he seemed entirely at Eliot's service, and was swept along with us on a brisk walk to Soho.

Eliot, too, seemed younger than when I had first met him in New York—more sensitive, more volatile, more alert. We stepped into a French restaurant, where we were swiftly seated, and I saw a wine list placed in Eliot's hands. For several seconds, he considered it gravely, consulted the waiter —then his face cleared, the trial and ritual over. With less caution, he gave orders for lunch to the scarcely visible waiter at his side.

The wine performed its miracles. Almost at once, the table, chairs, and floor were slightly elevated. Wherever I turned my head, things took on a rosy hue; everything looked preternaturally clear and bright. Eliot was saying how vehemently he detested the charms of *Elia*, the essays of Charles Lamb—he abhorred their everlasting *whimsy*. Whimsy was the curse of Lamb. (Years later, when I saw *The Cocktail Party* in New York, I realized that the side of Eliot that was uppermost in that Soho restaurant resembled Sir Henry Harcourt-Reilly, the victorious, lighthearted psychiatrist of the play.) He later asserted that the most heinous crime a writer could commit was dullness—all the other vices resulted in lesser offenses— and this prompted me to bring up the verses of T. Sturge Moore—which set Eliot off into an imitation of Moore and Robert Bridges, the two of them seated in a restaurant, tapping out each other's metrics on the edge of the table. "Sheep in sheep's clothing," he called them.

Eliot remarked that such pedantry and rules were not for him—that though he could never write a poem without the music of it running through his head, he could never remember the laws of scanning verse—the melodic theme of the poem was the thing!

He seemed moved and pleased when Marya spoke her admiration of "Ash Wednesday," for at that moment the poem had yet to receive the praise that it deserved. And then as if in fear of hubris, he reassumed the manner of a cheerful host, catching us off guard with talk of baseball, quoting batting averages and standing of the clubs, with particular reference to the St. Louis team. Read looked blank. The luncheon hour floated on toward four o'clock, and walking out of the restaurant, we emerged into a rare display of London's golden light.

Following that afternoon in Soho, I had many subsequent meetings with Eliot, but none is more vivid, more characteristic of his social charm than that occasion. I was to learn later, when I read Leonard Woolf's autobiographies, how appropriate the Bloomsbury setting was to Eliot's temperament. How sharply his Americanisms were set off against that background; how clearly his Tory politics were outlined against the Cambridge Leftism of the Bloomsbury literary circles; how "radical" in this environment his championship of Joyce and Ezra Pound must have seemed. His devotion to the Anglican Church was still another marked difference from the tradition of dissent inherited by the Cambridge-bred inhabitants of Bloomsbury! The advantage he secured from the associations of Russell Square was that of "difference"—and it was a difference that did not permit Bloomsbury to patronize him.

My associations of Bloomsbury during that summer had taken their color from the dusty, reddish-brown porticos of The British Museum. In memory, the scene has an unreal atmosphere surrounding it, as though its foundations had been reared out of Egyptian antiquity. The huge stone-sculptured head from Easter Island near the front door, probably, and with a dream's illogic, contributes to this impression. Surely remnants of the past seemed to perpetuate themselves in the shabby, unshaven familiars of the Museum who haunted the stone benches at the entrance, puffing earnestly on cigarettes. The figures appeared and vanished with furtive swiftness, and a second later, others of their kind took their places.

Because of the shade trees and aged squares, it was easy enough to repeople Bloomsbury with its well-to-do Victorian past, its polished door-pulls, its air of respectability. During that summer, odds and ends of legend, if not ghosts, still clung to the corners and buildings of the Museum's neighborhood—where Harold Munro's Poetry Bookshop once flourished, and

"Occult" bookshops still offered their dubious wares. Not far away were the second-floor rooms in Woburn Walk where Yeats once lodged—sat with lighted candle and a crystal ball, exploring the cults of Hermes Trismegistus. And it was from these same rooms, so it was said, that Yeats, in a moral rage, had kicked Alastair Crowley, "The Great Beast," down two flights of stairs. And was it in these surroundings that Eliot acquired his interest in Tarot cards and palmistry? Bloomsbury balanced, as it was, between its good and evil, was Manichaean. I detected a faint odor of brimstone in the air.

One day that summer we received an invitation to join Bryher and H. D. at a performance of *Escape Me Never!* Though we had met H. D. before that evening, I remember her most clearly, standing in the lobby of a Shaftesbury Avenue theater, waving me a greeting, with a cigarette in her hand. She was, so I thought, an American Aphrodite, taller and less sensuous than her Greek ancestress, but with the same powers to attract and charm: she moved with an ease and brilliance that outshone all those who surrounded our small company of four. In contrast to her, how middle-class, how drab other people in the lobby looked—how cumbersome and ill at ease they seemed in evening dress: how hopelessly *English*. H. D.'s talk was like her verse, angular and swift, with small rushes of words. Her accent, like Ezra Pound's, was British-American-on-the-Riviera. She spoke of poetry, the stage, and how Elizabeth Bergner's performance in the play had recreated the illusion of youth.

There was rather more than a touch of the transcendental Moravian Puritan in H. D. that lifted conversation off its feet, swaying in short flights, with a bright laugh, or a suspended sentence, wavering in air. Yet those who, even today, associate her solely with Pound's Imagist verse, are wrong. When I met her in 1934, she had been reading William Morris with her characteristic enthusiasm—and she was about to reread the devotional poets of the seventeenth century. She had probably reawakened her interest in the Pre-Raphaelites, and therefore, in William Morris, through her friendship with Violet Hunt. She insisted that we visit Violet Hunt, for she was among the most extraordinary of H. D.'s London friends. "I'll get in touch with her," she said, "so she can invite you over to her house for a drink at tea-time soon."

This proposal started off an elaborate series of three-way communications between H. D., Miss Hunt, and me. These were by phone and letter, Hilda calling up Violet, Miss Hunt writing me a cryptic note, then phoning me the next morning to apologize for her vagueness—would I ignore the note—she was writing another. Then the round would begin again. By the time there could be full agreement on a certain time, on a certain afternoon, we were in no mood to visit Miss Hunt—only H. D.'s pleas for us to keep the date sent us off one afternoon to Miss Hunt's house, South Lodge, Campden Hill Road.

I had known of Miss Hunt only through her biography, *The Wife of Rossetti*, the curious story of Elizabeth Siddal and her suicide, retold as if by a bright child who had overheard family gossip at hours when everyone thought she was safely tucked away in bed. Violet was the daughter, not of Holman Hunt, but another Hunt of the Pre-Raphaelite circle, William Henry Hunt, a sensitive water-colorist, a painter of flowers, who had been praised by Ruskin and Turner. It was generally known that she had assisted Ford Madox Ford in the editing of *The English Review*, that in her youth, she had enjoyed the fame of being a feminist, and was the author of several "problem" novels.

Half-dreading the ordeal, we set out for South Lodge on a summer's day. Campden Hill Road was chalky with dust, and the small garden plot in front of South Lodge looked withered and spent. Violet Hunt herself opened the door. At a glance, it was impossible to guess her age; here was the apparition of a slender, once beautiful woman—gray, wraith-like, light in movement. The dress she was wearing had been bought in Paris on a holiday; she was undergoing "rejuvenation" treatments, and her doctor had given her an injection earlier in the afternoon, which was why she couldn't sit down. She aimed a broad smile in our direction, then led us to a small sofa facing a portrait of herself as a girl; there we were seated, while she drew herself to one side, so that we could admire the portrait as she went on talking.

Her monologue flowed on and on, and as it entered full stream, she picked up two tall glasses, and filled them, three-quarters high, with soda from a syphon. "You do take soda-water, don't you?—oh, my God! I've forgotten the whiskey! D'ye mind if I pour it in now?" Which she did without prompting, leaning over us. Her smile was angelic, her manner protective. "Unlike most English," she went on, "I like Americans. My mother was partly Irish, and when I was young, I wanted to marry Oscar Wilde. He was handsome; so was I. Even if he was homosexual, I could have taken care of him. But my mother wouldn't let me—she was so Victorian! He was really enchanting! And the woman he married was a fool. She was *stupid*." Then, after a momentary pause: "How would you like to buy some William Morris wallpaper? I have rolls and rolls of it up in the attic. I can't use it all. You might as well buy it. It's very pretty, and I can let you have it cheap. William Morris designed all the furniture in this room. The ground floor is my William Morris floor, and the floor upstairs was partly redone by Wyndham Lewis. Let me take you there."

She led us up a short flight of stairs into the study. Dust had settled everywhere; two chairs were heaped with old magazines; the small desk was covered with loose papers. And surely enough, on one wall was the fading remains of a futuristic Wyndham Lewis mural. As one looked at it, the painting seemed to recede further into the plaster. Miss Hunt's attention was drawn to something on the desk, and when she turned to us again, a letter was in her hand, and her face had lost the pleasure that lit her features when she had spoken of Wyndham Lewis a few seconds ago. "I want to read you a letter I received from Henry James the other day. It hurt me, and I feel very sad about it." She took it out of its envelope and read it to us. James was saying that, though he had sent her an invitation to his house party at Rye, he had thought the matter over, and decided that she had better *not* come. She had been living with Ford without being married to him. She would have to accept the consequences of her social transgressions; she would have to pay the price. This was regrettable; but she would have to suffer the loss of his company and protection.

"The last time Henry called, he left his umbrella," she said, and this thought suddenly cheered her up again. "I must show it to you, before he comes back to claim it." She hurried us downstairs again into the small side parlor. And then, seemingly forgetful of the object of her quest, offered us instead: "Do you want me to tell you about the Ruskin divorce case? I know all the details!" We probably looked more dazed than encouraging, for she changed the subject: "It wasn't Ford who discovered D. H. Lawrence, it was I. I read his manuscripts, and saw to it that Ford published some of the poems. It was I who encouraged Lawrence."

At this she seemed to radiate joy, and proclaimed: "You *must* stay for dinner. You mustn't go now, for one of my last admirers will soon be here. He's a Canadian, you know, and frightfully dull, but he's loyal to me and very kind. His name is Shelley!" We must have looked as though we did not believe her. Then she laughed, "No, no, he's not *that* Shelley; he was one of the boys in the Oscar Wilde case!" (Later I found that in this she had been truthful enough.) But by this time we had edged near the door. She rushed before us, down the steps, and into her front garden. From a basket in one corner of it, she produced garden gloves and shears, slipped on the gloves, and cut a sun-scorched rose from a yellowed bush—"Carlyle planted these," she almost shouted, and thrust it at us. As we closed the gate of South Lodge behind us, we felt a bit alarmed. We were, of course, unused to Edwardian gestures, its showmanship, its bursts of candor. In respect to being in high Edwardian style—their only point in common— Miss Hunt was not unlike Rosa Lewis. She had once been beautiful; she was now tremendously vulnerable; Rosa Lewis could take care of herself—Violet Hunt, one felt, could not. As we reentered Campden Hill Road, I saw a portly, top-hatted elderly gentleman approaching South Lodge. He was certainly Edwardian in dress. Was he the Shelley Miss Hunt had in mind?

Friends, such as H. D. and Dorothy Richardson, still traveled to South Lodge, which, when Miss Hunt's mother was alive, had been the shelter of a literary salon. Now the few visits were in kindness to Violet, who seemed lonelier each season. In her autobiographical book, which I glanced through in a Charing Cross second-hand shop, her glittering moments were called *I Have This to Say: The Story of My Flurried Years*. Her descriptive candor remained unimpaired and was as insubstantial as a mayfly's wing. Her touches of madness, her loss of chronology had more color in them than could be found in her later writings. If she was haunted by ghosts of long past "literary evenings" at South Lodge, and if she "dropped" too many names, there was also something poignant in her yearnings for an immortality by way of associations. She was not a Philistine, and had inherited an artist's temperament.

My little book on D. H. Lawrence had recently appeared in London, and brought me two separate invitations to visit

Keats Grove in a far edge of Hampstead Heath. One was from a young writer who edited a new poetry magazine; the other was from Donald and Catherine Carswell. They were for the same day—tea and dinner—and the two houses were almost directly facing one another.

The beginning of our visit had a hint of transcendental experience in it, very like the sight of a vision while writing a poem. Our tea date was for four o'clock, and we alighted from a bus at four, about a quarter-mile from our destination. We had never been there before, yet, everything looked familiar— "I stood tip-toe up on a little hill," went through my head. I felt I knew exactly where we were going, and without hesitation turned the right corners, passed the right trees, and stopped precisely in front of the young editor's gate. Had I been unnaturally keyed up at the prospect of going to Keats Grove? I felt cool enough. Was I deceiving myself? I do not think so. Everything seemed so casually right, familiar, and actual. (Afterwards, when I had returned to America, I discovered in my library Edmund Blunden's biography of Leigh Hunt. In it I found an engraving, somewhat blurred, of the environs of Keats's house in Hampstead. Was this a clue to my experience?) Yet I believe today that the possible memory of a badly reproduced, dimmed version of an old engraving cannot explain away the sharpness of the vision I experienced that afternoon. The engraving was of a bird's-eye view of the place; what I saw had been a close-up, and each step I took had seemed inevitable.

The young editor was a heavy-shouldered, muscular, brisk, engaging host. As we entered his small house, he told us that he knew Americans liked coffee better than tea. And coffee he gave us—very strong, very black, and very bitter. I became aware that things that seemed American were fashionable among those who had just come down from Oxford and Cambridge. With quickening levity Auden had scattered a few Americanisms among the lyrical turns of his new poems, and our host confessed he now kept a notebook in which he wrote all the Americanisms he could find. He had been much impressed by James Cagney in the film, *Public Enemy*, particularly at the moment he smashed the freshly cut half of a grapefruit into his girlfriend's face at the breakfast table. He longed to visit Chicago, to see the gangsters, to see how they "operated," how they "ran the works" with their "Tommy guns." I was given to understand that they had real, masculine virility. They got things done. And they had authority.

I began to wonder if, and this by some mysterious process of "free association," Wyndham Lewis's little magazine, *The Enemy*, had become entangled with Cagney's *Public Enemy* in my host's mind—for he was a disciple of Lewis. And it was true enough, that both the magazine and the hero of the film were poised against the mores of middle-class society. By this time, other guests began to fill the room. Most of them were young men, newly arrived in London from Oxford and Cambridge, and, so it seemed to me, recent converts to authoritative thinking and Communism. Their clothes had a Bond Street air. They looked extraordinarily well-off, and athletic. I happened to mention to one of them that at dinner, across the way, I would probably meet Hugh MacDiarmid that very evening— did he know him? "O no," said he, without a trace of irony, "MacDiarmid is *not* a gentleman!" Evidently there was a bottomless schism between Oxford Communists and the Scots. When I mentioned the Carswells and the Edwin Muirs who were living near, eyebrows went up and lips closed. And the subject changed as to whether or not American multi-millionaires were "robber barons."

Yet my host did me a service I did not forget: he was characteristically dogmatic in explaining the excellence of Henry Moore. He was so forceful, so convincing in advancing the merits of Moore's early sculpture that I made a point of seeing it for myself, and was completely won over by the presence of Greco-Celtic imagination in Moore's art.

With Moore's name echoing in my ears, we crossed the path dividing Keats Grove from our host's tidy little house to the Carswells' cottage door, a few steps closer to the broad and rolling grasses of Hampstead Heath, and beyond them, the lanes and paths winding into shadows of deep green foliage. The cottage we were about to enter looked as though it had once possessed a thatched roof, and even as we approached, it seemed to exhale an air of smiling, shabby gentility. Mrs. Carswell, who opened the door to us, was cheerfulness itself; she had the figure of a young girl, and as she moved, her fox-colored hair seemed to flash fire. The large room around us looked as though its furnishings had not been changed since 1890—each piece was well-worn and polished by frequent use; the chairs looked lived in, and secure. Mrs. Carswell's early writings had been watched over and praised by D. H. Lawrence, and after his death, she reaffirmed her loyalty to him by writing *The Savage Pilgrimage*, a sharp, bright memoir of Lawrence as she knew him, a book that was all the better because she was far too quick-witted and intelligent to indulge herself in hero worship. She informed us that Hugh MacDiarmid would soon be dropping in, and she described him as a Scottish D. H. Lawrence, a bit wild, and looking somewhat like the photographs of the youthful Ezra Pound.

Before MacDiarmid arrived, Donald Carswell stepped into the room. His manner was that of the Edinburgh historian he actually was, his wit half-concealed by an air of gravity; this role complemented his wife's—which was that of the un-affected, absentminded hostess, who, though about to serve a meal at her own hearth, retained the privileges of a guest. Then MacDiarmid came in, looking very much as his hostess described him, hand in hand with a disheveled but very pretty Scots girl, in a thin, crumpled dress. When he sat down, she settled herself into his lap, put a slender, possessive arm around his neck, and listened intently to everything he said. That evening, MacDiarmid was in a high-spirited, Scottish Nationalist mood, and was all for Ezra Pound and Major Douglas's schemes for social credit; for that evening at least, Marx and Lenin were out of sight and out of mind. This may have been in deference to the Carswells, who, like Lawrence, were distrustful of Communist promises and claims. In contrast to the irrationality of Communist converts to a cause, the Carswells maintained an air of Scottish independence and sanity. Though far more "bourgeois" in their manners than MacDiarmid, the Carswells were neither prigs nor hypocrites.

It was soon revealed that the evening meal was to be less a dinner than a combination of "high-tea" and supper, elaborated and delayed by renewed pouring out of drinks and talk. After an hour or so, John Patrick Carswell, a student at Merchant Taylors' School, walked in and assisted at clearing the living room table to prepare resetting it for supper. As the fresh white cloth was spread across the top, an inspiration seized father and son. The white cloth was too much of a temptation: what a field for the Battle of Bannockburn! A salt-shaker stood up for Stirling Castle; spoons, knives, and forks, opposing one another, were lines of men. A small cream pitcher was the Bruce, and the heavier table silver were the English knights who fell into the pits and traps that Bruce had dug for them. I never saw a battle played so gallantly. The mock gravity of Donald Carswell had worked a spell: the Battle of Bannockburn went on with cheers from MacDiarmid. Another hour passed—it was appropriate to wait until a joint of lamb had been roasted to a turn.

When we rose from the table it was past midnight. MacDiarmid's barelegged girl, curled up on the living room sofa, had fallen asleep. In that neighborhood, the taxi-stands would be deserted, and the buses and underground had stopped running for the night. There was nothing else to do but to walk back to King Henry's Road with Donald Carswell and John Patrick as our guides. I remember a luminous full moon riding high in the sky above trees and houses, and it seemed we were following it as fast as my stick, a shilling ashplant, would allow.

The book on Lawrence was also responsible for my meeting Barbara Low, the psychiatrist, sister of the Soviet foreign minister Litvinoff's wife, Ivy Low, who was also one of Lawrence's friends. Miss Low was extremely fond of the Litvinoff children; she herself was an ardent "Janite"; therefore, so she told us, she was delighted by their interest in Jane Austen as "the most class-conscious of British novelists," which was why she was sending them, by special post to Moscow, Jane Austen's complete works in a fine edition. Today, I wonder if the Litvinoff children, now grown up—and known for their protests against the blind forces of Soviet literary dictatorship—inherited their courage and independence from a British source, Miss Low as well as the writings of Miss Austen?

In addition to Henry James's stories, Ede's memoir of Gaudier-Brzeska had become our guidebook of things to see in London, and at Charing Cross, it was Gaudier-Brzeska's eye that directed us to the statue of Charles I, mounted on his handsome little horse. Because Katherine Mansfield had been totally unaware of its existence, Gaudier pitched into a violent quarrel with her, accusing her of being insensitive to aesthetic values, and, in doing so, I believed him to be right. From where I sat on the top of a double-decked bus, the statue took on the character of a delicately cut cameo, a precious object in a case, rather than that of a public monument.

Even today, I remember Charles I of Charing Cross as having a transcendent quality, something that could be described as fitting to "an art without epoch." To my taste, it is in the select company of an anonymous Spartan Warrior, Rodin's Balzac, Epstein's monument to Oscar Wilde, Henry

Moore's Celtic Mask in silver, and Brancusi's torso of a young girl. All these seem guarded by an invisible presence standing near them. Is this the presence that the ancients called Apollo, and we are likely to call "an immortality"? I suspect it is. The examples I have chosen are among the carriers of whatever we think of when we speak of "Western Culture"; they are, quite literally, related to the "touchstones" we have in mind when we seek a definition for beauty in sculptural art.

Through Bryher and H. D., Marya and I were invited to have tea with Dorothy Richardson and her husband, Alan Odle, at their rooms in Queens Terrace, St. John's Wood. Queens Terrace was in a dreary neighborhood, almost a slum; the dry summer had burnt its grasses and had left the smell of yellow dust hanging in air. I had heard that St. John's Wood once had an art school at its center, but by 1934, the art school had become a memory of things past; many of its students had marched off to war against the Kaiser, and had not returned. At Queens Terrace, it looked as though the young and able-bodied had left that part of the world forever. The Terrace buildings seemed ready to fall to ashes: one might well imagine that winter winds rushed through them, and that summer suns had baked their rafters black. Certainly, they were precarious living quarters.

Feeble as the tenements looked, they did not seem very old. They resembled smirched and sallow Victorian teenagers, afflicted with rickets. They were probably built near the end of Victoria's reign, the evil work of contractors bent on making money in a hurry. This was the kind of housing for the "underprivileged" that gave substance to William Morris's brand of Socialism and had been cited as evidence in Bernard Shaw's prophecies of the British Empire's decline and fall.

After crossing an area of yellowed grass and leaves, I sounded the knocker on the half-opened door at 32—it had probably been left ajar to welcome us. At the knock Odle, on enormously long legs, leaped downstairs. The color of his skin was chalk-white; his long nose and jaw cast green shadows against his thin cheek and neck. As he stood before us, with a long and bony forefinger raised in greeting, he reminded me of an early Renaissance Angel of the Annunciation.

With exaggerated deference, he introduced himself, and said that Miss Richardson was lying down, but would be up in a few moments to join us at tea. He would serve the tea things in the living room upstairs. The room was divided by a wide-paneled screen, whose half-circle enclosed us at the table, and around one edge of it came Odle, moving sinuously, with a well-filled tray. A short time later Dorothy Richardson herself quietly emerged from behind the screen. Beside her husband, she seemed short and stout. Behind glittering, rimless eyeglasses, her hazel eyes shed good will and benevolence.

There was one feature of her appearance that struck us as odd. Her great mass of Anglo-Saxon golden hair had been gathered into a coarse, fish-net-woven, green snood, held fast by a green ribbon, tied in a bow beneath her chin. No doubt, the snood saved time in dressing her hair, but the bow beneath her chin gave her the look of wearing an invisible Victorian bonnet. (Though we saw her several times that summer, she was never without it.) It was obviously efficient in keeping her hair close to her head: her wearing it and her lack of concern for stylish dress made her seem curiously masculine.

Though kindly in her speech—and one had the impression she seldom felt the need of raising her voice—her conversation had a Johnsonian ring, and I suspected that she set herself out to shock us by saying that her favorite books were *Little Lord Fauntleroy* and *The Girl of the Limberlost*. She believed that both revealed interesting and little known aspects of the American psyche. For instance, little Lord Fauntleroy's passionate attachment for all things English was so very American! I refused to rise to her bait, and Odle intervened by remarking that he loved crime and had been wholly fascinated by *Sanctuary*.

Odle's observation was in very nearly perfect counterpoint to his wife's commentary: it was in the balance of Faulkner against Frances Hodgson Burnett; Odle entranced by American sadism, lawlessness, and savagery, and Miss Richardson intrigued by whatever she had seen of American innocence and childishness.

She then spoke of her meeting Hemingway in Paris, and of her being charmed by *In Our Time*, while he, in turn, had expressed his admiration for the early books of her *Pilgrimage*. This, I thought to myself, was a natural liking and affinity, for both had made an art of writing refreshed conversational prose —prose at an opposite pole from the writings of Virginia Woolf and Lytton Strachey. She had noted that in Paris Hemingway spent far less time than his compatriots did in the cafés of Montparnasse; he was too busy at his typewriter. She thought his adolescent emotions peculiarly American, which she had also discovered in the novels of Sinclair Lewis. Although she stopped short of saying so, it was clear enough that she thought of them as agile, gifted children.

Before we left Queens Terrace, Odle invited us to join them for drinks on an evening next week in a Baker Street night club.

Alan Odle had earned a precarious living as an artist, contributing caricature sketches of London's bohemia to *Vanity Fair*. His pen and ink drawings were reminiscent of the flowering, billowing style of Beardsley's illustrations, and before he married Miss Richardson, he had worn velvet jackets, and had kept late hours talking and drinking at the Café Royale, on Regent Street. Like Miss Richardson, he had made an "escape" from a suburban middle-class family. Yet he lacked her strength and self-discipline in coming to grips with daily living. He was far too much of a "gentleman" to be bohemian, and too much of a free spirit to tolerate suburban respectability. His vaguely salacious drawings were not naughty enough to draw the attention of censorship, and not good enough in their own right to redeem their naughtiness. I believe Miss Richardson's care and protection of Odle showed a maternal, and, perhaps, Puritanical bent, for she hoped, I think, to reform his more careless habits, and to modify his childish tendencies toward Satanism. The poverty in which they lived represented her ideas of thriftiness, for she put her money in savings banks to provide funds for Alan after her death.

The following week, at nine o'clock, we were in the street made famous by Sherlock Holmes. I had the impression of passing many storefronts. The street seemed as empty and as edged with fear as an urban scene in one of Chirico's early paintings. We found the number given to me by Odle. I pressed a button and a door swung open revealing a flight of carpeted stairs. Up we walked to enter a barn-like room, furnished with deep-pile carpet, small, round tables, and black, leather-covered club chairs, easy to sink into, and a difficult seat from which to rise again. Miss Richardson and Odle were waiting for us, an open pack of Gold Flakes on the table between them, a pitcher of water and two small glasses of whiskey within reach.

Seated here, Dorothy Richardson seemed more in her element, and primed for conversation, than at Queens Terrace. Here, she was mistress of a larger scene by virtue of a flow of talk. Here she seemed to resume the monologue of her many-volumed *Pilgrimage*, which told of her hard-won independence, of Beethoven and Bach, of the trials of translating Proust, of mischievous turns in the character of Gide, of the merits of Goethe, particularly in his novels: names floated up and down the firmament of her talk as if they were angels on Jacob's Ladder, bearing flaming or extinguished torches. It was talk the like of which was seldom heard anywhere, least of all in New York of the 1930s. (I was to read later in her letters that H. G. Wells, Havelock Ellis, and May Sinclair, all remarkable talkers themselves, had left their impress on the ranges of her conversational style.) She was poor and part of her earnings came from her translations, commissioned by publishers, of German and French fiction. Her only "sin against the light" was her belief that her translations (which were at best no more than glorified hack-work), were not a waste of energies that should have been given to *Pilgrimage*. Her temperament seemed very Anglo-Saxon: her convictions leaned neither to Mosley right nor to Communist left, but to deeply-rooted Toryism, colored pink by a tincture of anarchist feeling. Dorothy Richardson and Dame Edith Sitwell (whom I met some twelve years later) were, I thought, among the last of English eccentrics. In their boldness, in their lack of concern for public opinion, both were effective. They had behind them—though neither participated in it—England's violent suffragist movement, which, in moments of self-doubt, probably strengthened their ability to speak with authority and decision.

Something very like a sense of duty impelled me to turn my mind away from London to Dublin, to reinforce an earlier desire to visit the city that haunted my Irish grandfather's imagination. (In actuality, Dublin also haunted my father's dreams. He had once told me of a curious experience he had had after major surgery. He was then lying on his bed, hands folded across his chest. A voice told him he could now go wherever he wished. If he would raise his arms and clap his hands behind his head, as Peter Ibbetson did, his wish would come true. He obeyed the voice, and found himself walking through the gates of Trinity College. He saw the statue of Queen Victoria. He felt divinely happy and self-assured; he was carrying books under his arm. Throughout his days in bed whenever he felt unwell, he would return to Dublin.) It no longer mattered that my grandfather had supremely failed in almost everything he turned a hand to. Within family legend, his attractions had become irresistible. In a strange way, the very façades of Trinity College had become touchstones that I must test and know to keep myself alive.

With an introduction from Bryher I had already been in correspondence with a young woman novelist who agreed to sublet her rooms in Dublin to me, and while we (my wife, small daughter, and I—my son to be left in London with Miss Stevens) stayed in Dublin, she would be our casual, unofficial guide. So far, our arrangements were firm. Yet, when we went to the American Express in London to book our passage, the young clerk at the counter all but refused to sell us tickets. "You don't want to go to Ireland," he stated flatly. (A few days before, when I had talked to Eliot about the trip, he had said the same thing.) I took these warnings—which were unexplained by both Eliot and the clerk—as signs of embittered British prejudice against the Irish. I insisted on booking passage.

The clerk's behavior reminded me of what had happened the week before in King Henry's Road. H. D. had given my small son Patrick his favorite toys, a gentle-looking tawny-haired stuffed lion, and an appealing, sad-featured leopard of the same make, which he promptly named "King George." He carried the animals with him everywhere. He slept with them. One afternoon he ventured into a mews behind our house and came back, ten minutes later, looking fearfully upset, cradling King George tenderly in his arms, but the lion gone. We gathered it had been snatched from him by a little girl. "It's the Irish," said Miss Stevens, "they live in that filthy mews!" Surely enough, I remembered seeing a very dirty red-haired child, in a garish pink, short-skirted frock, running up and down the street. If anything went wrong, that child was clearly marked as guilty: her green eyes, impertinent grin, and dirty bare feet were sufficient evidence. Her denial of stealing the lion was proof that she was as unregenerate as ever. Stealing was natural to her, thought Miss Stevens. And if I planned to go to Ireland, warned Miss Hawkins, I was not to hang my coat over the back of a chair: it would vanish like that!

Curious portents against our going to Ireland continued to fall from the air as plans progressed. In Liverpool, while rushing to board a bus that was to take us to our boat, I somehow lost sight of our small daughter. She had been absorbed by the crowds milling around the various bus locations, and it was only by a running, gasping chance that I caught sight of her mounting the steps of the wrong vehicle; I threw my arms around her waist, and lifted her into the Dublin bus. Soon we found ourselves being herded onto the deck of what seemed to be an unseaworthy ferryboat, to discover that the American Express clerk had neglected to book a cabin for us. There were no deck chairs: I seated myself on a capstan, my wife on our suitcase, and alternately, we sat Joanna on our laps. Against channel breezes we covered ourselves with a present from Bryher, a rose and green steamer rug, very handsome and warm. With the rug pulled up to our shoulders, we half-deceived ourselves that the all-night voyage would be comfortable. Nothing could have been further from the truth.

The decks were jammed with Liverpool Irish on a weekend holiday. In spite of their modest behavior, the girls and women on board wore, it was all too plain, only two articles of clothing, a skirt and a shawl. The men wore jackets, boots, trousers; seldom a shirt. All seemed drunk, or nearly so; men and women sank to the deck and stretched themselves out side by side, gathering their rags and paper parcels around them as best they could. They were as near to nakedness as the ancient poor of Whitechapel in London's East End; certainly as noisome and unwashed. If they seemed less hopeless, it was because drink and the solace of a Woodbine blurred the edges of despair. Their bodies were not quite spent, and some of the girls, like those in nineteenth-century engravings of peasants, had clean features, white skins, and saintly smiles; their innocence seemed impregnable.

The moment the boat steered clear of the docks, it began to list from side to side—a slow, slithering motion. This was by no means restful, for we were in continual danger of losing our anchorage around the capstan, and of the suitcase sliding first toward the center of the deck, and on the next list, rolling off the deck into the sea; my wife's perch had become so precarious that I transferred her to the capstan. We dismissed all hope of sleep.

At four or five minute intervals throughout the night, keeping time with the listing of the boat, a great bear of a man, lying on his back, chanted "More beer, beer is best," dreamily echoing the slogan of a brewery poster. I remember my relief at seeing the first lavender tints of dawn and jade-green waves around the boat. This was certainly another island from the one we left behind us; eager to go ashore, I soon learned that we were at the beginning of a very long wait. On the march through the customs house, each passenger from the boat was being thoroughly searched for firearms. We stood five hours in line—even my small daughter's bag was searched by fumbling boys, one of whom gravely extracted a doll from it, examined the toy closely, and replaced it with seeming regret.

At last free of customs, I settled my family into a taxi, and after what then seemed a short ride (I had probably dozed in the cab), we came to the house where I had sublet rooms from a young lady novelist. At the door the landlady met us with, "I thought you were shot dead. Did you hear the Tommy guns? Several of my best friends were killed last night." In this way I was informed that "the troubles" which had assumed their violent character in 1916 were not yet over.

[243]

O'Duffy's boys, the Blue Shirts, still roamed the streets; so did members of a disbanded I.R.A.; so did detachments of De Valera's government troops in smartly tailored green uniforms; and when they clashed, there was sporadic Tommy gun fire. To complicate matters, newly active Labor unions were striking against the government. A newspaper strike was in progress: incoming English and American papers were burned at the quays. And since wireless sets, even as late as 1934, were comparatively rare in Ireland, the blackout of news if not complete, was general. In a rumor-ridden country, the strike permitted rumors to proliferate whenever and wherever a cup of tea or a glass of stout was served. Fascists were rumored to have taken over O'Duffy's Blue Shirts, while Communists were said to control the unions. In the newspaper union's bulletin, published once a week, Catholic priests defended Marx and Engels, and Maud Gonne assailed, with bitterest invective, William Butler Yeats, her youthful admirer. To someone stepping into Ireland as I did, the Irish seemed as unstable, as wild, as mad, as they were reputed to be.

After our night on the boat, the modest three rooms we had sublet, looked luxurious. Fully clothed, we slept till tea-time, and when we awoke, it was to the sight of a wonderful violet radiance, the Dublin twilight, pouring through the windows. With the glimmering haze of light shining everywhere, no wonder Ireland seemed visited by the supernatural, that it was known as "Holy Ireland." On such an evening, tall Gaelic crosses seemed to float above low-lying churchyards. From our windows, and as the mist shifted, we had glimpses of hills. We became aware of a druid-dark greenness of foliage and turf, refreshed and cooled by daily showers. This was my first sight of a city invaded by country greennesses and reaches of sky, for even the skies, with blackbirds sailing against the clouds, had become parochial and intimate.

As we were having tea, the young lady novelist dropped

by. She was angular, lithe, and gay; whatever she felt or thought was swiftly hidden behind a sharp smile, glancing eyes, and neatly-dressed, short red hair. I never saw a woman drink whiskey neat with more aplomb and fewer ill effects; as her glass refilled, her cheerfulness became a glittering cage around her. She had made a date for us to meet Oliver St. John Gogarty that evening at nine in a Dublin pub. She had even secured a promise from the landlady to take care of Joanna while we were out.

As the evening advanced, she briskly steered us out of the house, into the street, and onto the swaying upper deck of a tram. I had the sensation of weaving and reeling through half of Dublin's streets, precariously leaning over pedestrians and infrequent motor traffic. At a signal from our guide, we descended from the tram and went up the stairs onto the second floor of a pub where we waited for Gogarty in a small room. Gogarty had become a caricature of Joyce's Mulligan, a little more florid, a little more theatrical than even Buck Mulligan had dared to be.

In a flurry of haste, Dr. Gogarty a half-hour later arrived and rushed us down into the street, where we were instantly encircled by a group of ragged, grim, middle-aged men. "We know you, Gogarty," one said, "empty your pockets!" Which Gogarty, hands moving swiftly, promptly did; copper and silver and ten shilling notes were pressed into the beggar's hand. The men, so he informed us, were striking newsboys, and with the same breathlessness, he invited us to step into his car across the street, saying he would then take us to his house in Ely Place for a drink. As he pushed us into the car, a young man, with a gun in his hand, stepped before us and leveled the pistol at Gogarty's face, with, "We missed you last time, but we're going to get you now!" The doctor, however, was too alert for him; the car had begun to move; the young man leaped backward, while the doctor shouted at me, "One of O'Duffy's

Trinity Blue Shirt boys." At once we were purring along, as if we rode in a sewing machine, at something like thirty miles an hour.

The two incidents were so incredible that they seemed contrived during the doctor's less fortunate moments in telling an anecdote. Did he serve them up for our excitement and his own entertainment? One could almost believe he did. There was the same unreal character, the same incoherence as in his story of how De Valera's men had waked him up one night, had bundled him still in his nightshirt into a car, had said they were taking him for a ride, and then, as the car swerved round the corner near one of the quays, he had leaped out straight into the Liffey—and that was why he had given two swans, in gratitude, to the river. He went on to tell how he swam to the other side, how he then walked to De Valera's house, knocked, and said: "Dev, what do ye mean, setting your thugs on me?" And Dev, cool as always, had replied, "Och, Gogarty, so you're still alive!"

Our own ride with Gogarty took scarcely more than fifteen minutes, and before us stood Ely Place where we swiftly stepped inside. Through tall windows its back gardens glimmered in moonlight, and I had the impression of walking into a Regency drawing room, where the ghost of Tom Moore would have felt at home. The furnishings, slightly frayed and worn through daily use, created the illusion of recently departed splendors: they evoked memories of Adam and Chippendale. Gogarty steered us across the room, and there in a corner, on a sofa, we saw a slender man with a trim mustache, seated next to a woman, so pallid and silent as to be almost invisible. Throughout our stay, neither uttered an intelligible word. They gazed at Gogarty; they gazed at us. They were like apparitions, summoned up by Madame Blavatsky at a seance years ago, and, forgotten, had remained seated where they were. Indicating his two other guests by the merest inclination of his head, Gogarty whispered in my ear, "Be very careful what you say, be very careful. That is Percy Graves I introduced you to; he's one of the leading editorial writers on *The London Times*, and a half brother of Robert Graves—you must be very careful."

Dr. Gogarty, a host before his silent guests, told a number of anecdotes, most of them about Yeats. And his mimicry of his friend performing Hermetic rites fell particularly flat—he was then like a small boy trying to ridicule his elders and his betters.

Sentimentally, Dublin and its slums were called "dear dirty Dublin." Surely enough, broken fan lights over Georgian doors and thresholds as well as ragged, bare-legged women and children could be found, but Dublin, like Edinburgh, Venice, and Florence, which I came to know later, is a city of enchantment. And there is always the river Liffey flowing through it reflecting the fronts of eighteenth-century red brick houses in its stream. In Dublin, time seems to disappear in a confusion of ancient yesterdays against the promises of something that will be done tomorrow. I remember that I had caught the fever of mislaying time; I tended to drift, to walk half-asleep through the National Portrait Gallery out into the street again, only to hear the curses of old beggar women, whom I had not seen, tuning up against me: "Goddam bloody Britisher!"

Our unofficial guide, the young lady novelist, did her best to educate me in the mysteries of Irish behavior and politics; it was not her fault I learned them with great imperfection. It was in Ireland that at length I came to realize how unfit I was to understand political action, Irish or otherwise. One must love the game of politics to know it well; I had no love for it, and was likely to become bewildered at its changes of face and alliances. In reading the weekly strike edition of Dublin's only newspaper, I never understood how priests could write essays on Marx. To me, these actions of the church were as far out of joint as Gogarty's stories of his political adventures.

During the summer of 1934 few were aware of the great fame Yeats's writings were to achieve after his death in 1939. It is one of the ironies of fame that academic critics who had found him "too Romantic" when he was out of favor, converted analyses of his poems into the subject matter of countless papers and dissertations. In universities and colleges something very like a Yeats industry took root which made me think of his own lines on the scholars: "Bald heads forgetful of their sins . . . All think what other people think . . . Lord, what would they say / Did their Catullus walk that way?" His fame outgrew even such distinctions: in sight of Ben Bulben in 1969, a magnificent, if somewhat massive, wreath was laid upon his grave; it was inscribed—and probably because of his version of a few Noh plays—"From the Yeats Society of Japan."

In the strike newspaper I read that Yeats was giving a single performance of his heretical play, *The Resurrection*. We walked to the Abbey Theatre and, to my surprise, had no trouble in booking seats. A few evenings later we strolled into the half-filled house. The audience looked respectable and dull. Lord Longford, known as the fattest peer in Ireland, sat well up front, his pink flesh wrapped in a gray flannel suit; while before the curtain, also dressed in gray, stepped William Butler Yeats. I cannot remember the exact phrasing of his talk; it was to the effect that he welcomed "the happy few," that he hoped the press would stay away, as the newspaper strike was on. No critics would be sent to see the play; no riots would take place; and there would be no need for censorship to be enforced.

Yeats knew, of course, that Irish piety would have no mercy on his play, no matter how exalted it proved itself.

Christ as a living phantom would be difficult for a bigoted, literal-minded Catholic audience to witness, and indeed it would require unusual perception on the part of any theatergoer to assimilate the play's heady mixture of Yeatsian anthropology, skepticism, and spirituality. Too many people, as they take their seats in the theater, have become accustomed to letting their minds go blank, their emotions fall to emptiness.

As exhibited by Yeats, Christ was a life-in-death, death-in-life creation of warring supernatural opposites:

> Odour of blood when Christ was slain
> Made all Platonic tolerance vain,
> And vain all Doric discipline.

The elder Yeats remained a legend in Dublin, and to say his name aloud was like summoning the Devil. The longer I stayed in Ireland, the more I was haunted by the songs of his *Words for Music, Perhaps*, the songs of "Crazy Jane," who stood for Ireland. Yeats's portrait of Crazy Jane was that of a satire-inspired heroine, for his associations and references were those of a self-taught, well-read Dubliner brought up in an Ascendency household. His father, John Butler Yeats (as letters between them show), was no less resourceful, witty, and cultivated.

With *Words for Music, Perhaps* sounding in my ears, we traveled by bus to suburban Wicklow and took up residence in a battered, rambling roadside hotel. The son of the landlady tended bar and did the porter's chores. He had a gift for making himself scarce, and, for most of the day, completely invisible. Under the bar, he had contrived a lair, where he could half-recline in peace, reading a smuggled Paris edition of Joyce's *Ulysses*. Of all Joyce admirers I had met, this boy's devotion seemed deepest and most unwavering. He would come up for air slowly, blind to the anger of his patrons, his face glowing with adoration of "the master." I doubt if he knew the irony implicit in the fact that his worship of Joyce withheld drinks from thirsty customers, a turn of fate that would have amused the author of *Finnegans Wake*.

Of Wicklow I remember signs of deep-grained poverty in the faces of its peasants—with their blank, inward-looking eyes. I remember cottages with roses twined sentimentally around each doorway, with earthen floors, and the stench of human excrement rising from them—did places like these contribute to Dean Swift's scatological fixations? One might well think so. For Swift, when an infant, captured by his wet-nurse, probably entered dwellings as fair to look at and as noisome as these were. I remember a beautiful grass-grown churchyard on a hill overlooking the sea where mariners lay buried, and I had images of sea-captains and their men washed up on the pebbled beach below the churchyard. And why did this funereal setting seem so beautiful? The beauty, I suspect, was in the dark green turf at my feet, in the salt-wind in my hair, and in the shifting sunlight on the jade-green sea below me. The impressions were those of life and rebirth in nature, not those of death.

I had the feeling, there in Wicklow, of opening my eyes after a long sleep. And when we had tea in the ragged garden behind our not-very-clean hotel, even the rooks settling to rest on the cornices of an old church tower took on a semblance of timeless beauty. Within a brief walk from the hotel, an abandoned Georgian house, slowly sinking into the waist-high weeds and grasses around it, had the same marks of survival from another world. Instead of depressing me, these melancholy scenes sent me back to writing again. At last I felt I must begin where my ancestors had left off. However romantic this intuition may have been (for, after all, my United States passport was in my breast pocket), I felt I belonged to the English Pale of a rain-rilled ancient island. I felt I could write, and write I did, in the uncomfortable, dusty little sitting room of the hotel, my table covered with a rough, tasseled wool cloth, whose original Turkey red color had begun to fade many years ago.

In Ireland, I became aware that the two poverties, earthly and spiritual, closely resembled each other. It was the latter that had caused such bitter destruction among the people. It affected both Catholics and Protestants alike, and in addition had a singularly inbred provincialism. Yeats was well aware of this, and that was why, so I believe, he schooled himself to break through local dogmas into another world. This led him into a dubious universe indeed, one that was bounded by the teachings of Madame Blavatsky and Gaelic mythology, and the writings of Homer, the Greek tragic dramatists, Blake, Shelley, Landor, Dante Gabriel Rossetti, Arthur Symons's French Symbolists, and William Morris. And if this scheme of things seems fantastic (which it was!) it liberated him from in-grown Irish pettiness, and was buoyant enough to lift him above small desires and party politics. If, at times, he allowed himself to be skeptical of his own beliefs as well as those of others, the largeness of his design precluded his retreat into cynicism—and that could be taken as a measure of the distance between him and the Gogartys of Irish intellectual life. In his later poems, Yeats thought of his "intellectual passions" as being descended from Swift, Burke, and Berkeley. Obviously he had placed himself on the side of greatness as it moved against the "intellectual hatred" of smaller men.

The people of Dublin and Wicklow I saw were the people of Ireland's long Civil War, and all seemed to speak in the same language that one overheard in Yeats's *Words for Music, Perhaps*. I saw them all around me. In them I heard much of the same discontent, the same slant-eyed distrust of one another, and, when they spoke of public figures, they invented transparent nicknames for living personalities. *Words for Music, Perhaps* had for its background an atmosphere not unfamiliar to all men and women of a distracted twentieth century.

Although I had been too shy to write to poets I admired, in the case of Yeats, I overcame my usual diffidence, and wrote a short letter, not asking to see him, but expressing, as best I could, my pleasure at reading his recent poems. Early in the morning on the day that followed the posting of my letter, I received a phone call from Yeats's wife. She informed me that Yeats had had a vision of my grandfather standing on a stairway in Trinity College, that he must meet me before I left Ireland. I would see him that very afternoon for tea at the Kildare Street Club in Dublin. I must not fail him: her words were given as a command. This tone in her voice may have been her way of putting at ease an all-too-reserved-and-formally-stiff young man who hesitated to impose his presence on a famous poet.

Since we had planned to sail back to London that evening, we left Wicklow precipitously for lunch in Dublin; then Marya decided, with characteristic modesty (here her own diffidence came forward), not to join me in meeting Yeats, but to treat Joanna to a movie, while I had tea at the Kildare Street Club. I left them in the lobby of a shabby cinema theater, Joanna radiant, for in Wicklow, movies were then shown in shelters that looked like abandoned barns—this place had the dignity of a tiled floor at its entrance.

On Kildare Street, the building that housed the Club rose up before me as though it were a jagged, red-brick hill of Victorian-Gothic-Gingerbread, resembling the German-made stone-block building toys I owned in childhood. Dublin's violet atmosphere shone through the mist around it. I crossed its threshold into a grotto-like lobby, the vast room lit by a single, naked, dim electric light bulb hanging above the chief porter's desk. I seated myself on a large, leather-covered sofa that faced the door. The air was chilled. I half-expected invisible stalactites, suspended from high, darkened ceilings, to drip before me, or tap my knees.

I had been seated but a moment or two, when Yeats, with a long, vigorous stride, swung open the door, and approached me, extending his right hand. He seemed far taller, more robust, than I had seen him at a distance on the Abbey Theatre stage. With one sweep of his arm, he was out of his macintosh and seated beside me, a finger of his right hand raised to summon a porter from the darkness behind the sofa to serve us tea, biscuits and cigarettes. "Your grandfather," he began, "from the stairs of Trinity, instructed me to see you. What do you think of the world today? I find it living in garrets and cellars; the young are Communists—are you a Communist?" Before he hurried on, I had scarcely breath to say that I was *not*, yet it was true that I was still sympathetic to Left causes, that . . . He handed me an admirable Turkish cigarette, and I was caught up in the spell he cast around me. I heard, and could almost see, his sentences and paragraphs take form: commas appeared, then semi-colons, then colons, then periods. It was wonderful eighteenth-century eloquence, overlaid with the merest echoes from Walter Pater's prose: whatever one thought of it—it was *style;* wit flashed, and cadences floated in air. Aside from listening to recordings of John McCormack's songs and James Joyce's *Anna Livia Plurabelle,* I had heard nothing to equal the beauty of Yeats's Dublin speech and accent.

On the afternoon that Yeats talked to me, in a monologue that lasted almost two hours, he had probably been ruminating over an essay he was in the process of writing, titled "Cellars and Garrets"; now he was pleased at having someone, who was not a Dubliner, listening to him. He spoke of Swift and Burke, Giovanni Battista Vico, Polybius, Sorel, Marx, Croce, Spengler, and Frobenius. "Sorel and Marx . . . have preached a return to a primeval state, a beating of all down into a single class that a new civilization may arise with its Few, its Many, and its One." For that moment, and with myself as his audience, Yeats played the role of Swift, echoing Swift's discourse on the tyrannies of the Few, the Many, and the One. Then, with a rapid change of persona, he spoke of "the tragedian Parnell . . . the symbol that made apparent . . . that epoch's contrary: contrary—not negation, not refutation; the spring vegetables may be over, they have not been refuted. I am Blake's disciple, not Hegel's: 'Contraries are positive. A negation is not a contrary.'"

All of this was, of course, of far more relevance to poetry's meanings than anything I was likely to hear in New York where ideas of writing were still overshadowed by the dogmas of Marx, Freud, and Lenin. In conversation, however wild some of his talk may have sounded, Yeats skillfully rode above the nonsense in which political directives were confused with the values of poetry. So much was clear. And he spoke with the authority of an elder poet who had been a Senator of the young Irish Free State, who knew the limitations and treacheries of political action, and who yet remained a poet of the first order. I was not merely impressed by what he said, but ready to be warned against deeper connection with Leftist causes and totalitarian beliefs.

When Yeats paused to light a cigarette, I asked him why no recent book of his could be found in Dublin bookshops. "Don't you know why?" said he. "No one in Ireland can read poetry today!" This last remark was with an air of triumph, as though his ready answer had achieved some sort of obscure victory.

The meeting with Yeats at the Kildare Street Club was, as it should have been, my last sight of Dublin. It made me feel that a journey begun many years ago in those visits to my grandfather's house on Jefferson Street had completed its cycle, and that my own progress toward self-knowledge had begun. I felt I had made a late start in life, but at least I could accept the fact that my maturity would be slow; I felt that the poems I had completed in London and in Wicklow, *Chorus for Survival*, expressed a faith that my native country would survive the darkness of the passing hour, and that I was ready to face the world again.

After my Irish visit, almost everything in London came as an anti-climax. My new duties at Sarah Lawrence began with the fall term, and even now August, 1934, was drifting toward September, and the grasses on Primrose Hill were turning grayish brown. I was brought up short by discovering I lacked the money to buy our passage home. I had indulged myself by living too fully within and for the moment. I then sat down and wrote an article for *The Atlantic Monthly* on London's National Portrait Gallery.

The check I received in payment was so generous that it not only secured our booking on the last voyage of the gaunt and stripped *Leviathan*, but a few dollars were left over with which Marya and I celebrated our ninth wedding anniversary in a Regent Street restaurant. I remember her gaiety, her light step across the threshold, her small, tapered hands and fingers, her wide, innocent eyes, and the radiant air that encircled her as she seated herself opposite me at the table.

The *Leviathan*, her rusted steel ribs showing, her decks in disarray, was a moth-eaten, cobweb-strung, gray hulk. She rode the waves with a huge, lop-sided pitch. It was as though she had outlived her time and knew it, and instead of being the floating, gaudy, middle-class hotel that she once was, she had now fallen into a night-haunted world—a ghost ship on uneasy waters. Storms fell from the sky; winds and rain tore at her. Her passengers seemed to take on contagious pallor and were helplessly sea-sick. At meals the dining rooms were three-quarters empty. Torn and rotten silk drapes swayed overhead and against the walls. Yet she made fairly good time; we were not to be delayed on our journey back to the States. Within five days, through gray clouds of rain and spray, the lights of Long Island came into view.

Epilogue

O N MY RETURN to New York in 1934, I felt that the era
through which I had lived and survived so precariously
drawing to a close. I had not long to wait: Hitler's Germany
had become a visible danger to Europe; war loomed ahead of
us. "Fellow travelers" like myself were soon to discover that
Stalin's Russia had become a scene of terror. In Moscow as
well as in Berlin, freedom of thought and speech had become
a crime: as we know today, a new hypocrisy, nursed by the
state, came into being. For the artist as well as the intellectual,
the Wheel of Fortune was slowly turning toward disillusionment. I felt that I had been very slow to learn that a single
humane act outweighed all the pretensions of humanitarian
causes and beliefs.

When during 1936, an editor of the *New Masses* phoned
me demanding that I sign a statement approving the verdicts
in the Moscow Trials, at last I found it easy to say: "No." I
told him to send me a transcript of the trials in English—at
which he became angry and hung up the phone. I was shown,

clearly enough, that Communist editors merely followed orders from Moscow—and that these orders had no relationship whatsoever to truth as I saw it, or to the arts.

By 1938 my relationships to the Left movements in writing had become very tenuous indeed. And in politics, whatever I heard of the Spanish Civil War gave me a sense of horror, rather than sympathy for the Loyalist cause. In New York, at a dinner given to raise money for the Loyalist partisans, my wife and I listened to shouted speeches that sounded as though the intellectuals of our time had gone insane. The excitement generated seemed either fanatical—which some of it was—or inspired by those who condoned Communist firing squads and party purges. My wife and I left early, so deeply shaken by the experience that we consciously declined future invitations to parties given for the defense of Loyalist Spain. We were not pro-Fascist. We were anti-totalitarian; and I thought then, and still believe that the Communists were no better than the Fascists—and, of course I was not alone in thinking so. Sir Osbert Sitwell was among the first to appear in print with the statement that the Spanish Civil War was the dirtiest war in history: its actual victims were the Spanish people, the poor, the helpless—Sir Osbert had succeeded for me at least in breaking through the fog of dialectical hypocrisy. The era of the early 1930s had given way to a new war generation. The time for misplaced optimism had come to an end.

But the theme of the preceding chapters is not political. For I believe that in every age political deserts are bleached white with the bones of their poets and intelligentsia. My theme is that of exile—and beyond it there is the debt I owe to a Middle-Western, Anglo-Irish tradition. Within that heritage, and powerfully I think, stand the examples of Catullus, Horace, and Lucretius who celebrated the themes of love and death—and who did not fear to question the morals of their

day. And as I have mentioned earlier, there was also the haunting presence of Hardy's *Satires of Circumstance,* and it was
Hardy's influence on D. H. Lawrence that led me to reading
the younger writer with so much interest. I rejected those to
whom the solutions of large questions came too easily. For
me, the cross-grained sturdiness of Veblen's discontent had
more conviction than Marxian formulas. To my mind Pragmatism had become as superficial as Zola's "Naturalism," now
dwindling among the theories of the past. The material findings of one age are often the mere keepsakes of curiosity during
the next.

A reminder of Hardy's presence took place at Twickenham, one day in August 1951. The encounter came about this
way: my wife, my son, and I received an invitation for tea
at Walter de la Mare's apartments overlooking a cricket-field.
The house we entered was probably Victorian, but the green-
ery around it, and, perhaps, De la Mare himself, had invested
it with an atmosphere of druidic fastness. Although the second
floor where he received us had all the protective warmth of a
sitting-room-parlor, I felt we were being entertained among
the higher branches of an elderly oak tree. Aside from ourselves, there was another guest, a famous surgeon, a large-
boned man, who like us, had made the journey up from
London.

De la Mare seated himself leaning forward—a posture that
seemed retained from an early habit—looking *up* at his visitors
as though moved by a youthful impulse to ask them questions.
He turned to the large man seated at his side, fixing attention
with a quick dark eye, and the question came: "What is the
first thing *you* think of when you wake up in the morning?"
The doctor flushed slightly: he was silent.

He had come to de la Mare that afternoon to ask him
questions concerning the imaginative life of children. De la

Mare had scored by taking the initiative, but this once done he went to some pains to restore the doctor's ease. His voice was softer, and looking up again he offered another question: "Why do some children at the age of nine or so write such inimitable notes and letters, as if touched by genius? And a few years later write nothing but empty words? The genius gone. Is the human vessel so quickly overturned? And completely emptied at eight or nine or ten? Is that the fate of some?"

De la Mare was, of course, as in a game of chess, moving his questions in the direction of the "creative process," to which the ancients referred when they gave credit to the Muses for gifts possessed. Ancient poets, with the thought of hubris near their hearts, made no claim to having a source of genius within themselves, and were wary of attracting the gaze of an evil eye. These rules of conduct were less superstitious than indicative of a humility, one which contained a deeper wisdom than attempts to analyze the "creative process" with all-too-human, and rapidly outmoded, scientific formulas. Scientific analysis is one thing; synthesis, particularly in the arts, is another. To explain the second by use of the first is a common error. Analysis of a poem or a painting is seldom more than a teacher's effort to instruct the ignorant. The Athenians knew the psyche well and respected its aesthetic mysteries.

But to return to that afternoon in August above the green cricket-field at Twickenham. De la Mare would not, of course, allow himself to come closer to the mysteries of writing verse than a knight's leap in speculation. He spoke of his delight as a young man, at reading Henry James's *The Turn of the Screw*. Here de la Mare neared the provinces of his own stories, his "Seaton's Aunt," his "Physic," even his anthology of writings recollecting childhood, *Early One Morning*—but he spoke of none of these. He continued to talk of James and *What Maisie Knew*.

The conversation glided from James to Thomas Hardy, from prose to poetry. "If anything is wrong with poetry today," de la Mare went on, "it is because it lacks compassion, the kind of human passion felt in reading Hardy's poetry, passion that has an understanding of human errors and their fatality."

"I remember," said de la Mare, "when I was young and made a pilgrimage to Hardy's home. In answer to my ring, he met me at the door, and stepping forward, said, 'Come, we shall take a walk.' And walk we did. He led me through a graveyard, and as we entered aisles of uncut grass, with tombstones on either side, he stroked the heads of the worn stones with his hand. They seemed to be his familiars, and he caressed them as though they were beloved creatures at his side. 'These are my friends,' he said, 'Bend down and read their names. Do you see them? And here is one you must read carefully. She is a girl, a year younger than I, someone I wronged.' The girl had died, aged thirteen, over forty years ago. 'Shortly before her death,' said Hardy, 'I had quarreled with her. It was in the schoolhouse on a winter afternoon. I thrust her against a white-hot stove and burnt her horribly. From another cause, some childhood infection, a few months later she was dead. Since that day of her death, I have never forgiven myself: and she is with me now, today.' He gave the headstone a last caress, and then moved on among the others, assuring me that they were all his friends."

By this time, the apparition of Hardy's figure strolled through the room, weaving between the chairs and tea-table, the shadow of a short, slender old man slowly fading in the path between headstones and graveyard grasses. As de la Mare told it, the story was less an anecdote, with its attendant moral, than the creation of a visionary episode, suspended in mid-air.

The vision reminded me of Wordsworth's gift to English poetry—the clear yet elusive simplicities of speech and action that Hardy sustained and furthered into the poetry of our time. Surely Wordsworth's "still, sad music of humanity," his "trailing clouds of glory . . . from God who is our home," had undergone a metamorphosis into Hardy's ghosts who people the wind, who return to Nature speaking from grasses and the lips of flowers. In many of Hardy's poems the re-enactment of the Fall of Man is very like the Fall from a Wordsworthian Eden. It is this likeness in holding a mirror up to life that gives Hardy's poetry its endurance, its poignancy.

I also felt that as a direct heir of Hardy's pantheism de la Mare had gained the authority to speak of time, and its passage from human birth into an after-life, as though they were among the ironies of Fate. These ironies were always present and were shared, as some of us believe, by future generations. On the occasion of another visit de la Mare had looked up at us brilliantly to say, "We shall probably live in this room forever, or shall we haunt it?" With this he smiled at his handsome, lion-haired granddaughter.

If I have given the impression that de la Mare had been merely charming in an early Georgian manner, that would be wrong. In that association his unglossed portrait of Hardy would not have been so effective. The peculiar quality of de la Mare's art of conversation had a touch of the Devil in it, not a boyish Devil but one of well-established, seasoned antiquity, one who had a kinship to the Serpent, whom Adam had come to know through Eve, and who invaded the dark rooms where Seaton's aunt, though blind, had made herself mistress of her nephew's fortunes. If, for over fifty years, de la Mare had written lyrics with the grace of a Bernini angel piercing the heart of St. Theresa, it was his Devil who purged the best of them of an overplus of sweetness.

It was then fitting of de la Mare to talk of Purcell's music, and of Herrick, Campion, and Lovelace, for in his poems, he combined the Wordsworth-Hardy tradition with the purest strains of music in English poetry. Within this union of enduring, yet elusive forces, the secret of de la Mare's magic worked its spell.

As we left the house, an instinct made me turn to look back at its second-floor windows. A sash flew open, and de la Mare leaned across the sill and waved a hand, then pointed upward through the rain to green leaves swaying above his roof. In his druidic shelter, he was Prospero waving goodbye through twilight.

The Twickenham meeting brought to a double close the English cycle of my heritage. When I returned to New York, I concluded that both Hardy and Robinson Jeffers—that solitary figure on the California coast—were poets of mature accomplishment, heirs of whatever we choose to call "Western Culture"—heirs of a Greco-Roman-Biblical tradition. In this it was also of moment that a number of Jeffers's early poems showed traces of Wordsworthian pantheism and turns of speech. Certainly neither Hardy nor Jeffers offered facile or optimistic definitions of man's place in the universe.

Although as far back as I can remember poetry has been an essential portion of my experience, I believe the writing of poems comes from a deeper source than that of physical reflex and personal being. For me, at least, the source is of a voice directing actors in a human scene, in which even my own voice is that of an inspired character in a play. I feel that my poems are actually dramatic poems overheard beyond the footlights of that scene. I think it significant that before I did any writing at all, I invented plays and players to speak of whatever moved my imagination. When I began to write, poetry then took over. Beyond this book my poems should be allowed to speak for themselves.

I think that if we talk too much about "the art of poetry" we are actually drifting toward too much "shoptalk," or a narcissistic version of "art for art's sake," which D. H. Lawrence described as "art for my sake." And Kipling wrote: "The Devil whispered behind the leaves, 'It's pretty, but is it Art?' "

The poem, whether inspired by the Comic Muse, or the Tragic, is usually relevant to the central forces that guide our lives, and these are of a world that elemental philosophers defined as "Not Myself." That was long ago, but it is still true that in the universe of "Not Myself" the actual work of the Muses, and therefore, of the poet, is to endow abstract ideas, beliefs, and emotions with the life of the senses. Although a poem may embody an idea, there is no such thing as an abstract poem. That is why the recital of slogans (or good intentions) cannot make poems, and why didactic verse is so seldom poetry. This is also why the rhetoric of politicians is so distinctly not the speech of poetry.

During the twentieth century the Muses, as the Greeks knew them, have seldom appeared wearing their ancient names. In Hardy's *The Dynasts*, they ride above the battles and are disguised as The Ironies. No doubt they inspired Hardy. They are overheard as the haunting Angels in Rilke's *Duino Elegies*. Or they are rediscovered in the shadowy presences of Yeats's cosmos in *A Vision*. They are by no means lost or strayed. Nor have they lost their meaning, their power to reveal the hidden recesses of the human psyche.

To the poet—and this should be evident to everyone—the Muse-inspired reaches of historical imagination, from Homer's day to this, are of living importance. And so is memory. As History—the Daughter of Memory—shows us, every poet need not be an intellectual. The flaws of Edmund Spenser, Tennyson, and Robert Bridges may be traced to a lack of intellectual firmness and probity. That was their weakness, not their distinction. (In any art mere fools and dullards are not to be suffered gladly.) But the Muses do insist that those whom they befriend possess more than a usual share of human intelligence.

I also believe that the artist has the responsibility, whatever the hazards, of carrying through the demands of his art till death overtakes him; in so doing, he reaffirms his allegiance to life. In this, I am reminded of the elderly Renoir. The painter suffered a stroke that had disabled an arm. He instructed an assistant to tie a paintbrush to his hand and wrist, so as to allow him to complete the canvases waiting for him in his studio. The results of such spiritual strength may not be sad: one remembers Hardy's "An Ancient to Ancients," and the old age of Sophocles and Yeats.

As one speaks of History, and more specifically Memory, my symbol of this is the house on Jefferson Street, that stood for whatever I learned during childhood and youth. Through its associations, both conscious and unconscious, the house is a signature of my existence—other signs are in my verse, my translations, my critical writings—and all these are my very life, however it may take form. Today, the visible being of the house is gone. It belongs to Memory, yet I like to fancy that the roots of the small lilac forest behind the house will stir to life again, and that, somehow, however difficult the effort may be, new shoots will flower into another generation.

On the few visits I made to it since 1934, the house looked increasingly weather-beaten and sooty. Its unbalanced cream-brick front, with high roof turrets at the top, had grown dark and yellowed, and it still created the illusion of leaning forward over those who rang its front door bell. Its last inhabitants were Cousin Marian and Cousin Paul. Since Marian was the elder, she had been instructed at my uncle's deathbed, to look after her brother, who was then over sixty, fixed in his habits, and a bachelor.

Paul's life had been devoted to enormous readings, interrupted by rare intervals of writing; writing at night, reading by day. Following the example of Des Esseintes, Paul draped his bedroom in black, and then went beyond it, by having bed sheets and pillow slips of black-dyed cotton—which, he said, effected economies in laundering and protected his eyes from glare and dazzle. He believed in the efficacy of social reform through the Single Tax; he admired Edgar Saltus's *Imperial Purple,* and the wanderer Simplicissimus. When asked why he did not write more frequently, Paul would reply, "The dead hand of Dostoevski covers all literature." He had sharp blue eyes and fiery hair, brushed straight up from his forehead. Out of respect for his English grandmother, so he said, he wore rubbers, and carried an umbrella, in all weathers.

Since sister and brother lived alone in the large house, Marian on the second floor, Paul on the third, the place began to assume the air of an abandoned hotel; layers of dust obscured the glazed and framed Piranesi engraving of Cestius's pyramid that had hung for years in my uncle's study on the second floor. While her brother spent his afternoons at the public library where the statue of Washington stood guard, Marian painted, as the fancy took her, water colors or oils, in the manner of Edmund Dulac, in a north-lit bedroom. On fine days during the spring and fall, Marian would set up her easel in a city park, or in the lilac-haunted back yard on Jefferson Street, braving the soot that floated from the red skies of the factories in the valley, a mile away. Slowly the rooms fell into general disorder, for Marian and Paul considered themselves owners of an inherited estate, not its caretakers. Marian, however, was not unindustrious: as long as she could mount a ladder once a year, the walls of the front parlor were covered with a fresh coat of paint, and she took pride in this annual activity. In the neighborhood around them, the flood of Italian immigration was replaced by that of Puerto Rican. Spanish became the language of the streets, and since Marian and Paul distrusted foreign shopkeepers in buying food, they subsisted on well-known brands of canned goods, which Paul assured me were excellent, and preserved his health. He observed that the hours of the day could still be heard in the ringing of the Convent bells. And did this Convent house the Little Sisters of the Poor? If so, it would have been appropriate. His grandmother's sturdy Church of England Protestantism, and his Irish grandfather's disgrace in being converted to the Roman Church, forbade Paul making definite inquiries concerning the order of sisters heard singing behind Convent walls.

Three years ago I heard that the house on Jefferson Street no longer stood its ground, and indeed after Cousin Paul's death, its existence was scarcely justified. It had lived its century: books piled in hallways and on unused stairs, closets filled with moth-frayed clothes, and heaps of newspapers stacked anywhere had turned the premises into a firetrap. A high wind through an open door and up a chimney behind a mantelpiece would be enough to carry the house away in flames. Cousin Marian began to feel that its brick façade, so much like that of an outmoded fortress, no longer protected her. The house was unfit to shelter her grandfather's treatise on geometry, published in Dublin before he landed on these shores, and certainly it was ill-equipped to preserve in safety the box that contained the gold medal that Queen Victoria handed to her great-grandfather Goadby for his services to science. The world was more scientific now than it had ever been; the medal was too valuable to sell. The evidence of Dr. Goadby's merit would be better off with her as its keeper in a small apartment. The house was condemned, and the land on which it rested was bought by the city.

Index

187, 191, 205–206, 211,
223–225, 241
Ellis, Havelock, 106, 240
Emerson, Ralph Waldo, 3,
22, 177, 206, 212, 221
Episcopal Church, 53, 84,
103, 173

F

Faber and Faber, 205, 223
Farrell, James T., 200–201
Faulkner, William, 112, 115,
238
Fearing, Kenneth, 120–122,
123, 163, 168
Ferber, Edna, 117
Fitzgerald, F. Scott, 112, 118,
162
Forbes-Robertson, Sir
Johnston, 60
Ford, Ford Madox, 227, 229
Freeman, Joseph, 169, 183
Freud, Sigmund, 106, 109,
167, 254
Frost, Robert, 65–66, 191

G

Gale, Zona, 116, 117, 118,
122, 163
Galsworthy, John, 78
Gauguin, Paul, 71–72
George, W. Lloyd, 124–126

German-English Academy,
71, 74–75
Gibbs, Willard, 188
Gide, André, 115, 239
Goadby, Henry Addison, 8,
24, 25–27, 30–31, 39, 267
Gogarty, Oliver St. John,
245–247, 248, 251
Gonne, Maud, 244
Graves, Percy, 247
Graves, Robert, 86, 247
Gregory, Anna Catherine
Henkel (mother), 3,
14–15, 22, 35, 47, 66,
73, 84, 93; and HG,
16–18, 21, 50–51, 137–
138, 158–159
Gregory, Bulwer Lytton, 30
Gregory, Caro, 2, 6
Gregory, Elizabeth Goadby
(grandmother), 5, 7, 21,
24–26, 29–33, 35, 212–
213, 215, 266
Gregory, Elizabeth (cous-
in), 2–3, 12, 21, 38,
40–41, 45, 67–68
Gregory, Florence (half-
sister), 53, 60, 194
Gregory, George, 26, 29,
43–45, 55, 60
Gregory, Henry Bolton
(father), 13–15, 22, 33,
37, 47, 49, 73–74, 83–
85, 98, 101–103, 138, 241